AOS SERIES

VOLUME 100

THE *SŌUSHÉN HÒUJÌ*

LATTER NOTES ON COLLECTED SPIRIT PHENOMENA ATTRIBUTED TO TÁO YUĀNMÍNG (365–427)

AOS SERIES

VOLUME 100

AOS

NEW HAVEN, CT

2022

THE *SŌUSHÉN HÒUJÌ*

Latter Notes on Collected Spirit Phenomena Attributed to Táo Yuānmíng (365–427)

An Annotated Translation

by

RICHARD VANNESS SIMMONS

AOS

NEW HAVEN, CT

2022

Library of Congress Cataloging-in-Publication Data

Names: Tao, Qian, 372?-427, author. | Simmons, Richard VanNess, editor.
Title: The Sōushén hòujì : latter notes on collected spirit phenomena attributed to Táo Yuānmíng (365- 427) / an annotated translation by Richard VanNess Simmons.
Other titles: Sou shen hou ji. English
Description: New Haven : American Oriental Society, 2022. | Series: American Oriental series; 100 | Includes bibliographical references and index.
Identifiers: LCCN 2021056394 (print) | LCCN 2021056395 (ebook) | ISBN 9781955357012 (paperback) | ISBN 9781948488976 (pdf)
Subjects: LCSH: Tao, Qian, 372?-427,--Criticism and interpretation.
Classification: LCC PL2665.T3 S613 2022 (print) | LCC PL2665.T3 (ebook) | DDC 895.11/24--dc23/eng/20220113
LC record available at https://lccn.loc.gov/2021056394
LC ebook record available at https://lccn.loc.gov/2021056395

The paper used in this publication meets the minimum requirements of the American National Standard for Information Sciences—Permanence of Paper for Printed Library Materials, ANSI Z39.48-1984. ♾™

To the Memory of Alan J. Berkowitz

CONTENTS

ABBREVIATIONS

Bslt Bó Jūyì 白居易 (772–846). *Bó shì liùtiě shìlèi jí* 白氏六帖事類集. Taibei: Xinxing shuju, 1971.

Btsc Yú Shìnán 虞世南 (558–638). *Běitáng shūchāo* 北堂書鈔. N.p.: Nanhai Kongshi sanshi you sanwan juan tang, 1888.

Cxj Xú Jiān 徐堅 (659–729). *Chū xué jì* 初學記. Beijing: Zhonghua shuju, 1962.

Fyzl Dào Shì 道世 (fl. 668). *Fǎyuàn zhūlín* 法苑珠林. *Sìbù cóngkān* edn.

Gsz Huìjiǎo 慧皎 (497–554). *Gāo sēng zhuàn chū jí* 高僧傳初集. Taibei: Taiwan yinjingchu, 1970.

Sbck *Sìbù cóngkān* 四部叢刊.

Slf Wú Shú 吳淑 (947–1002), ed. and comm. *Shì lèi fù* 事類賦. N.p.: n.d.

Sshj *Sōushén hòujì* 搜神後記. *Xuéjīn tǎoyuán* 學津討原 edn.

Ssj Gān Bǎo 干寶 (d. 336). *Sōushén jì* 搜神記. Edited by Wāng Shàoyíng 汪紹楹. Beijing: Zhonghua shuju, 1979. (Based on the *Xuéjīn tǎoyuán* edn.)

Ssxy Liú Yìqìng 劉義慶 (403–444). *Shìshuō xīnyǔ* 世說新語. Edited by Wāng Zǎo 汪藻 (fl. 13th c.). Beijing: Zhonghua shuju, 1962.

Tpgj Lǐ Fǎng 李昉 (925–996), ed. *Tàipíng guǎngjì* 太平廣記. Taibei: Xinxing shuju, 1958.

Tpyl Lǐ Fǎng, ed. *Tàipíng yùlǎn* 太平御覽. Beijing: Zhonghua shuju, 1960.

Xjsshj *Xīnjí Sōushén hòujì*, in *Xīnjí Sōushén jì Xīnjí Sōushén hòujì* 新輯搜神記新輯搜神後記. Edited by Lǐ Jiànguó 李劍國. 2 vols. Beijing: Zhonghua shuju, 2007.

Xssj *Xù Sōushén jì* 續搜神記.

Ywlj Ōuyáng Xún 歐陽詢 (557–641), ed. *Yìwén lèijù* 藝文類聚. Taibei: Xinxing shuju, 1969.

INTRODUCTION TO THE PUBLISHED EDITION OF THIS TRANSLATION

In the many years since this translation was first completed as a Master's thesis at the University of Washington in 1986,[1] we have seen the production of a good deal of fine scholarship about the *zhìguài* 志怪 genre and its social, cultural, and religious context. This new scholarship has greatly developed our understanding of the many collections of 'records of anomalies', including their intended uses and readership. This new scholarship generally surpasses the fairly rudimentary overview of the *Sōushén hòujì* 搜神後記 (*Sshj*) and its genre that the present volume provides in its introductory discussion. The interested reader who wishes to explore beyond the stories and anecdotes in this volume and seek out a deeper understanding of the *Sōushén hòujì* and related texts in their time and place will find much of value in this later scholarship.

One significant recent advance has been the collation of the text in light of the many piecemeal variants and fragments preserved in various historical texts. Our opening discussion of the textual history of the *Sshj*, which still accurately characterizes the essentials of what is known about the general arc of the traditional text's formation and evolution, notes that "if verification of authenticity and origin for any given section of the *Sshj* is to be at all accurate and useful with regard to the historical context of that specific section, such verification must be undertaken individually for each entry in question."[2] That task has since been meticulously completed by the hand of Lǐ Jiànguó 李劍國 in his *Xīnjí Sōushén jì Xīnjí Sōushén hòujì* 新輯搜神記新輯搜神後記 (2007). Lǐ has painstakingly sorted through all extant versions of the anecdotes of both *Sōushén jì* and *Sōushén hòujì* and developed what is considered to be the new authoritative version of both texts.[3] Lǐ's second volume attends to the *Sshj* and argues that twenty-four entries in the received text, which is derived from the *Mìcè huìhán* 祕冊彙函 edition, are invalid inclusions while restoring another twelve entries from other sources that Lǐ judges should be included. Lǐ also identifies five *Sshj* stories that he asserts should be in the *Sōushén jì*. Finally, Lǐ undertakes a major reordering of the entire contents of the *Sshj*, while also editing many entries in light of trusted versions in other sources. The result is a ten-*juàn* version that contains a total of ninety-nine anecdotes. Appendix 2 of this volume lists all the *Sshj* entries by title and provides Lǐ Jiànguó's collation decisions, indicating what he includes in his *Xīnjí Sōushén hòujì* (*Xjsshj*), which twelve stories he has added, which he rejects for inclusion, and which he reassigns to Gān Bǎo's 干寶 (d. 336) *Sōushén jì*. New translations for the twelve passages restored by Lǐ Jiànguó in *Xjsshj* are added to the main text

1. See also the Translator's Postface below.
2. See p. 9 below.
3. Campany, *A Garden of Marvels: Tales of Wonder from Early Medieval China* (Honolulu: Univ. of Hawai'i Press, 2015), 61.

following the *Sshj* translation. However, this volume maintains all entries from the *Sshj* and does not eliminate those that Lǐ Jiànguó did not include in *Xjsshj*.

It is of note that Lǐ's *Xjsshj* excludes the one entry that is independently identifiable as a composition by Táo Qián 陶潛 (365–427), "The Peach Blossom Wellsprings" (j. 1, no. 5). Yet though Lǐ Jiànguó does not think this story belongs in *Sshj* he nevertheless maintains the identification of Táo Qián as the author of *Sshj* (and of the stories he includes in *Xjsshj*). Thus Lǐ adds one story that was clearly attributed to Táo Qián in *Gāo sēng zhuàn* 高僧傳, "The Hemp Frocked Monk" (X7).

Aside from these additions, this translation presents the text mostly "as is," so to speak, and does not restructure it to match Lǐ Jiànguó's new collation. This allows modern readers to experience the text as a whole, in the shape it took under the hand of traditional editors, the good stories and the mediocre ones, the longer and the shorter, unmitigated by the preferences and selection choices of modern scholars. Thus, the present translation serves to represent a kind of time-capsule of the traditional take on the text and its original arrangement, or at least the arrangement received by late tradition, while also including the twelve additional passages restored by Lǐ Jiànguó. Certainly, the various details provided in the notes to each translated passage remain quite accurate and useful and generally have not been superseded by the few representative translated passages that occur in recent anthologies and studies in English.

Other significant advances have been made in our understanding of the *zhìguài* genre and its social, cultural, and religious milieu. Among the most penetrating scholarship in the field is found in the abundant collection of studies by Robert Ford Campany, whose rich work spans the decades between the original completion of this translation in 1986 and the present day. In *Strange Writing: Anomaly Accounts in Early Medieval China*, published in 1996, Campany includes the *Sōushén hòujì* in a study of over sixty other *zhìguài* collections from the fourth to sixth centuries. Campany's *Strange Writing* provides a comprehensive new perspective on, and interpretation of the *zhìguài*. Indeed, Stephen Teiser calls this volume "the definitive treatment" of the *zhiguai* genre.[4] Campany moves away from the view that the *zhìguài* represent an early, nascent form of fiction and emphasizes their documentary nature, which aligns well with the conclusion in the present volume regarding the essentially historical character of the *Sōushén hòujì* stories. Acknowledging the historical and evidentiary elements of the stories, Campany shows us how the *zhìguài* can provide a window on medieval Chinese culture, particularly with regard to the popular and spiritual elements of that culture. The texts can thus be read for what they tell us about religion in medieval China. Campany undertakes that approach quite deftly in chapters 7 and 8 of *Strange Writing* wherein he approaches the texts and the stories they contain in the development of a kind of ethnography of early Chinese religion. Much of Campany's subsequent work continues fruitfully in this direc-

4. Teiser, review of *Strange Writing: Anomaly Accounts in Early Medieval China*, by Robert Ford Campany, *History of Religions* 39.3 (2000): 310.

tion, for example, his 2012 *Signs from the Unseen Realm: Buddhist Miracle Tales from Early Medieval China.*

In the same year that Campany came out with *Strange Writing*, Kenneth J. DeWoskin and J. I. Crump produced a complete translation of Gān Bǎo's *Sōushén jì*, titled *In Search of the Supernatural: The Written Record.* Campany's review of this volume chides it for continuing to treat the *zhìguài* "as precursors of the later 'birth of fiction' in China."[5] Yet he nevertheless acknowledges that it is a competent and readable translation. It is certainly a fine representative in English of the text to which the source for the present volume was intended to be the sequel.

A notable and useful dedicated study of the *Sōushén jì* is found in *Rémi Mathieu's Démons et merveilles dans la littérature chinoise des Six Dynasties: Le fantastique et l'anecdotique dans le Soushen ji de Gan Bao*. In his review of Mathieu's volume, Wolfgang Behr tells us:

> Mathieu's *Démons et merveilles* serves as a kind of essayistic companion to [. . .] translations of the *Soushen ji*. Its primary aim is to elaborate on certain recurrent topics of the collection in the form of a close reading and thematic synopsis of the sources, to reconstruct the dense network of intra-textual relationships between the respective short accounts as well as their inter-textual indebtedness to Classical predecessors and to other less well-known representatives later subsumed under the *zhiguai* and *xiaoshuo* labels, in a very learned and heavy footnote apparatus.[6]

In addition to DeWoskin and Crump, the translations of the *Sōushén ji* to which Behr refers here include those by Rémy Mathieu et al. (1993) and L. N. Men'šikov (1994).

Other recent translations of *zhìguài* include Zhang Zhenjun's 2018 translation of the *Yōumínglù* by Liú Yìqìng 劉義慶 (403–444), which follows upon Zhang's earlier study of the same collection. For an excellent broad selection of *zhìguài* stories in English, the reader is referred to Campany's *zhìguài* collection titled *A Garden of Marvels: Tales of Wonder from Early Medieval China* (2015). This is an eminently readable anthology of tales and anecdotes from a variety of sources, including *Sōushén hòujì*, thus placing this volume and its stories among its peers and providing background perspective and a raised-relief look at the *zhìguai* genre as a whole.

5. Campany, review of *In Search of the Supernatural: The Written Record*, tr. by Kenneth J. DeWoskin and J. I. Crump, *China Review International* 4.1 (1997): 118.

6. Behr, review of *Démons et merveilles dans la littérature chinoise des Six Dynasties: Le fantastique et l'anecdotique dans le Soushen ji de Gan Bao*, by Rémi Mathieu, *Oriens* 36 (2001): 362.

SELECTED POST-1986 SCHOLARSHIP ON *ZHÌGUÀI* AND THE *SŌUSHÉN HÒUJÌ*

Alimov, I. Concerning 'Records of Searching for Spirits' of Gan Bao. *Manuscripta Orientalia* 18.1 (2012): 3–14.

Behr, Wolfgang. Review of *Démons et merveilles dans la littérature chinoise des Six Dynasties: Le fantastique et l'anecdotique dans le* Soushen ji *de Gan Bao*, by Rémi Mathieu. *Oriens* 36 (2001): 361–64.

Campany, Robert Ford. Ghosts Matter: The Culture of Ghosts in Six Dynasties *zhiguai*. *Chinese Literature: Essays, Articles, Reviews* 13 (1991): 15–34.

———. Notes on the Devotional Uses and Symbolic Functions of Sutra Texts as Depicted in Early Chinese Buddhist Miracle Tales and Hagiographies. *Journal of the International Association of Buddhist Studies* 14.1 (1991): 28–72.

———. Buddhist Revelation and Taoist Translation in Early Medieval China. *Taoist Resources* 4.1 (1993): 1–29.

———. *Strange Writing: Anomaly Accounts in Early Medieval China*. Albany: State Univ. of New York Press, 1996.

———. Review of *In Search of the Supernatural: The Written Record*, tr. Kenneth J. DeWoskin and J. I. Crump. *China Review International* 4.1 (1997): 118–21.

———. Living off the Books: Fifty Ways to Dodge *Ming* in Early Medieval China. In *The Magnitude of Ming: Command, Allotment, and Fate in Chinese Culture*. Ed. Christopher Lupke. Pp. 129–50. Honolulu: Univ. of Hawai'i Press, 2005.

———. Two Religious Thinkers of the Early Eastern Jin: Gan Bao 干寶 and Ge Hong 葛洪 in Multiple Contexts. *Asia Major* 3rd ser., 18 (2005): 175–224.

———. *Making Transcendents: Ascetics and Social Memory in Early Medieval China*. Honolulu: Univ. of Hawai'i Press, 2009.

———. Religious Repertoires and Contestation: A Case Study Based on Buddhist Miracle Tales. *History of Religions* 52 (2012): 99–141.

———. *Signs from the Unseen Realm: Buddhist Miracle Tales from Early Medieval China*. Honolulu: Univ. of Hawai'i Press, 2012.

———. *A Garden of Marvels: Tales of Wonder from Early Medieval China*. Honolulu: Univ. of Hawai'i Press, 2015.

———. Miracle Tales as Scripture Reception: A Case Study Involving the Lotus Sutra in China, 370–750 CE. *Early Medieval China* 24 (2018): 24–52.

Chan, Timothy W. K. A Tale of Two Worlds: The Late Tang Poetic Presentation of The Romance of the Peach Blossom Font. *T'oung Pao* 94.4 (2008): 209–45.

Chiang, Sing-chen Lydia. Visions of Happiness: Daoist Utopias and Grotto Paradises in Early and Medieval Chinese Tales. *Utopian Studies* 20.1 (2009): 47–76.

DeWoskin, Kenneth J. and J. I. Crump, tr. Gan Bao, *In Search of the Supernatural: The Written Record*. Stanford: Stanford Univ. Press, 1996.

Georgieva, Valentina. Representation of Buddhist Nuns in Chinese Edifying Miracle Tales During the Six Dynasties and the Tang. *Journal of Chinese Religions* 24.1 (1996): 47–76.

Holzman, Donald. *Immortals, Festivals, and Poetry in Medieval China: Studies in Social and Intellectual History*. Aldershot: Ashgate, 1998.

Knechtges, David R., and Taiping Chang, eds. *Ancient and Early Medieval Chinese Literature: A Reference Guide*. 4 vols. Leiden: Brill, 2010–2014.

Lǐ Jiànguó 李劍國. *Xīnjí Sōushén jì Xīnjí Sōushén hòujì* 新輯搜神記新輯搜神後記. 2 vols. Beijing: Zhonghua shuju, 2007.

Mathieu, Rémi, et al. *A la recherche des esprits, recits tires du Sou Shen Ji*. Connaissance de l'Orient, Serie chinoise. Paris: Gallimard, 1993.

Mathieu, Rémi. *Démons et merveilles dans la littérature chinoise des Six Dynasties: Le fantastique et l'anecdotique dans le* Soushen ji *de Gan Bao*. Paris: Editions You-feng, 2000.

Men'šikov, L. N. *Gan'Bao: Zapiski o poiskax duxov [Sou šen' czi]*. St. Peterburg: Centr Peterburgskoe Vostokovedenie, 1994.

Swartz, Wendy, et al., eds. *Early Medieval China: A Sourcebook*. New York: Columbia Univ. Press, 2014.

Teiser, Stephen F. Review of *Strange Writing: Anomaly Accounts in Early Medieval China*, by Robert Ford Campany. *History of Religions* 39.3 (2000): 308–10.

Xuē Huìqí 薛惠琪. *Liùcháo fójiào zhìguài xiǎoshuō yánjiū* 六朝佛教志怪小說研究. Taibei: Wenjin chubanshe, 1995.

Yáng Yì 楊義. *Zhōngguó lìcháo xiǎoshuō yǔ wénhuà* 中國歷朝小說與文化. Taipei: Yeqiang, 1993.

Zhang, Zhenjun. *Buddhism and Tales of the Supernatural in Early Medieval China: A Study of Liu Yiqing's (403–444)* Youming lu. Leiden: Brill, 2014.

Zhang, Zhenjun. *Hidden and Visible Realms: Early Medieval Chinese Tales of the Supernatural and the Fantastic*. New York: Columbia Univ. Press, 2018.

Zhōu Cìjí 周次吉. *Liùcháo zhìguài xiǎoshuō yánjiū* 六朝志怪小說研究. Taipei: Wenjin chubanshe, 1990.

Zhōu Jùnxūn 周俊勛. *Wèi Jìn nánběicháo zhìguài xiǎoshuō cíhuì yánjiū* 魏晉南北朝志怪小說詞彙研究. Chengdu: Ba Shu shushe, 2006.

PART ONE

CHAPTER 1

History of the *Sōushén hòujì* Text

The collection of anecdotes that exists today under the title *Sōushén hòujì* 搜神後記 (Latter Notes on Collected Spirit Phenomena), though attributed to the authorship of Táo Qián 陶潛 (365–427) in the early fifth century, actually only survives in a collection of fragments culled from various sources sometime after the Sòng and most likely in the late Míng. Moreover, the greater part of the material in the collection existed only under a different title prior to the Sòng, a title that was never, so far as can be discerned from preserved records, connected with Táo Qián's name. Yet there is an early record of the *Sōushén hòujì* title and that of another "*sōushén*" ('collected spirit phenomena') collection that are both given under Táo Qián's name. Though there is no definite connection between these two texts and the third title, and little evidence that what they contained is preserved in any substantial form in the present text, it is probably because of these early listings under Táo's name that the present text is also attributed to him. For this reason, the following account of the transmission of the received *Sōushén hòujì* begins with a discussion of these titles and their connection to Táo Qián.

The earliest reference we have to a "*sōushén*" collection by Táo Yuānmíng 淵明 is in Huìjiăo's 慧皎 (497–554) preface to his *Gāo sēng zhuàn* (Biographies of Eminent Monks):

> *Xuānyàn jì* 宣驗記 and *Yōumíng lù* 幽明錄 by [Liú] Yìqìng 劉義慶, Prince of Línchuān 臨川, *Míngxiáng jì* 冥祥記 by Wáng Yǎn 王琰 of Tàiyuán, . . . and Táo Yuānmíng's *Sōushén lù* all incidentally bring up various monks and discuss their finer character. Yet all [such discussions] show up as appendages, and there are a great deal of omissions and oversights.[1]

Huìjiăo, of course, was concerned with the quality of biographical material these works contained, but his mention here of a *Sōushén lù* 搜神錄 by Táo, just one hundred years after Táo's death is strong evidence that such a text existed.[2] There is little reason to suspect that Huìjiăo doubted that Táo Qián was the author, and much less reason to suspect that he deliberately attributed a text to Táo he might have known to be forged. For though Huìjiăo was a devout Buddhist, this reference is simply that of a historian complaining about the adequacy of his sources. He is not trying to praise or elevate the texts he mentions.

---

1. Huìjiăo, *Gāo sēng zhuàn chūjí* 高僧傳初集 (Taibei: Taiwan yinjingchu, 1970) [hereafter *Gsz*], ii.

2. Arthur Wright estimates that the *Gāo sēng zhuàn* was completed in "about 530." See his discussion of the text, "Biography and Hagiography: Hui-chiao's Lives of Eminent Monks," *Silver Jubilee Volume of the Zinbun-kagaku-kenkyusyo Kyoto University* (1954): 383–432, esp. 400.

Huìjiǎo's contemporary, Wáng Mànyǐng 王曼穎 (n.d.), also mentions a "narrative by Yuánliàng" when surveying previous biographical literature on Buddhists in a letter he wrote to Huìjiǎo appended to the *Gāo sēng zhuàn*.[3] Though he does not mention it by name, Wáng Mànyǐng was presumably referring to the same text by Táo Qián that Huìjiǎo mentions in his preface, for the letter evinces that he was quite familiar with most of the sources Huìjiǎo used in his study.[4] This reference is confirmation, albeit rather weak, that as early as the sixth century there was a text under Táo Qián's name that contained, among other things, incidental information on Buddhists.

This text is mentioned again in the early Táng. Yet the references are still only within the context of Buddhist scholarship. Dào Xuān 道宣 (596–667) and Fǎ Lín 法琳 (n.d.), early Táng monks, both list a *Sōushén lù* by Táo Yuánliàng in bibliographies of texts that provide information on early Buddhists.[5] However, neither Dào Xuān nor Fǎ Lín provide any information on the length of the text or on its specific content. This is where the trail ends for this title. If a *Sōushén lù* by Táo Qián did once exist, it has been lost today, leaving us only to guess at what it might have contained and its relationship to the *Sōushén hòujì*.[6] Lacking further evidence, it is also impossible to speculate any further than I have above on the veracity of the attributed authorship.

The earliest listing of a *Sōushén hòujì* (*Sshj*) is in the *Suí shū* 隋書 "Monograph on Literature" (Jīngjí zhì 經籍志) (submitted to the emperor in 656).[7] Here Táo Qián is credited as the author of a ten-*juàn* work under this title. The only other early catalogue listing is found over two centuries later in Japan where the *Nihon-koku genzaisho mokuroku* 日本國見在書目錄 compiled by Fujiwara Sukeyo 藤原佐世 (d. 898) also listed a ten-*juàn Sōushén hòujì* by Táo Qián.[8] The other early references to the work are found in Xú Jiān's 徐堅 (659–729) *Chū xué jì* 初學記. Xú's work attributes three passages to Táo Qián, two as from "Táo Qián's *Sshj*" and one as from "Táo Qián's *Sōushén jì*,"

3. *Gsz*, 379. Yuánliàng 元亮 was a sobriquet of Táo Qián's.

4. For a discussion of Huìjiǎo's sources for the *Gsz* and Wáng Mànyǐng's comments concerning them, see Wright, "Biography and Hagiography," 408–29.

5. For Dào Xuān's listing, see his *Sānbǎo gǎn tōng lù* 三寶感通錄 in *Taishō shinshū daizōkyō* 大正新修藏經, ed. Takakusu Junjirō 高楠順次郎 (1866–1945) and Watanabe Kaigyoku 渡邊海旭 (1872–1933) (Tokyo: Taishō issaikyō kankōkai, 1924–32) [hereafter *Taishō*], LII, no. 2106, C.431a. For Fǎ Lín's listing, see his *Pòxié lùn* 破邪論 in *Taishō* LII, no. 2109, B.485b. Dào Xuān also once attributed the title *Sōu shénlù* to Gān Bǎo. See his Dào Xuān *lǜshī gǎntōnglù* 律師感通錄 in *Taishō* LII, no. 2107, p. 435.

6. There is a possibility, for example, that the *Sshj* story concerning Fótúdèng (j. 2, no. 18) was among the material that Huìjiǎo gleaned from the *Sōushén lù* for his *Gsz*. See Wright, "Biography and Hagiography," 420, and Paul Pelliot, "Autour d'une traduction sanscrite du *Tao tö king*," *T'oung pao* 13 (1912): 418 n. 3.

7. *Suí shū*, comp. Wèi Zhēng 魏徵 (580–643) (Beijing: Zhonghua shuju, 1973), 33.980.

8. In Kobase Keikichi 小長谷惠吉 (1865–1944), *Nihon-koku genzaisho mokuroku kaisetsu kō* 解說稿 (Tokyo: Komiyamu shoten, 1976), 10.

the latter probably a copy error for the *Sshj*.[9] The attribution to Táo Qián is indirectly verified for one of Xú's citations where the *Tpgj* preserves a passage from Xiāo Jí's 蕭吉 (d. 614) *Wǔxíng jì* 五行記, which gives a version of j. 9, no. 98 under the heading "Táo Qián Sōushén *jì*."[10] These are the only, and all, references to a *Sōushén hòujì* (or a *Sōushén jì*) by Táo Qián that can be found before the Míng. Significantly, every single one of these references explicitly identifies the author. This is a clear indication that a collection attributed to Táo did exist in the seventh century. Yet because the only entry in the received *Sshj* that we can be reasonably certain Táo Qián wrote, "Táohuā yuán jì," is cited even in the *Cxj* as "Táo Qián's 'Táo yuán jì'," the credibility of Táo's authorship of a *Sshj* collection remains uncertain.[11]

Beyond the fact that it was probably ten *juàn* long, the form of this seventh-century *Sshj* collection is unclear. For the bulk of the entries in the received *Sshj* that are found cited in the *lèishū* 類書 ("books of sources arranged by category") are attributed to a collection called the *Xù Sōushén jì* 續 (*Xssj*) and in no case is that title ever attributed to Táo Qián. *Cxj*, which as noted above attributes three citations to Táo Qián, also cites four entries from the *Xssj* that can be found in the present *Sshj* but does not once identify an author for them.[12] Moreover, two of the entries that *Cxj* identifies as Táo Qián's are cited as *Xssj* in other *lèishū*.[13] This leads one to believe that in the seventh century this *Xssj* was an additional sequel *Sōushén jì* collection into which the *Sshj* was at some time conflated, thus eventually to disappear as an independent text. What percentage of this *Xssj* would have been from the *Sshj* and how much of it is material from other sources is impossible to determine.

Toward the end of the Táng it appears that the identity of this *Xssj* also became obscured in a process where it was somehow confused with, or appended to, Gān Bǎo's *Sōushén jì* 搜神記 (*Ssj*). The suggestion of this possibility was first raised by Toyoda Minoru 豐田穰 and the idea was later more fully elaborated by Morino Shigeo 森野繁夫.[14] Bibliographic evidence for a conflation of the *Ssj* and its sequel (or really sequels)

9. See *Cxj*, 28.681 and 29.715 where passages from j. 5, no. 52 and j. 9, no. 98 are cited as *Sshj*, as well as *Cxj*, 29.712 where a passage from j. 9, no. 100 is cited as *Sōushén jì*. (Ordinal numbers given for passages refer to entries in the received *Sshj* according to their order in the *Xuéjīn tǎoyuán* edition. Following the example of Wāng Shàoyíng's edition of the *Sshj* [Beijing: Zhonghua shuju, 1981], I have used this system to organize the translation and will give the number when referring to passages in the present *Sshj*.)

10. *Tpgj*, 443.3314.

11. See *Cxj*, 28.674. Also refer to j. 1, no. 5, n. 18 below.

12. See *Cxj*, 1.21 (*Sshj* j. 5, no. 55), 2.38 (*Sshj* j. 7, no. 78), 25.608 (*Sshj* j. 9, no. 105), and 26.638 (*Sshj* j. 6, no. 77).

13. See *Sshj* no. 52 (j. 5) cited in *Fyzl*, 78.3b–4, and no. 55 (j. 5) cited in *Fyzl*, 59.17b and *Ywlj*, 2.81.

14. My understanding of the transmission of the text at this point is very much indebted to the work of these two Japanese scholars. See Morino, "*Sōjinkōki* no tsūkōbon" 搜神後記の通行本, *Shinagaku kenkyū* 27 (1962): 17–26; Toyoda, "*Sojinki, Sojinkoki* genryuko" 搜神記搜神後記源流考, *Toho gakuho* 12.3 (1941): 43–66. For a translation of Toyoda's study into Chinese, see Yí Ān

can be found shortly after the Táng, when we have listings for a ten-*juàn Sōushén zǒngjì* 總記 (Combined Records of Collected Spirit Phenomena) in *Chóngwén zǒngmù* 崇文總目 and later in the *Sòng shǐ* 宋史 "Yìwén zhì" 藝文志.[15] Separate listings for *Ssj*, *Sshj*, or *Xssj* cannot be found in these catalogues or others contemporary with them. Toyoda and Morino, through detailed comparisons of the contents of the received text of the *Ssj* with that of the *Sshj* and with *lèishū* citations of both texts, were able to confirm that such a conflation did occur. Morino then went one step further and examined the process through which the present texts were later reconstructed on the basis of the conflation and *lèishū* citations. Since an understanding of the confusion of the *Ssj* with its sequel and the process of reconstruction that took place in the wake of that confusion helps explain the form of the present *Sshj*, we will briefly summarize Morino's main arguments.

Morino first establishes that the received text is not a direct descendant of an 'original text' (*genbon* 原本). He comes to this conclusion as the result of two observations: One, there are at least nine citations of the *Xssj* in the *lèishū* for which no counterpart can be found in the *Sshj*.[16] Two, a comparison of the content of the received entries with their *lèishū* versions shows a great deal of variation and that in some cases it is the *Sshj* stories that are the least detailed.[17] Hence, he says that the more terse entries are "abridged citations from various texts which were edited in at some point during the formation of the received text."[18] Moreover, since all Sòng and earlier references to the contents of the *Sshj* are to the *Xssj*, with the exception of only a very few, the text could only have appeared in its present form after the Sòng.

頤安, "*Soushen ji, Soushen houji* yuanliukao," *Zhōnghé yuèkān* 3.5 (1942): 40–51 and 3.6 (1942): 45–57. For a full examination of the textual history of the *Sōushén jì*, see Kenneth J. DeWoskin, "The 'Sou-shen-chi' and the 'Chih-kuai' Tradition: A Bibliographic and Generic Study" (PhD diss., Columbia Univ., 1974).

15. See Wáng Yáochén 王堯臣 (1011–1056), ed., *Chóngwén zǒngmù* (N.p.: *Yuèyǎtáng cóngshū*, 1824), 3.37a; *Sòng shǐ*, comp. Tuō Tuō 脫脫 (1313–1355), et al. (Beijing: Zhonghua shuju, 1977), 206.5219. Wáng Yáochén's listing indicates that the authorship of this collection is not given and that though some attribute it to Gān Bǎo, that is incorrect. The *Sòng shǐ* lists the collection under Gān Bǎo's authorship without reservation. (Note: The editors of the *Sòng shǐ* "Yìwén zhì" explain, in 202.5033, that they consulted the *Chóngwén zǒngmù* in compiling the bibliography. Hence, their entry for a *Sōushén zǒngjì* may simply repeat that of Wáng Yáochén.)

16. Here and following, all references to the *Sshj* mean the received text. Because of the overwhelming correspondence between the *Sshj* and the *Xssj*, which we noted above, Morino deals with the text referred to as *Xù Sōushén jì* in early citations as the prototype (i.e., the *genbon*) for the present *Sshj*. Wáng Guóliáng 王國良 in his edition has identified a full eighteen of these citations, which include Morino's nine plus nine others. See Wáng Guóliáng, *Sōushén hòujì yánjiū* 搜神後記研究 (Taibei: Wenshizhe chubanshe, 1978), 17, 123–32.

17. Morino specifically compares no. 76 (j. 6) with *Fyzl*, 76.11a–b, and no. 98 (j. 9) with *Tpgj*, 443.3314.

18. Morino, "*Sōjinkōki* no tsūkōbon," 19.

Morino then goes on to observe that there is a striking amount of confusion and duplication between the entries in the present *Ssj* and *Sshj* (as the *Xssj*) and the identification of citations from those entries in the Sòng *lèishū*.[19] He found:

1. From the *Sshj*,
   A) tweve found identified as both *Xssj* and as *Ssj* in various citations;[20]
   B) eight only found cited as *Ssj*.[21]
2. From the *Ssj*,
   A) three found identified as both *Xssj* and as *Ssj* in various citations;[22]
   B) three only found cited as *Xss*j.[23]
3. From both the *Sshj* and the *Ssj*,
   A) four found identified as both *Xssj* and as *Ssj* in various citations;[24]
   B) one found cited only as *Xssj*.[25]

Hence, Morino concurs with Toyoda's conclusion that "the original text [*genbon*] upon which the *Tpyl* and the *Tpgj* depended was something that in content rather notably overlapped both the *Ssj* and the *Sshj*, and also it is likely that later hands added emendations and the overlapping portions were deleted."[26]

Such extensive overlap does not show up in the *lèishū* from the early Táng, despite the fact that there are plenty of citations in texts from that period. This would seem to indicate that the division between the *Ssj* and the *Xssj* is much more clearcut prior to the Sòng. Morino concludes that a conflated text combining parts of the *Ssj* and the *Xssj* had appeared by the Sòng, citing the *Chóngwén zǒngmù* and *Sòng shǐ* listings for a *Sōushén zǒngjì* as affirmation of this possibility.

Comparing different Sòng *lèishū* citations of the same story under different titles, *Ssj* and *Xssj*, Morino finds significant variation in their content. From this variation, he demonstrates that the *lèishū* could not have been the sole source for the reconstruction of the present texts, some form of the conflated text must also have been used, and that

19. By Sòng *lèishū*, Morino is referring for the most part to *Tpyl* and *Tpgj*.

20. *Sshj* j. 2, nos. 12, 23, 24; j. 5, no. 55; j. 6, no. 62; j. 7, no. 86; j. 8, no. 94; j. 9, nos. 98, 106; j. 10, nos. 113, 115, 117. For the specific locations of the various citations, please consult Morino, "*Sōjinkōki* no tsūkōbon," 20–21, or Wāng Shàoyíng's editions of the *Sshj* and the *Ssj*.

21. *Sshj* j. 3, no. 38; j. 5, nos. 49, 53; j. 6, no. 69; j. 7, nos. 78, 79; j. 8, no. 88; j. 9, no. 109.

22. *Ssj* j. 10, no. 262; j. 16, no. 379; j. 18, no. 428. (Numbering follows Wāng Shàoyíng's *Ssj* [Beijing: Zhonghua shuju, 1979]; all following references to the *Ssj* will be to this edition.)

23. *Ssj* j. 1, no. 26; j. 10, no. 261; j. 20, no. 460.

24. *Sshj* j. 2, no. 22; j. 5, no. 52; j. 6, nos. 60, 61.

25. *Sshj* j. 4, no. 48.

26. Toyoda, "*Sojinki, Sojinkoki* genryuko", 57. Morino differs with Toyoda's use of *genbon* here. He feels that by the Sòng the continued existence of an intact prototype (his understanding of *genbon*) is very much in doubt. But I believe Toyoda is simply using the term here to refer to the text or texts that the Sòng *lèishū* were citing from, without presumption as to their status as prototypes.

the *lèishū* citations were citing from more than one source for the *Sōushén* texts.[27] But in all cases where they cited the conflated text, the entry was cited as *Ssj*.[28]

Morino maintains that by the time the *Tpgj* and the *Tpyl* were compiled, the *Xssj* was already lost, and all citations attributed to the *Xssj* in the Sòng *lèishū* are thus from secondary sources. Whether this is true or not, it is clear that in the situation where all entries from the conflated text are cited *Ssj*, those entries in the Sòng sources that are identified as *Xssj* would be from the *Xssj* originally, even if they were cited as from the *Ssj* elsewhere in Sòng period sources. Moreover, if later reconstruction was based partially on the conflated text, or a remnant thereof, then it would be only natural that a *Xssj* entry surviving in the *Sshj* or the *Ssj* would more closely match even that cited in the Sòng *lèishū* as *Ssj*, because that entry in any case would have originated in the conflated text.[29]

Finally, Morino compares the duplicates between received texts of the *Ssj* and the *Sshj*. Examining *Sshj* j. 5, no. 52 and j. 6, no. 61, he finds that pre-Sòng *lèishū* list both as *Xssj* but that there are Sòng *lèishū* citations for each under both *Ssj* and *Xssj*.[30] This means that the Sòng *lèishū* cited these two from the conflated text as *Ssj* and similar entries identified as *Xssj* are from secondary sources. Yet significantly, the early *Fyzl* citation for each (cited *Xssj*) are quite detailed and match the received *Ssj* version closely whereas the *Sshj* versions are much more terse. This indicates that, in deciding whether an entry in the conflated text they had (in whatever form it was) should be *Ssj* or *Sshj* when that text was identified as both among various *lèishū*, those reconstructing the *Ssj* made a decision based on the completeness of the entry in question. The more complete story was placed in the *Ssj* even if an early Táng source had identified it otherwise. Later,

27. For example, *Sshj* j. 7, no. 86 has the *lèishū* citations *Tpgj*, 319.2354 (as *Xssj*) and *Tpgj*, 438.3264 (as *Ssj*). Neither of these matches the received *Sshj* exactly and the one that comes closest is the one cited as *Ssj*. If the editors had been using the *Tpgj* in their reconstruction of the *Sshj*, the entry cited *Xssj* should match the present *Sshj*. But it does not. So there must have been a third source, Morino concludes, and this third source would be the conflated *Ssj-Xssj*. Refer also to *Sshj* j. 4, no. 48, n. 109.

28. For instance, see *Sshj* j. 6, no. 61, n. 141. Also compare the circumstances surrounding j. 5, no. 52, n. 120.

29. As we see in the example cited in n. 27 above. Among other examples Morino points out, is *Ssj* no. 428 (j. 18) found cited in *Tpyl* 909.4031 as *Ssj* and in *Tpyl* 32.153 as *Xssj*. The present *Ssj* version is virtually an exact duplicate of the *Tpyl* entry cited *Ssj* but the entry cited *Xssj* is a bit longer and slightly variant in detail. So, Morino argues ("*Sōjinkōki* no tsūkōbon," 24) although the story was originally found in the *Xssj*, a fact confirmed by a citation of this entry also as *Xssj* in Chén Yuánliàng's 陳元靚 (n.d.; of the Sòng) *Suìshí guǎngjì* 歲時廣記 (*Cóngshū jíchéng chūbiān* 叢書集成初編 edn.) (Shanghai: Shangwu yinshuguan, 1929), 36.399. It was cited as the *Ssj* in *Tpyl*, and later found its way into the received *Ssj*, in both cases by virtue of its inclusion in the conflated text. However, it is plausible, to take issue with Morino on this example, that there were actually two versions of this story circulating. If that had been the case, the above circumstance could have occurred whether there was a conflation text or not.

30. These correspond to *Ssj* j. 5, no. 95 and j. 6, no. 397, respectively. Consult Morino's study and Wāng Shàoyíng for locations of specific *lèishū* citations.

when the *Sshj* was reconstructed, a terse entry cited in some other source was then chosen to avoid duplication with the *Ssj*.[31]

Out of this analysis, then, comes Morino's conclusion:

> The received edition of the *Sshj* was essentially compiled from the stories of the *Xssj* that had been mixed into a conflated edition of the *Ssj* and the *Xssj*, supplemented with *Xssj* entries from the Táng and Sòng *lèishū*, divided into ten *juàn* following the *Suí shū* "Jīngjí zhì," and assigned the designation "Táo Qián's *Sōushén hòujì*."[32]

Hence, Morino's analysis makes clear that behind the formation of the existing *Sshj* text was a confused and circuitous process that can be traced only on the basis of individual entries in the text. If verification of authenticity and origin for any given section of the *Sshj* is to be at all accurate and useful with regard to the historical context of that specific section, such verification must be undertaken individually for each entry in question.[33] But, as Morino explains in his conclusion, we can generalize a few main points concerning the transmission of the book as a whole up to the Sòng: One, the bulk of the text was in origin material gathered under the title *Xù Sōushén jì*. Two, much of the contents of this once autonomous *Xssj* text was eventually preserved only in various Táng and Sòng *lèishū*. Yet three, some of the material seems to have been transmitted directly, though most likely in a form that allowed it to be confused with the *Ssj* during the Sòng, i.e., transmitted by means of what Morino has termed the 'conflation text' (*gōhen* 合篇).

It should be noted that in its broad features, the history of the *Sshj* looks quite similar to that of the *Ssj*. DeWoskin has concluded that "a large part if not all of the 20C SSC [i.e. 20 *juàn Sōushén jì*] appears to have been lost and then reclaimed from other books, and that many of its stories were possibly not part of the original *Sou-shen-chi* at all."[34] Yet he observed "there are indications that a certain core of material was in fact transmitted directly."[35] On the whole, DeWoskin's findings on the transmission of the *Ssj* do not conflict with the above conclusions concerning the *Sshj*.

At some point after the Sòng, the text we have today took form. Since the earliest and best editions of the *Sshj* are all found together with the *Ssj*, it seems likely that the

---

31. Wāng Shàoyíng has made a similar observation. See his notes to *Sshj* j. 2, no. 22; j. 5, no. 52; j. 6, no. 61.

32. Morino, "*Sōjinkōki* no tsūkōbon," 26. Wáng Guóliáng has also observed tremendous confusion in the identification of *lèishū* citations from the *Ssj* and the *Xssj* as well as the frequent contradictions between the present *Ssj* and *Sshj* and between both texts and the *lèishū*. Beyond blaming the compilers of the present text for a lax attitude, however, he does not draw any general conclusions concerning the reason for this confusion. See his *Sōushén hòujì yánjiū*, 19.

33. Wáng Guóliáng has done so for forty-one cases where the source—*Ssj* or *Xssj*—is uncertain. Twenty-nine of these cases concern entries found in the *Sshj*. See *Sōushén hòujì yánjiū*, 19–27.

34. DeWoskin, "'Sou-shen-chi'," 134.

35. DeWoskin, "'Sou-shen-chi'," 87.

recension of the *Sshj* text closely parallels that of the *Ssj*.[36] It would thus seem proper to briefly review the presumed circumstances of the recension of the *Ssj*.[37]

What appears to be the earliest witness to the present form of the *Ssj* (and here I assume of the *Sshj* as well) is Hú Yīnglín's 胡應麟 (fl. 1590) discussion of the *Ssj* text with his friend Yáo Shúxiáng 姚叔祥 (n.d.). Yáo had discovered the text in Hú's library catalogue and was delighted to find that this text did in fact exist. When Yáo questioned Hú about it, Hú cautioned that "this is merely copied from among the *Fǎyuàn* [*zhūlín*], [*Tàipíng*] *yùlǎn*, *Yìwén* [*lèijù*], *Chūxué* [*jí*], and the [*Běitáng*] *shūchāo*."[38] So though he does not say so directly, Hú Yīnglín himself might very well have undertaken the reconstruction.[39] But whether it was Hú or someone else it seems almost certain that the text he is discussing here is the one that was collected in *Mìcè huìhán*, the earliest extant edition of both the *Ssj* and the *Sshj*.[40] Yáo Shúxiáng was involved in the editing process of this collection, and it is probable that through his introduction the *Ssj*—and the *Sshj*, which must have been appended to it—found its way into the hands of the principal editors.[41]

Unfortunately the editors of the *Mìcè huìhán*, Hú Zhènhēng 胡震亨 (*jǔrén* 1597) and Shěn Shìlóng 沈士龍 (n.d.), mention nothing concerning the source of the texts in their prefaces to the *Ssj*. As far as concerns the *Sshj* they do no more than question the authenticity of the text and the attribution to Táo Qián on the basis of details in the contents,

36. This appears to have been first suggested only recently by Lǐ Jiànguó 李剑国 in his *Táng qián zhìguài xiǎoshuō shǐ* 唐前志怪小说史 (Tianjin: Nankai daxue chubanshe, 1984), 345. The editions I am referring to here are the *Mìcè huìhán* 祕册彙函 and the *Jīndài mìshū* 津逮秘書.

37. My review here is based on the more complete discussions of the recension that can be found in Fàn Níng 范宁, "Guānyú *Sōushén jì*" 关于《搜神記》, *Wénxué pínglùn* 1964.1: 86–92; DeWoskin, "'Sou-shen-chi'," 73–87, 180–92; and Lǐ Jiànguó, *Táng qián zhìguài xiǎoshuō shǐ*, 279–90.

38. Hú Yīnglín's recollection of the conversation is preserved in his *Jiǎyǐ shèngyán* 甲乙剩言, *Bǎoyántáng mìjí* 寶顏堂秘笈 edn. (n.p.: Wenming shuju, 1922), 16a. Yáo Shúxiáng also recorded the conversation, see his *Jiànzhībiān* 見只編, in *Yányì zhìyán* 鹽邑志言, ed. Fán Wéichéng 樊維城 (*jìnshì* 1616) (Shanghai: Shangwu yinshuguan, 1937), B.10b–11a.

39. Fàn Níng believes that it was Hú, see his "Guānyú *Sōushén jì*," 90–91. DeWoskin ("'Sou-shen-chi'," 188–90) doubts Hú had the resources to do so. But there is no concrete basis on which to prove that Hú, a richly endowed bibliophile, was at all lacking in the necessary resources to undertake a recension. Nor should it be considered that Fàn Níng was accusing Hú of trickery, as DeWoskin seems to imply, for Fàn Níng surely knew well that Hú would not have had any compunction in reconstructing the text—especially if he was saving a lost book by means of what remained of it in other sources. Nor did Hú claim that the book was anything other than what it clearly appears to be: largely a collection of passages preserved in *lèishū*.

40. Convenient and easily available reprints of the *Mìcè huìhán* editions of the *Ssj* and the *Sshj* has been published by Wáng Yúnwǔ 王雲五, et al. (*Cóngshū jíchéng chūbiān* edn.) (Shanghai: Shangwu yinshuguan, 1936).

41. Fàn Níng, "Guānyú *Sōushén jì*," 91. On Yao Shuxiang's connection with the *Mìcè huìhán* and its editors, see DeWoskin, "'Sou-shen-chi'," 74, 188.

albeit a valid argument.[42] This leaves the whole matter of the origin of the recension upon which the present texts are based still shrouded in heavy uncertainty, though the fact that Shěn and Hú mention both the *Ssj* and the *Sshj* in the same preface is a further clue that the transmission of both texts is closely connected at this point. How, when, and why the title *Sōushén hòujì*, as well as the consequent attribution to Táo Qián, was attached to the recension of what is for the most part a text that was called *Xù Sōushén jì* also remains a glaring question.

In conclusion, all we can be certain of is that the *Sshj* we have today is a reconstruction probably made in the Míng of material gathered from various sources that can, for the most part, be traced along one path or another back to the *Xssj*, a text with no connection to Táo Qián.[43] Though there is no direct bibliographic evidence dating the *Xssj* to the Six Dynasties, there can be little doubt that it was compiled prior to the Táng and that most of the material it contained originated in the Six Dynasties. This is demonstrated by the extensive duplication and similarity of material found in the collection with material from the *Ssj* and many other texts from that period.[44] The narrative style of the *Sshj* also confirms that the text is from the Six Dynasties, a fact first pointed out by the editors of the *Sìkù quánshū zǒngmù*.[45]

Besides the *Mìcè huìhán*, the only other complete surviving edition of the *Sshj* is the *Jīndài mìshū* edition and the latter is a copy of the former.[46] Except for minor copy variants, and the addition of one story (j. 4, no. 48), Zhāng Hǎipéng's 張海鵬 (1755–1816) *Xuéjīn tǎoyuán* 學津討源 Qīng edition of the *Sshj* is identical to the *Mìcè huìhán* edition and is the base text used for this translation.

---

42. The *Mìcè huìhán* preface is also preserved in Máo Jìn's 毛晉 (1594–1659) *Jīndài mìshū* edition of the *Ssj* and *Sshj*. For a discussion of the preface as it pertains to the *Ssj*, see DeWoskin, "'Sou-shen-chi'," 75–79. Concerning Shěn Shìlóng's discussion of the *Sshj*, see the *Sìkù quánshū zǒngmù tíyào* 四庫全書總目提要 entry for the text, which is translated in Appendix 1.

43. See Table 1 for an outline of the history and genealogy of the *Sshj* described in this discussion.

44. This evidence is overwhelming and there is no need to discuss it here. Wāng Shàoyǐng's and Wáng Guóliáng's editions of the *Sshj* contain complete collations of the surviving duplicated material for each *Sshj* entry and the locations in other texts.

45. See the discussion of the style of the *Sshj* in the following section.

46. For a complete list of extant texts of the *Sshj*, the reader may consult Lǐ Jiànguó, *Táng qián zhìguài xiǎoshuō shǐ*, 345; as well as Yán Màoyuán 嚴懋垣, "Wèi Jìn Nánběi cháo zhìguài xiǎoshuō shūlù fù kǎozhèng" 魏晉南北朝志怪小說書錄附考證, *Wénxué niánbào* 6 (1940): 51, and Fù Xīhuá 傅惜華, "Liùcháo zhìguài xiǎoshuō zhī cúnyì" 六朝志怪小說知存逸. *Hànxué* 1 (1944): 183–85.

Table 1. The Genealogy of the *Sōushén hòujì*: Witnesses and Possible Sources

	Sōushén lù	*Sōushén jì*	*Sōushén hòujì*	*Xù Sōushén jì*	*Sōushén zǒngjì*	(Gān Bǎo's *Sōushén jì*)
Six Dynasties	Huìjiǎo's preface to *Gāo sēng zhuàn** (and Wáng Mànyǐng's letter*)					
Suí		Xiāo Jí's *Wǔxíng jì** (in *Tpgj*)				
Táng	Listings of Dào Xuān* and Fǎ Lín*	*Cxj**	*Suí shū* "Jīng jí zhì"* *Cxj** Fujiwara Sukeyo's Listing*	*Btsc* *Ywlj* *Fyzl* *Cxj*		
Sòng				*Tpgj* *Tpyl* *Slf*	(Possible conflation appears) *Chóngwén zǒngmù*	
Yuán					*Sòng shǐ* "Yì wén zhì"	
Míng			*Mìcè huìhán** *Jìndài mìshū**			
Qīng			*Xuéjīn tǎoyuán** *Sìkù zǒngmù* (other editions)			

*Attributes authorship to Táo Qián (365–427)

CHAPTER 2

Characterizing the *Sōushén hòujì*

The preceding discussion of the history of the text has helped us to begin to identify the *Sshj* by examining its historical origins. It is now necessary to pursue its identity in terms of the character of the text itself. Below we shall discuss the *Sshj* with regard to its nature (or form), technique (or style), and contents (or subject matter).

2.1. THE *SŌUSHÉN HÒUJÌ* AS A *ZHÌGUÀI* TEXT

We might well begin by asking what genre the *Sshj* belongs to. In the orderly schemes of twentieth-century histories of Chinese literature, it is considered to be in the genre *zhìguài* 志怪 ('recorded anomalies') under the broader generic category *xiǎoshuō* 小說 ('minor narratives').[1] Though these are probably the most satisfactory genre designations for the *Sshj*, it is important to keep in mind that the formal assignment of the *Sshj* and related texts to the *zhìguài* and *xiǎoshuō* genres came well after the Six Dynasties, the period in which most *zhìguài xiǎoshuō* ('minor narratives recording anomalies') were produced.

The earliest identification of the *Sshj* as a *xiǎoshuō* was not until the Qīng when it was classified among *xiǎoshuō* in the *Sì kù quánshū zǒng mù* and it was not identified as a *zhìguài* until the twentieth century in Lǔ Xùn's *Zhōngguó xiǎoshuō shǐlüè*.[2] As

1. See, for example, Yóu Guóēn 游国恩, et al., *Zhōngguó wénxuéshǐ* 中国文学史 (Beijing: Renmin wenxue chubanshe, 1980), 297–98; and Lǔ Xùn 魯迅, *Zhōngguó xiǎoshuō shǐlüè* 中國小說史略, 1923, rpt. from Taiwan (n.p., n.d.) [hereafter Lǔ Xùn, *Shǐlüè*], 47–52. The term *xiǎoshuō* is now used as an equivalent for the modern English word 'fiction'. But this Chinese term has been invested with the full implications of the English only in recent times and to translate it as such is misleading in historical discussions.

2. See *Sìkù quánshū zǒngmù tíyào*, 139.2946; and Lǔ Xùn, *Shǐlüè,* 51. Other Six Dynasty works now classified as *zhìguài*, including the *Ssj*, were listed as *xiǎoshuō* earlier, but not until the Sòng, in the "Yìwén zhì" 藝文誌 of Ōuyáng Xiū's 歐陽修 (1007–1072) *Xīn Táng shū* 新唐書 (Beijing: Zhonghua shuju, 1975), 59.1539–43. See Chéng Yìzhōng 程毅中, ed., *Gŭ xiǎoshuō jiānmù* 古小說間目 (Beijing: Zhonghua shuju, 1981), 1–7. The term *zhìguài* did not become clearly established as a generic designation until the publication of Lǔ Xùn's *Shǐlüè,* though it was used to describe certain *xiǎoshuō* as early as the Táng in Duàn Chéngshì's 段成式 (d. 863) preface to his *Yǒuyáng zázŭ* 酉陽雜俎 and further refined in that role during the Míng by Hú Yīnglín in the third j. of "Jiŭ liú xù lùn" 九流緒論, in his *Shǎoshì shānfáng bǐcóng* 少室山房筆叢 (Beijing: Zhōnghuà, 1958), 374. The history of the term *xiǎoshuō* as a generic designation is much older and still more complex. For comprehensive surveys of both terms in Chinese literary history, see Lǐ Jiànguó, *Táng qián zhìguài xiǎoshuō shǐ*, 1–11, and Tán Fèngliáng 谈凤樑, "Shìlùn Zhōngguó gŭdài xiǎoshuō gàiniàn de yǎnbiàn" 试论中国古代小说概念的演变, *Wenyi luncong* 10 (1980): 67–93. Also see Chéng Yìzhōng (as cited above); and DeWoskin, "'Sou-shen-chi'," 193–259.

such, the designations are descriptive and there can be no assumption that the authors of *zhìguài* intentionally created works to fit within the *zhìguài xiǎoshuō* genre as it is known today. For this reason, our examination of the *Sshj* cannot be limited to evaluating the work as a representative of the pre-defined type, but must include a close inspection of the *Sshj* to see how it serves to outline and illustrate what are now classified as *zhìguài xiǎoshuō*. This is true for other reasons also, as our attempt to delineate the *zhìguài* genre will presently show.

A glance at the contents of the *Sshj* and other Six Dynasties *zhìguài* reveals that they are composed of discrete stories or anecdotes. Lǐ Jiànguó has outlined three categories that characterize the sources for the stories and anecdotes found in the *zhìguài* as part of his attempt to flesh out the nature of the genre as a whole:

> One, myths and legends that had already taken form during the primitive stages of various peoples which later continued to be transmitted and moreover which continued to be enriched in content; two, superstitious and religious traditions concerning supernatural beings, calamities, divination, dream prognostication, *yīn-yáng* theory and five phases theory; three, fantastic folklore about geographical and [other] natural phenomenon.[3]

Broad as this description may seem, it in fact leaves much out. For example, the *zhìguài* also often contain anecdotes about historical persons, which are many times fantastic but which do not fit neatly into any of the three categories Lǐ Jiànguó outlined. In the *Sshj*, these make up a substantial portion of the contents. Hence, Lǐ's description may actually be too narrow. Indeed, without producing an encyclopedic laundry list, it may be impossible to describe definitely all that can be found in the *zhìguài*. Kenneth DeWoskin tells us:

> In the corpus of surviving examples of *chih-kuai* writing, one finds everything from a one-line comment on a hedgehog to long and carefully structured stories, complete with elaborating description, love poetry, and the "telling" presence of the narrator. As a genre, the *chih-kuai* is difficult to delineate. Bibliographies seem inclined to include in the *chih-kuai* any narrative items that simply did not fit well elsewhere. The amount of writing transmitted from the Six Dynasties is substantial, but far from infinite.

3. Lǐ Jiànguó, *Táng qián zhìguài xiǎoshuō shǐ*, 17. Several studies have been done that discuss most aspects of the genre much more thoroughly than can be done here, where we attempt only to provide a general outline as a basis for our examination of the *Sshj*. Besides Lǐ Jiànguó and DeWoskin, the reader may consult the *zhìguài* bibliographies by Yán Màoyuán and Fù Xīhuá. In addition, see Kenneth J. DeWoskin's more recent work "The Six Dynasties *Chih-kuai* and the Birth of Fiction," in *Chinese Narrative: Critical and Theoretical Essays*, ed. Andrew H. Plaks (Princeton: Princeton Univ. Press, 1977), 21–52; Karl S. Y. Kao, *Classical Chinese Tales of the Supernatural and the Fantastic* (Bloomington: Indiana Univ. Press, 1985), 1–21; and Lawrence Chapin Foster, "The *Shih-i chi* and Its Relationship to the Genre Known as *Chih-kuai hsiao-shuo*" (PhD diss., Univ. of Washington, 1974).

> There is nonetheless, no consensus whatsoever on exactly what works lie with in the boundaries of the *chih-kuai* genre.[4]

It seems clear that the genre designated '*zhìguài*' cannot be easily identified by definition but rather must be discerned through an examination of the works that are generally accepted as representatives of the genre. The *Sshj* is one work that most studies mention when discussing texts central to the *zhìguài* and thus serves well to illustrate them.

2.2. THE HISTORICAL NATURE OF THE *SŌUSHÉN HÒUJÌ*

The earliest listing for the *Sshj*, in the *Suí shū* "Monograph on Literature," well before the text was gathered up among the works known as *zhìguài xiǎoshuō*, classified it among the *zázhuàn* 雜傳 ('miscellaneous biographies') in the history section (*shǐ bù* 史部). The *Sshj* is found there together with many other works now classified as *zhìguài*.[5] This listing is significant because it is closest in time to when the *Sshj* and other *zhìguài* were actually produced—hence, possibly a more accurate reflection of how they were conceived of in their own time.

In their brief discussion of the works listed in this section, which includes Gān Bǎo's *Ssj* and Liú Yìqìng's 劉義慶 (403–444) *Yōumíng lù* 幽明錄 as well as the *Sshj* and many others, the editors of the "Monograph on Literature" concede that all contain "empty, baseless, strange, and nonsensical narrative." They add however, that they "surmise their original sources were probably leftover bits of trivia [collected by] the historian's office out of which writers selected the more important pieces."[6] For this reason they included them among the *zázhuàn* in the history section.

The *Suí shū* editor's sense was clearly that the *Sshj* and the other works listed were primarily of an historical interest, and that despite their often farfetched content, emphasizing all aspects of supernatural beliefs, they had been deemed worthy of preservation by earlier writers. This was probably because, as Shigezawa Toshio 重澤俊朗 has suggested, Six Dynasties historians often believed that ghostly and anomalous events in the supernatural realm had a direct impact on events in the world of men and so were worthy of preservation just like any other kind of history.[7]

---

4. DeWoskin, "Six Dynasties *Chih-kuai*," 22.
5. See *Suí shū*, 33.980.
6. *Suí shū*, 33.982.
7. See Shigezawa, "Bunken mokuroku o tsujite mita rikuchō no rekishi ishiki" 文獻目錄を通して見た六朝の歴史意識, *Toyōshi-kenkyū* 18 (1959): 11. We assume here that the main task of the Chinese historian at that time was to document and maintain a record of what was considered significant out of all that took place in the human realm. The human realm had been considered to include the supernatural from very early on. For according to Lǐ Jiànguó, offices of records and history undertook the observation and recording of myth, legend, superstition and manifestations of supernatural as well as natural phenomenon even well before the Former Hàn (206 BCE–23 CE), by which time such activities were actually established practice.

The author of the largest and most widely known *zhìguài* collection, Gān Bǎo, had been a historian in the Eastern Jìn court and besides his now lost *Jìn jì* 晉紀 also wrote the *Sōushén jì* in that capacity. His preface explains that he undertook the *Ssj* in the tradition of scholars of history, and moreover, that what he recorded therein is "sufficient to express and make clear that the way of the spirits is not false."[8] It is impossible to know whether the situations of most other *zhìguài* writers are accurately reflected by the single fairly well preserved example that Gān Bǎo represents, nor is there a preface or other external evidence that provides any direct clues to the underlying impetus behind the compilation of the *Sshj*.[9] The lack of any concrete evidence concerning the actual authorship of the bulk of the *Sshj* further clouds the picture. But to read through the stories contained in this text tends to verify the connection of *zhìguài* with the historian's profession suggested by the *Suí shū* "Monograph on Literature" and by Gān Bǎo's preface.[10]

The majority of the anecdotes are set in real, identifiable time frames. When a location is given, it is in most cases a historically identifiable place. Quite often the stories center on characters who were actual historical persons for whom there are still records—most of the other unidentifiable names were probably actual people as well, there is just no longer any way of verifying their existence. The great majority of the entries start out in the formulaic manner of the historian, usually stating the 'when', 'where', and 'who' of the anecdote right in the first sentence. There is nothing to disprove the characterization that the entries are "the leftover bits of trivia of the historian's office." The only easily discernable qualitative difference between what is found in the *Sshj* and the more standard histories is the difference between the minor narrative (*xiǎoshuō*) and history as described by Wáng Yáo 王瑤: With history writing, the focus is purely on the people involved, whereas with *xiǎoshuō* (by which Wáng was really referring to the *zhìguài*), the focus is on the strange nature of the events and incidents the people were involved in.[11]

It may be argued that the farfetched and implausible nature of the stories disqualifies them as history. Perhaps this is true from a modern perspective, but the supernatural and fantastic that they depict was taken seriously by many historians and others in the Six

8. The preface is preserved in *Jìn shū* 晉書, comp. Fáng Xuánlíng 房玄齡 (578–648) et al. (Beijing: Zhonghua shuju, 1975), 82.2150–51. For a complete translation, see DeWoskin, "Six Dynasties *Chih-kuai*," 32–33.

9. A succinct investigation of the general motivation behind the compilation of the Six Dynasties *zhìguài* collections can be found in Kao, *Classical Chinese Tales*, 16–27.

10. Besides Gān Bǎo, there are other well known Six Dynasty period authors associated with the historian's office known to have been interested in the supernatural and contemporary occult practices, including Guō Pú 郭璞 (276–324) and Zhāng Huá 張華 (232–300). See Wú Hóngyī 吳宏一, "Liù cháo guǐshén guàiyì xiǎoshuō yǔ shídài bèijǐng de guānxì" 六朝鬼神怪異小說與時代背景的關係, *Xiàndài wénxué* 44 (1971): 43. DeWoskin ("Six Dynasties *Chih-kuai*," 21–52) discusses the relationship between the Six Dynasties historian and the *zhìguài* in general.

11. See Wáng Yáo, "Xiǎoshuō yǔ fāngshù" 小說與方術, in *Zhōnggǔ wénxuéshǐ lùnjí* 中古文學史論集 (Shanghai: Gudian wenxue chubanshe, 1956), 109.

Dynasties. Gān Bǎo, for one, appears to have believed in the existence of the supernatural, the "way of the spirits," so abundantly illustrated in his *Ssj*. He was not alone.

From early in the Hàn there had been a strong interest among intellectuals and the ruling elite in the practices and beliefs of the shamans and early Daoists as viable pursuits, whether for immortality or for more profound spiritual needs. These trends became even stronger and more widespread during the time of the Three Kingdoms (220–265) and later in the Jìn, which naturally lead to an increased faith in the occult and supernatural.[12] Jī Kāng 嵇康 (223–262), for instance, is one intellectual whose belief in Daoism is well known. He was also a firm believer in the supernatural.[13] In addition there were many writers from poorer, less elite backgrounds whose convictions concerning the occult and the fantastic were stronger still.[14] Though their names are not known, this kind of person was probably responsible for much of the *zhìguài* writing.

Moreover, even as late as the Táng, the compilers of the *Jìn shū* often did not question the veracity of stories of the type found in the *Sshj*. For example, the *Jìn shū* biographies of Huán Wēn 桓温 (312–373) and his son Huán Xuán 桓玄 (369–404) include versions of the material found in *Sshj* j. 2, no. 16 and j. 3, no. 27.[15] The likelihood that writers from the earlier Six Dynasties period considered these stories plausible is surely greater than for the Táng and later periods and we can assume that many, if not all, did believe them.

It is frequently pointed out that *zhìguài* were often written to promote various schools of religious thought, for instance, by Daoists to promote Daoist practices, by Buddhists to promote Buddhism, or by either Daoists or Buddhists to disparage the other.[16] The *Sshj* does contain entries of a strongly religious tone. But the fact that the stories were written out of religious motivation, or that authorship was falsely attributed to well known persons to make the stories more credible in the eyes of their intended readers, does not, as Wáng Yáo reminds us, invalidate the assertion that their actual authors, known or anonymous, considered them credible representations of reality.[17]

The point here is not to evaluate Six Dynasties history writing but to show that with the *Sshj* and other *zhìguài* we are dealing with collections of anecdotes that were never written as outright fabricated or invented stories but simply as stories in the most basic

---

12. On the relationship of *xiǎoshuō* and *zhìguài* to intellectual trends in the Hàn through the Six Dynasties, besides Wáng Yáo and Wú Hóngyī, cited above, see Fàn Níng 范宁, "Lùn Wèi Jìn zhìguài xiǎoshuō de chuánbò hé zhīshìfēnzǐ sīxiǎng fēnhuà de guānxì" 論魏晉志怪小說的傳播和知識分子思想分化的关系, *Běijīng dàxué xuébaò* 1957.2: 75–88.

13. Fàn Níng, "Lùn Wèi Jìn zhìguài xiǎoshuō," 78.

14. Wú Hóngyī, "Liù cháo guǐshén guàiyì xiǎoshuō," 42.

15. See *Jìn shū* 98.2576 and 99.285. The *Jìn shū* use of what were later considered to be questionable sources is extensive. For further reference, see nn. 2 and 3 in Appendix 1.

16. See, for example, Tán Zhèngbì 譚正壁, *Zhōngguó xiǎoshuō fādá shǐ* 中國小說發達史 (Taipei: Qiye shuju, 1978), 116–30.

17. Wáng Yáo, "Xiǎoshuō yǔ fāngshù," 101–2.

sense of the word: accounts of incidents or events.[18] These accounts, moreover, were recorded for their interest as real, or at least genuinely believed, events or incidents. Though now considered fictional, they have a strong historical character.

The line between fiction and history is, of course, hard to draw. As Robert Scholes reminds us, history is where fiction and fact come together: when the facts of history cease to exist with the passage of time, they become a kind of fiction.[19] What we want to keep in mind here is that while some things are written as fiction from the start, the *zhìguài*, like most histories, were not. Hence, the role that *zhìguài* played in the later development of purer forms of fiction is parallel to that of history. The only difference being that, by emphasizing events that were primarily supernatural and fantastic, they enriched the choice of media that later authors had at their disposal.

This being the case, in order to be properly understood the *Sshj* and other *zhìguài* should not simply be combed for the stories that present the most interesting plot development, the fullest characterization, or other strengths as works of fiction. Though such efforts are valuable in helping to understand the influence of *zhìguài* on the development of later "pure" fiction, their historical tone as narrative records of anomalous events can only be understood by taking a broad look at all the different kinds of stories and anecdotes contained in *zhìguài* collections. Examining them this way will also provide a great deal of insight into the society and culture of the time when the *zhìguài* flourished. Our reading of the *Sshj* shows that this text as a whole displays well the latently historical character of the texts we now classify as *zhìguài*.

Before discussing the actual contents of the *Sshj*, which will bring these facts into sharper focus, we shall briefly turn our attention to its narrative style.

2.3. THE STYLE OF THE *SŌUSHÉN HÒUJÌ*

Most discussions of the *zhìguài* pay little attention to the style and the language they are written in. When they do, it is usually quite cursory, simply noting that they are written in the "classical language."[20] This classification puts the *zhìguài* among the first representatives of quasi-fictional prose narratives written in the *wényán* 文言, or literary, language, later to be followed by the Táng *chuánqí* 傳奇 and then by imitations of the *zhìguài* and *chuánqí* up through the Míng and Qīng.[21] The implication is to leave them excluded from the category generally identified as "vernacular fiction," which did not

18. See *Webster's New Collegiate Dictionary* (Springfield, MA: G. & C. Merriam Company, 1977), 1147.

19. Scholes, *Elements of Fiction* (New York: Oxford Univ. Press, 1968), 2–3.

20. See, for example, Kao, *Classical Chinese Tales*, 1.

21. The most well known representative of the latter being Pú Sōnglíng's 蒲松齡 (1640–1715) *Liáozhāi zhìyì* 聊齋誌異.

flourish until the Sòng and later, and whose earliest representatives are usually thought to be the Táng *biànwén* 變文.[22]

This characterization is essentially correct but it obscures the fact that the so-called classical language did not have a recognized and defined norm until the *gǔwén* movement in the Táng—that is not until the time when the *chuánqí* began to be written—and that the term vernacular is relative with regards to the language and time period in question. The form of language that was vernacular in the Sòng, Míng, or even Qīng is somewhat archaic in the present. At the same time, the language of the pre-Hàn period, the later accepted standard for the classical language, exemplified by, for example, the *Mèngzǐ*, was already to a certain extent archaic as early as the later Hàn. Wáng Chōng 王充 (27–ca. 97) observed that "the language of the present and past is different" and is known to have made a conscious attempt to include the vernacular of his own time in his writing.[23]

It is true that from the perspective of the present day, the language used in most plain narrative works from the Six Dynasties is in a form of classical, or at least ancient, language.[24] Yet while this language is often similar or basically the same as that of the pre-Hàn and early Hàn narrative, it is nevertheless sometimes significantly different from its antecedent.[25] These differences are due to the influence of new trends and usage in the spoken language of the day as they are reflected in the written narrative. Probably because the plain written narrative, even including vernacular elements, was still quite similar to the pre-Hàn language in many aspects, a dichotomy between two forms of written narrative—one classical and the other vernacular—similar to that which arose with the *gǔwén* movement in the Táng and the Sòng did not develop during the Six Dynasties.

Of course the picture is much more complex than we let on here. It is possible, for instance, that the role played by *piánwén* in the Six Dynasties through Táng and that played by *gǔwén* especially after it was well established in the Sòng were opposite sides of the same coin: Just as *piánwén* was something only the well educated could master,

---

22. For a discussion of the history and characteristics of vernacular narrative fiction, see Patrick Hanan, *The Chinese Vernacular Story* (Cambridge, MA: Harvard Univ. Press, 1981), 1–27.

23. See Wáng Chōng, "Zì jì piān" 自紀篇, in his *Lùn héng* 論衡 (Shanghai: Renmin chubanshe, 1974), 30.451. Also see Wáng Lì 王力, *Hànyǔ shǐgǎo* 漢語史稿 (Beijing: Zhonghua shuju, 1982), 2: 354.

24. By 'plain narrative' I refer to the language used for the most part to write the standard and non-standard histories of the period, as Shěn Yuē's 沈約 (441–531) *Sòng shū* 宋書 and Huì Jiǎo's *Gāo sēng zhuàn*, the works generally classified as *zhìguài*, and other treatises on various subjects, as Liú Yìqìng's *Shìshuō xīnyǔ* 世說新語. I exclude from this discussion the elaborate and stylized forms of writing, the *piánwén* 駢文, for example, that were prevalent at the time.

25. The explicit nature of these differences is discussed by Wáng Lì in his *Hànyǔ shǐgǎo* and by Yoshikawa Kōjirō 吉川幸次郎 in "*Seisetsu shingo* no bunshō" 世說新語の文章, in his *Chūgoku sambun ron* 中國散文論 (Tokyo: Chikuma shobū, 1966), 74–99. There is an abridged translation of Yoshikawa's article by Glen W. Baxter; see "The *Shih-shuo hsin-yü* and Six Dynasties Prose Style," *Harvard Journal of Asiatic Studies* 18 (1955): 124–41; rpt. in *Studies in Chinese Literature*, ed. John L. Bishop (Cambridge, MA: Harvard Univ. Press, 19660, 166–83.

gǔwén had to become very different from the spoken language, and thus limited to the domain of the literati, before it could be fully accepted in all circles of the educated elite.

In short then, we can see why the language of the *zhìguài* in general and the *Sshj* in particular is at once both classical and vernacular. Their authors were using the language that they spoke in what they wrote and, hence, their narrative is as vivid and lively as the vernacular of any period. Yet to the eyes of readers centuries later, the works they produced also glow with the patina of the classical language. Understanding this, we know what the Qīng editors of the *Sìkù quánshū tíyào* meant in their entry for the *Sshj* when they said "the diction and style of this book are anciently elegant."[26] They were referring to the plain narrative style of the Six Dynasties in which the *Sshj* is written.

What are some of the characteristics of this style? In one of the rare studies devoted solely to this question, Yoshikawa Kojiro has outlined the essential features of the Six Dynasties plain narrative with his examination of the style of the *Shìshuō xīnyǔ*.[27] Yoshikawa finds that the narrative language of the Six Dynasties, as exemplified by the *Shìshuō xīnyǔ*—but which he notes is also seen in texts such as the *Sǒushén jì* and the *Gāo sēng zhuàn*—is characterized by a prolific use of auxiliary words, or particles ('*jyoji*' 助字).[28] He explains that the heavy use of particles is in contrast to Sīmǎ Qiān's 司馬遷 (145–86 BCE) *Shǐ jì* 史記 or Bān Gù's 班固 (32–92) *Hàn shū* 漢書, which, he maintains, are rather sparing in their use of such auxiliary words. Yoshikawa also points out that by the Six Dynasties many words have new meanings or a different usage when compared to early Hàn and pre-Hàn texts.[29] These changes are due, as noted earlier, to influence from developments in the spoken language and show up most clearly in passages with a lot of direct dialogue, which by their very nature more consciously try to imitate speech. Hence, because the *Shìshuō xīnyǔ* is for the most part a collection of dialogues, it provides the most abundant examples of the Six Dynasties stylistic characteristics Yoshikawa outlined.[30]

Now, we have said that the *Sǒushén hòujì* was also written in this narrative style. Although it is not our point to provide an exhaustive study here of the Six Dynasties

---

26. See Appendix 1.

27. Among the few other studies directly concerned with Six Dynasties grammar and style that I have so far run across is a study on the use of pronouns in the *Ssj*, *Sshj*, and other texts by Ogawa Tamaki 小川環樹, "Koshosetsu no goho: Toku ni ninsho daimeishi oyobi gimon daimeishi no yoho ni tsuite" 古小說の語法：特に人稱代名詞および疑問代名詞の用法について, in *Chūgoku shōsetsu no kenkyu* 中國小說史の研究 (Tokyo: Iwanami shoten, 1968), 274–92. Also see, Zhān Xiùhuì 詹秀惠, "Nánběi cháo zhùshì shū sì zhǒng yǔfǎ yánjiù" 南北朝著釋書四種語法研究 (PhD diss., National Taiwan Univ., 1975).

28. By *jyoji* he is excluding the category of what the Chinese have traditionally called "full words" (*shí zì* 實字), which are mainly nouns, verbs and adjectives, and referring most of all to grammatical particles and adverbs. See Yoshikawa, "*Seisetsu shingo* no bunshō," 77–79.

29. For examples, see Yoshikawa, "*Seisetsu shingo* no bunshō," 77–85.

30. Patrick Hanan, *Chinese Vernacular Story*, 6, also allows that the dialogue in the *Shìshuō xīnyǔ* contains "elements of a distinctive vernacular."

plain narrative, we can demonstrate our claim that it is the style of the *Sshj*, and at the same time provide concrete examples of some of the features we have just alluded to, by turning at this point directly to the text. This will also allow us to confirm that the *Sshj* is made up of material that dates from the Six Dynasties.

In pure classical Chinese, the graph *shì* 是 was used only as a demonstrative pronoun.[31] But by the Six Dynasties it had begun to be used as the copula, similar to the way it is used in modern Chinese.[32] Examples of its use as the copula can be found in the *Sshj*, including:

1) *Wǒ shì Qīngxī mìao zhōng gū.* 我是清溪廟中姑。(j. 5, no. 50)
   'I am a lady of the Qingxi temple'.
2) *Cǐ shì wǒ nǚ.* 此是我女。(j. 6, no. 58)
   'This is my daughter'.
3) *Bèi zhōng rén gāo-zhěn-nán-qǐn zhèng shì qí xíng.* 被中人高枕安寢正是其形。(j. 3, no. 38)
   'The person inside the covers serenely and restfully sleeping was exactly his image'.

This use of *shì* as the copula (usually translated by the verb 'to be') is one feature of Six Dynasties narrative style that sets it apart from pure classical style.

If Yoshikawa's claim is correct that an increased frequency of the use of many particles is a defining feature of Six Dynasties style, this is evident in the *Sshj* as well. We find fairly frequent use of some of the particles that Yoshikawa specifically pointed out, for example, the use of *xiāng* 相 as a reflexive pronoun:

4) *Sì rén yún: Bù xiāng shā.* 四人云：不相殺。(j. 6, no. 66)
   'The four men said, "We won't kill you."'
5) *Xiān yǔ jūn yào xiānsǐzhě xiāng bào, gù lái xiāng yǔ.* 先與君要，先死者相報，故來相語。(j. 6, no. 76)
   'Formerly I made a pact with you that the first to die would report to the other, thus I have come to speak to you'.

The adverb *zhé* 輒, 'always', is also used many times in the text. Examples include:

6) *Jiā zhōng jíxiōng zhé huà zhī.* 家中吉凶輒話之。(j. 4, no. 42)
   '[He] had always talked to her about the good and the bad fortunes of the family'.
7) *Wàngzǐ xīn yǒu suǒ yù, zhé kōngzhōng xià zhī.* 望子心有所欲，輒空中下之。(j. 5, no. 52)

---

31. By 'pure classical Chinese' I refer only to the language (especially the lexicon and grammar) used in pre-Hàn texts, specifically those of the Spring and Autumn and Warring States periods (770–221 BCE).

32. See Wáng Lì, *Zhōngguó yǔfǎ lǐlùn* 中國語法理論 (Beijing: Zhonghua shuju, 1957), 1: 232; and his *Hànyǔ shǐgǎo*, 2: 353–54.

'Whenever Wangzi desired something, she would get it immediately out of thin air'.

8) *Sòng jiǔquán jūn měi Tàishǒu dào guān, wújǐ zhé sǐ.* 宋酒泉君，每太守到官無幾輒死。(j. 9, no. 109)

'During the Sòng, every time a Grand Administrator came to office in Jiǔquán commandery, he would always die in no time'.

And *fù* 復, as an adverb meaning 'again', is frequently found, for instance:

9) *Hǔ qù shù shí bù hūrán fù sòng ér guī.* 虎去數十步忽然復送兒歸。(j. 2, no. 12)

'The tiger went about ten paces then suddenly brought the boy back'.

10) *Fù bù gǎn fù zhuó.* 婦不敢復著。(j. 4, no. 44)

'[His] wife did not dare wear [it] again'.

11) *Shǎoshí fù huán wéi rén.* 少時復還為人。(j. 4, no. 47)

'Shortly, [he] then returned to being a man'.

One adverb particle that seems to have come into frequent use from the Three Kingdoms period and after is *xún* 尋 in the sense of 'shortly'. The *Sshj* provides many examples of this usage, among them:

12) *Xún shī tóng jìng.* 尋失銅鏡。(j. 2, no. 23)

'Soon he was missing a copper mirror'.

13) *Àn guà yán zhī, qīng suǒyàng xún yù.* 案卦言之，卿所恙尋愈。(j. 2, no. 25)

'According to what the hexigram says, your illness will shortly be followed by recovery'.

14) *Qí fū xún yì chū wài.* 其夫尋亦出外。(j. 3, no. 38)

'Her husband soon also went out'.

Another form that came into common usage by the Six Dynasties that was not seen in pure classical Chinese was the class of verbs of completion such as *bì* 畢 or *qì* 訖, meaning 'finished' or 'done'.[33] These are also found in the *Sshj*. Examples include the following:

15) *Xíng xíng jì bì, cǐ rén nǎi yu*è. 行刑既畢，此人乃說。(j. 2, no. 24)

'Once the execution was finished, he was cheerful'.

16) *Jì qì jué guān chū.* 祭訖掘棺出。(j. 3, no. 41)

'When the sacrifice was over, he dug up the coffin'.

17) *Yán qì hūrán bú jiàn.* 言訖忽然不見。(j. 6, no. 76)

'When he finished speaking, he suddenly disappeared'.

---

33. See Mei Tsu-lin [Méi Zǔlín] 梅祖麟, "Xiàndài Hànyǔ wánchéngmào jùshì hé cíwěi de láiyuán" 现代汉语完成貌句式和词尾的来源, *Yǔyán yánjiū* 1 (1981): 68–69, from where we also adopt the term 'verbs of completion' (*wánchéng dòngcí* 完成動詞).

Finally it is necessary to mention that a very productive form in modern Chinese, the complement of result (*jiéguǒ bǔyǔ* 結果補語), first began to be widely used in the Six Dynasties.[34] This form, which consists of a verb modified by another following verb indicating the outcome of the action of the first verb, commonly occurs in the *Sshj*.

Among the many examples are:

18) *Kè wèn yán, suì biàn wéi dàorén zhī róng.* 客問言，遂變為道人之容。(j. 2, no. 17)
'When the traveler heard this story, he changed into the guise of a Daoist'.

19) *Yī shuāng wúgōng . . . biàn yú pánzhōng tiào zǒu.* 一雙蜈蚣 . . . 便於盤中跳走。(j. 2, no. 20)
'A pair of centipedes . . . jumped out of his plate and crawled away'.

20) [*Míng*] *biàn xī hùnrán cóng kǒuzhōng yǒng chū.* [茗] 便悉混然從口中涌出。(j. 3, no. 35)
'[The tea] then all came spurting out of its mouth in a gush'.

21) *Wú yì mèng jiàn qīng wéi zú.* 吾亦夢見卿為卒。(j. 3, no. 36)
'I also dreamed you were a foot soldier'.

22) *Wǒ jīnrì jì dǎ huài nú gānluó.* 我今日既打壞奴甘羅。(j. 6, no. 65)
'Today, then, I shall forthwith smash your *gānluó*'.

A whole separate study could be devoted to a thorough enumeration and explication of the stylistic forms peculiar to the Six Dynasties that are reflected in the *Sshj*, something we can only rather superficially attend to here. Yet the summary above is sufficient to show some of the characteristic features of style in the *Sshj* and how that style reflects some general stylistic trends found in the plain narrative of the Six Dynasties. Some of the ways in which the Six Dynasties narrative differs from the earlier pure classical style should also be apparent from the preceding discussion. In addition, we can see how the style of the *Sshj* confirms that it does in fact trace its origins back to the Six Dynasties, as observed by the editors of the *Sìkù quánshū zǒngmù*.

2.4. THE CONTENTS OF THE *SŌUSHÉN HÒUJÌ*

From the review of the textual history of the *Sshj* we have seen that it is the fragmented and reconstructed remains of more than one Six Dynasties collection. We have also already noted in passing that the text we have today is composed of discrete stories and anecdotes, as are most *zhìguài* collections. The net effect of this state of affairs is to render the present *Sshj* text essentially a random collection of *zhìguài* stories and thus a fair representative of the *zhìguài* genre.

Reading through the entire contents of the *Sshj*, it is easy to see that a common feature of the stories is that most contain elements of the supernatural and the fantastic. Beyond

34. See Wáng Lì, *Hànyǔ shǐgǎo*, 405–6; and Liú Lìchuān 刘丽川, "Shì lùn *Sōushén jì* zhōng de jiéguǒ bǔyǔ" 试论《搜神记》中的结果补语, *Yǔyán yánjiū* 1984.4: 33–39.

this however, it is difficult to classify the collection as a set of any particular type of supernatural story. Yán Màoyuán has listed the *Sshj* among Buddhist collections in his study.[35] But this is difficult to defend. Wáng Guóliáng, out of ninety-three stories from the present edition that he evaluated, found only six that could be identified as Buddhist.[36] Only a few more could be added to that, which still leaves the collection only slightly representative of Buddhism.[37]

Within the context of early Chinese society, it is hard to identify given stories as specifically Daoist in content. If an attempt is made, only a few in the *Sshj* can be shown to have a definite Daoist origin. For instance, Wáng Guóliáng finds only five.[38] The rest of the stories reflect myth, popular belief, and legend from any number of sources and often display a syncretism of various traditions. Thus on the whole we agree with Wáng Guóliáng's conclusion that "this text is the product of Six Dynasties men of letters and is not the work of Daoists or Buddhists written to propagate their faith."[39] Keeping this conclusion in mind, together with our earlier assertion that the *Sshj* is a kind of historical account, we shall next quickly survey the stories.

The *Sshj* does contain entries that are entirely plausible even from a modern perspective. For example, "Eye Crag" (j. 1, no. 8) is a simple piece about an unusual landmark feature.[40] Two of the stories about dogs, "Black Dragon" and "Yáng Shēng's Dog" (j. 9, nos. 100 and 101), are perfectly credible accounts of the benefits and wonders of owning a dog—no doubt man's best friend from early on.

But wild dogs can be treacherous. The record shows that they can change form. In "The Old Yellow Dog" (j. 9, no. 104), a tricky cur takes advantage of one of Mr. Wáng's young wives by impersonating him. In "The Dogs at the Traveler's Hut in the Mountains of Línlǜ" (j. 9, no. 105), a group of gambling scoundrels turns out to be a pack of dogs who were probably also responsible for the deathly illness travelers contracted at the mountain hut.

Yè Qìngbǐng 葉慶炳 argues that because the two dog stories we mentioned first are reasonably credible, in contrast to these latter two which are of course not believable today, they are thus not "orthodox *zhìguài*."[41] But the fact that the *Sshj* includes stories

---

35. Yán Màoyuán, "Wèi Jìn Nánběi cháo zhìguài xiǎoshuō," 51.

36. These were j. 2, no. 17; j. 6, no. 76; j. 9, no. 106; j. 10, nos. 114, 115, 117; see Wáng Guóliáng, *Sōushén hòujì yánjiū*, 28–30.

37. We should add, for example, j. 2, nos. 16, 18. Lǐ Jiànguó, *Táng qián zhìguài xiǎoshuō shǐ*, 351, argues that the *Sshj* was the earliest text to contain a significant number of Buddhist entries. But since the text cannot be dated as accurately as Lǐ assumes (to within Táo Qián's lifetime) this observation is without a valid foundation.

38. Wáng Guóliáng, *Sōushén hòujì yánjiū*, 28. They are j. 1, nos. 1, 3; j. 2, nos. 12, 13, and 14.

39. Wáng Guóliáng, *Sōushén hòujì yánjiū*, 30.

40. For convenience and interest, in this section I will refer to the entries by both their numbers and their conventional titles. A complete list of the entries by title can be found in Appendix 2.

41. Yè Qìngbǐng, "Zhìguài xiǎoshuō zhōng de jī hé quǎn" 志怪小說中的雞和犬, *Zhōnghuá wénhuà fùxīng yuèkān* 9.5 (1976): 46.

of this type is an indication that Six Dynasties standards of selection were different from the modern ideas about *zhìguài* stories. All four stories were considered credible at the time they were written. In light of this situation, if we do not dismiss the *zhìguài* simply as works of fiction, we can understand how what we now call superstition reflects some of the actual beliefs about dogs and other things in the Six Dynasties. Hence, once we allow that the stories were believed by their authors and others at the time of writing, they reveal a great deal of information concerning popular culture in the Six Dynasties.[42]

For example, from *Sshj* stories we learn of a faith in the power of mirrors: they can reveal the true form of disguised beings. The dogs in the last story mentioned above were discovered by their reflection in a mirror; and a mirror reveals two women to be deer in "Deer Woman Jerky" (j. 9, no. 98).[43] The story "A Woman Marries a Snake" (j. 10, no. 16) helps to illustrate Six Dynasty marriage customs while at the same time revealing the terror many a young bride must have had about the occasion. A short set of entries about Jiǎng Zǐwén (j. 5, nos. 51–53) fills out a few details about the deification of this man of the Eastern Hàn (25–220). In fact the source for most of what is known about Jiǎng Zǐwén is the model for the *Sshj*, Gàn Bǎo's *Ssj*.[44] We learn from the *Sshj* that some believed that thunder was produced by a young woman in "The Grand Administrator of Línhè" (j. 5, no. 55); while the Daoist deity responsible for thunder, lightning, wind, and rain, the Duke of Thunder, is shown to listen to reason in "Chopping at the Duke of Thunder" (j. 10, no. 113).[45]

The pervasiveness of the belief in a lifespan determined by the heavenly bureaucracy is also underscored when we learn that a death that did not coincide with one's alloted time can be reversed, as it is in "The Daughter of Xú Xuánfāng" (j. 4, no. 41) and in "Chén Liáng" (j. 4, no. 43). Life may be regained also, it turns out, by bribing the officials in the other world, an act exposed in "Lǐ Chú" (j. 4, no. 44). It appears that the Daoists of the time did not have a monopoly on the methods for prolonging life.[46]

42. For a study of many aspects of popular thought and culture in the Six Dynasties based primarily on the *zhìguài*, see Lǐ Fēngmào 李豐楙, "Liù cháo jīngguài chuánshuō yǔ dàojiào fǎshù sīxiǎng" 六朝精怪傳說與道教法術思想, in *Zhōngguó gǔdian xiaoshuo yanjiu zhuanji*, ed. Sili jingyi wénlǐ xuéyuàn Zhōngguó gǔdiǎn xiǎoshuō yánjiū zhōngxīn (Taipei: Lianjing chubanshe, 1981), 3: 1–36.

43. A thorough discussion of mirrors and the beliefs surrounding them in the Six Dynasties culture can be found in Lǐ Fēngmào, "Liùcháo jìng jìan chuánshuō yǔ dàojiào fǎshù sīxiǎng" 六朝鏡劍傳說與道教法術思想, in *Zhōngguó gǔdiǎn xiǎoshuō yánjiù zhuānjí* 中國古典小說研究專集, ed. Sīlì Jìngyí wénlǐ xuéyuàn Zhōngguó gǔdiǎn xiǎoshuō yánjiù zhōngxīn 私立靜宜文理學院中國古典小說研究中心 (Taipei: Lianjing chubanshe, 1980), 2: 1–28.

44. See the notes to the *Sshj* entries.

45. On the Duke of Thunder and the Daoist bureaucracy, see Henri Maspero, *Mélanges posthumes sur les religions et l'histoire de la Chine: Le Taoïsme* (Paris: Civilisations du sud, 1950), 31.

46. For a description of the purely Daoist view of the predetermined lifespan and the methods for prolonging life, see Maspero, *Mélanges posthumes*, 15–41.

Concerning ghosts and demons, the most fascinating fact illustrated in the *Sshj* is their mortality.[47] "The Demon in his Abdomen" (j. 6, no. 68) and "The Ghost in the White Cloth Pants" (j. 6, no. 77) reveal that *guǐ* 鬼 can be killed with the proper medicine or poison. But the trouble that ghosts cause can sometimes be cured by simply offering them something to eat, as we learn in "Accidentally Hitting a Ghost's Foot" (j. 6, no. 74).

Several stories in this collection show us that conceptions about the experience of love between people of this world and beings from the other world can be as varied as those where both parties are ordinary people. In one story we mentioned above, "The Daughter of Xú Xuánfāng," a meeting in a dream leads eventually to a happy marriage and successful progeny. But another encounter that begins similarly, "The Daughter of Lǐ Zhòngwén" (j. 4, no. 46), ends in tragedy. From the latter story, we also see that lovemaking between a man and a ghost can be very physical. In other stories we learn the first meeting may take place in the real world. The unwary clerk Wú Xiáng in "The Maiden Zhāng" (j. 6, no. 59) meets a woman in the countryside only to learn later that the abode of the maiden he had dallied with was really a grave. However, in "The Daughter of Adjutant Hé" (j. 5, no. 56), the woman whom one Liú Guǎng meets in the countryside turns out to be a goddess. This is also the case with the woman in the well-known story represented in the *Sshj* in "The Fair Maiden of Pure Waters" (j. 5, no. 49).

In the five stories just discussed, the supernatural partner was the female half of the couple. But women of this world may also have their lives directly affected by the supernatural. Chén Jì's wife Qín falls in love with a dazzling and attractive man in "A Man Transformed from a Rainbow" (j. 7, no. 78), a story that is evidence of a folk association of rainbows with illicit sexual union that has very early origins.[48] Also, we can never be sure whether the fellow mentioned earlier that took advantage of Mr. Wáng's young wife in "The Old Yellow Dog" was really a dog, or whether he was some kind of demon.

It is the entries about hidden paradises that distinguish the *Sshj*.[49] Among them, "The Peach Blossom Wellsprings" (j. 1, no. 5) is the most well known. It is the one entry in the *Sshj* text that can be traced directly to Táo Qián, a result of its inclusion in his collected works.[50] However, it fits well among the other entries in this collection of *zhìguài*. The narrative style is quite similar to the rest of the *Sshj*, although the "Peach Blossom Wellsprings" is marked by a more vivid use of description and greater attention to detail than most of the other entries. Significantly, it is often read for what it can reveal about

---

47. For a useful discussion of the many facts about ghosts and demons revealed in the *Sshj* and other *zhìguài*, see Yè Qìngbǐng, "Wèi Jìn Nánběi cháo de guǐxiǎoshuō yǔ xiǎoshuō guǐ" 魏晋南北朝的鬼小說與小說鬼, *Zhongwai wenxue* 3.12 (1975): 100–119.

48. For a study of this association as reflected in the *Shī jīng* 詩經, see "Appendix II" in Marcel Granet, *Festivals and Songs of Ancient China*, tr. E. D. Edwards (New York: E.P. Dutton & Company, 1932), 254–58.

49. On hidden paradises, or the "lands of immortals," as reflected in Six Dynasties literature in general, see Ogawa Tamaki, "Gi Shin jidai igo (san seiki ikō): Senkyō ni asonda setsuwa" 魏晉時代以後 (三世紀以降)：仙鄉に遊んだ說話, in *Chūgoku shosetsushi no kenkyu*, 264–73.

50. See the notes to the entry.

Six Dynasties culture. Many argue that such secluded groups did exist in Táo Qián's time. Others maintain he was picturing a utopia-like world to express the need people felt for more stability in that troubled age.[51] Either way, the value of this entry as an historical source, in addition to its literary value, is clear.

Other entries about hidden paradises in the *Sshj* include "Scarlet Wall in Shān Prefecture" (j. 1, no. 3), which weaves together several strands of mythology in a story about a mystical mountain fairyland, and "The Sháo Dance" (j. 1, no. 4), in which a dancing man leads the way to a hidden land of fertility. The fantasy of unlimited abundance betrays the probability that much of the material in this collection is of a peasant origin. The theme shows up again in another story, "The Hairy Man" (j. 7, no. 82) as well as in the short piece "The Grain Comes to Fullness" (j. 3, no. 29).

The duplication of many story lines between the *Sshj* and other collections further underscores the fact that the *zhìguài* represent part of a much larger body of Six Dynasties popular mythology. A story very similar to "Scarlet Wall in Shàn Prefecture" can be found in Liú Yìqìng's *Yōumíng lù*.[52] "Huá Xīn will be a Duke" (j. 3, no. 36) shares major features with versions of a story that are attributed to *Yōumíng lù* and with two similar tales found in the *Ssj*.[53] These are clearly genetic mutations of a popular legend. Differences between the versions rule out the possibility that the *zhìguài* texts were merely copying from each other.

Before concluding, we recall our earlier observation that there are many stories on historic persons in the text. Among them, a story that tries to explain why the great dictator Huán Wēn never ultimately usurped the Jìn throne, "The Buddhist Nun" (j. 2, no. 16), is one of the few blatantly Buddhist entries. "A Divine Appearance" (j. 5, no. 57), another entry about Huán Wēn, illustrates popular conceptions about Jìn court factionalism. "Wáng Dǎo's Son Yuè" (j. 5, no. 51), explains how the young man died at the peak of his career. "Zhūgě Chángmín" (j. 8, no. 89) tells how this man was haunted by demons after he became rich. There also a few pieces on Guō Pú, as "Guō Pú Revives a Horse" (j. 2, no. 22) and "The Mirror in the Vase" (j. 2, no. 23).

The stories on Guō Pú and others on divination and magic, for instance, "Xiè Yǔn" and "Dù Zǐgōng" (j. 2, nos. 13 and 14), illustrate the connection between the *zhìguài* and the practices of shamanism and Daoism that many have noted.[54] But our look at

---

51. For a representative of the former opinion, see Chén Yínkè 陳寅恪, "'Táohuā yuán jì' pángzhèng" 桃花源記旁證, in *Chén Yínkè xiānshēng lùnwénjí* 陳寅先生論文集 (Taipei: Sanrenxing chubanshe, 1974), 2: 467–76. On the latter view, see Wú Yǐng 吳穎, "Táo Qián de 'Táohuā yuán jì'" 陶潛的《桃花源記》, *Yǔwén xuéxí* 56 (1956): 17–21; and Zhào Kèyáo 赵克尧 and Xǔ Dàoxūn 许道勋, "'Táohuā yuán jì yǔ shī' yǔ lìshǐ shíjì"《桃花源记与诗》与历史实际, *Fùdàn xuébào: Shèhuì kēxué* 1981.4: 52–55.

52. See Lǔ Xùn, *Gǔ xiǎoshuō gōuchén* 古小說鈎沈 (Beijing: Renmin wenxue chubanshe, 1951), 205–6. A translation can be found in Kao, *Classical Chinese Tales*, 137–39.

53. For the *Yōumíng lù* stories, see *Tpgj* 137.967, 316.2327. For the others, see Wāng Shàoyíng, *Ssj*, 9.116, no. 242, and 19.235–36, no. 448.

54. Wáng Yáo, Wú Hóngyī, and Lǐ Fēngmào, for instance.

the whole *Sshj* makes it clear that these types of stories make up only one rather small part of the whole collection, which contains far more entries concerned with popular mythology, superstition and legend. Unless we abandon all scholarly rigor and label all popular beliefs as Daoist or shamanistic, we can only conclude that Daoism is merely one source of the popular beliefs reflected in this collection, and when it is the source it is often not the prior or primary source.

Read with an eye to the history that they can reveal then, *zhìguài* such as the *Sshj* can help us gain a better understanding of the wide range of sources and types of popular mythology, superstition, and legend of the Six Dynasties. In this way we will be able to gain a richer view of the popular culture of the period and a more complete picture of the early stages of Chinese society. It is here we find the greatest interest of the majority of the *Sshj* entries, though there are several that stand well on their own simply as stories too. Every one has something to reveal to the investigative reader. We have not attempted to catalogue it all here, but only to point out the possibilities and then leave one to discover for oneself according to one's needs.

PART TWO

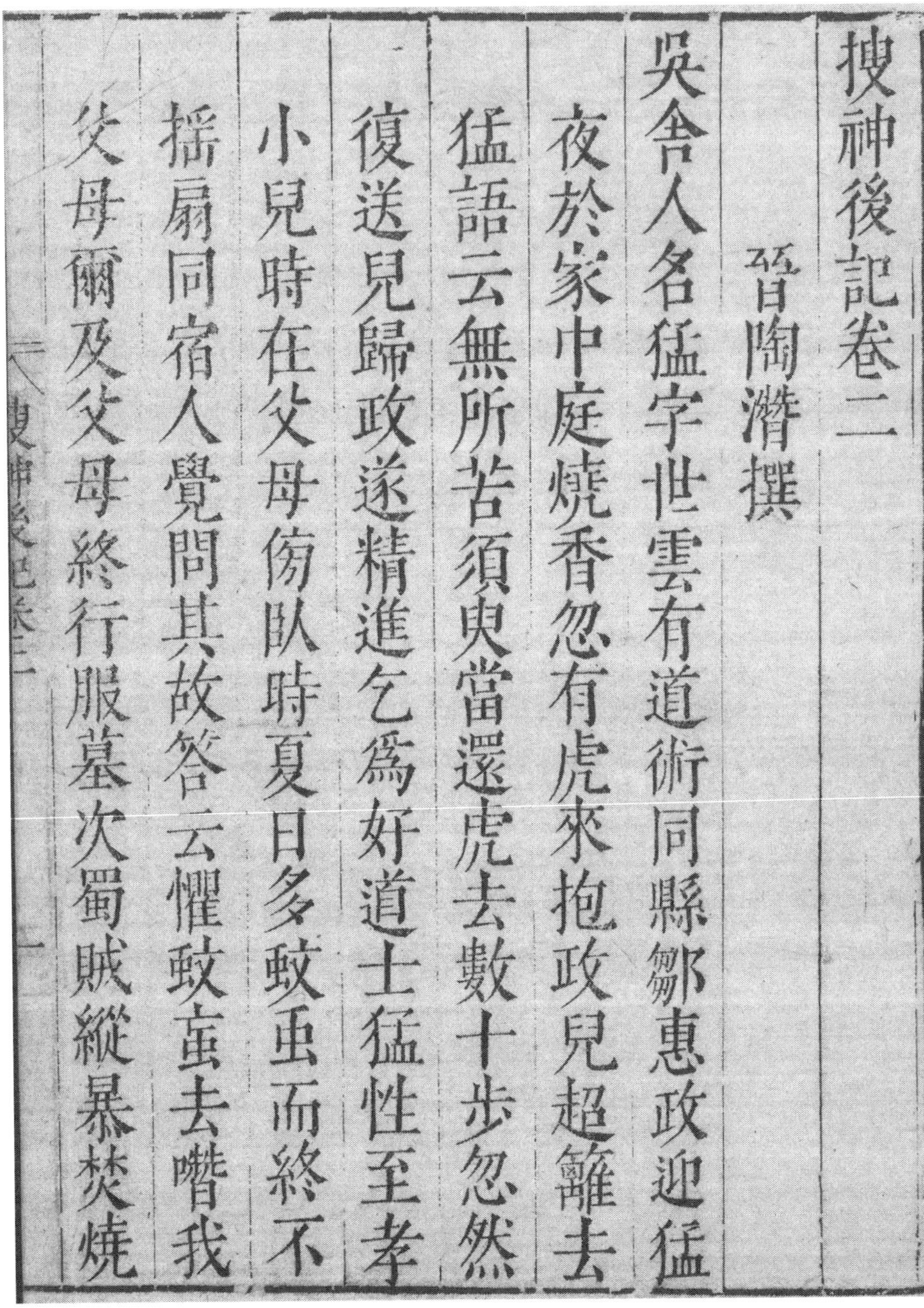

搜神後記卷二

晉陶潛撰

吳舍人名猛字世雲有道術同縣鄒惠政迎猛
夜於家中庭燒香忽有虎來抱政兒超籬去
猛語云無所苦須臾當還虎去數十步忽然
復送兒歸政遂精進乞爲好道士猛性至孝
小兒時在父母傍臥時夏日多蚊虫而終不
搖扇同宿人覺問其故答云懼蚊虫去嚙我
父母爾及父母終行服墓次蜀賊縱暴焚燒

搜神後記卷二　一

First page of *juàn* 2 of the *Mìcè huìhán* 秘册彙函 edition of the *Sōushén hòujì* from the Míng 明 Chóngzhēn 崇禎 reign period (1627–1644), held by Harvard Yenching Library

TRANSLATION OF THE *SŌUSHÉN HÒUJÌ*

Notes on the Translation

1) The following translation of the *Sshj* is based on the *Xuéjīn tǎoyuán* 學津討原 edition, with additional chapters based on *Xīnjí Sōushén hòujì*.
2) Romanization throughout the text is in *Hànyǔ pīnyīn* 漢語拼音.
3) In the translation of measurements, either a rough English equivalent or the Romanization for the original Chinese term is given, whichever seemed appropriate for the context.
4) Annotations are intended to provide reference for further understanding of the historical, cultural and textual nature of the entries.
5) Chinese characters are provided once for all Chinese terms and proper nouns that are Romanized. As much as possible, this is done in the footnotes, so as to provide them in close proximity to the relevant explanations. In cases where there is no cause to discuss a term or name in the footnotes (such as for names not found in historical records), the characters are provided within the translation in their first occurrence.
6) Traditionally the stories were not given a title but convention now assigns a title to each entry. We include translations of the conventional titles as found in the Wáng Shàoyíng and Wáng Guóliáng editions. Subtitles are sometimes added to the translations of the titles to further characterize the nature or content of the story where it seemed useful.

Sōushén hòujì: Juàn 1

1. Dīng Lìngwēi: The Transcended One
Dīng Lìngwēi, originally a man of Liáodōng, studied the Dào at Língxū Mountain.[1] After a while he transformed into a crane and returned to Liáodōng where he perched on an elegantly surfaced pillar at the city gate. At that time, there was a young rascal who raised a bow and was about to shoot it when the crane flew up and hovered about in the air talking. It said:

> There is a bird, there is a bird, Dīng Lìngwēi.
> I've gone away a thousand years and only now returned.
> The city walls are as before; but the people are different.
> Why not learn immortalhood; the grave mounds are piled high.

After that it flew high, soaring through the sky. Today all the Dīngs of Liáodōng say that among their ancestors there is one who rose to immortality. They just don't know his name is all.

2. An Immortal's Abode and Jade Elixer
North of Sōnggāo Mountain there is a large cavern.[2] None has fathomed its depth. The common people wander by to view it every season of the year. During the early Jìn [365–420], there was once a man who accidently tumbled into the cavern. His peers, hoping perhaps to avert his death, tossed food into the cavern. He got it and set out in search of an opening [from which he could get out]. In about ten days or so, he suddenly saw light and a grass hut in which two men sat facing each other playing encirclement chess. Beneath the chessboard was a cup of some whitish drink. The man who had tumbled into the cavern told them he was hungry and thirsty.

"You can drink this," a chess player told him.

He drank it and his energy returned tenfold.

A chess player asked, "Do you want to stay here?"

"I don't wish to stay," he replied.

---

1. Liáodōng 遼東 is in modern Nánníng. *Xū* 虛 should read 墟. Língxū 靈墟 Mountain is 35 *lǐ* northeast of Dāngtú 當塗 *xiàn* 縣, Ānhuī. See Wáng Xiàngzhī 王象之 (*jìnshì* 1196), *Yǔdì jìshèng* 輿地紀勝 (n.p.: Yueyatang 粵雅堂, 1855; rpt. Taipei: Wénhǎi chubanshe, 1962), 18.6b. Both *Yǔdì jìshèng* and *Jiāqìng chóngxiū dàqīng yītǒng zhì* 嘉慶重修大清一統志 (*Sbck* edn.), 120.5a, also indicate that Dīng Lìngwēi 丁令威 studied the Dào and obtained transcendency at Língxū Mountain. *Jiāqìng chóngxiū dàqīng yītǒng zhì* notes that "Cinnabar Cave" and "Cinnabar Well" (*dāndòng* 丹洞, *dānjǐng* 丹井) are found here as well. Lǐ Bái 李白 immortalized this location in his poem "Língxū shān" 靈墟山 (*Tōdai no shihen* no. 8644), which also speaks of the Dīng Lìngwēi legend.

2. Sōnggāo 嵩高 Mountain is Mt. Sōng. Located north of Dēngfēng 登封 *xiàn* in modern Hénán, it is the central of the Five Peaks (Wǔ yuè 五嶽).

"Go west from here and there will be a large well with many *jiāo* dragons inside," the chess player said.[3] "All you have to do is jump into the well and you will get out as a matter of course. If you get hungry, gather food in the well."

The fellow did as the [chess player] said and in about a half a year he came out somewhere in Shǔ.[4] After returning to the lower Luò [Luòyáng], he asked Zhāng Huá [about this adventure].[5]

Huá said, "that place is the abode of immortals. What you drank, sir, was a jade elixir and what you ate was stone marrow from Dragon Cavern."[6]

3. Scarlet Wall in Shàn Prefecture

Two men of Shàn Prefecture in Guìjī, Yuán Xiàng 袁相 and Gēn Shuò 根碩, were both hunting when they passed into some deep mountains where the overlapping peaks were quite numerous.[7] They spotted a flock of six or seven goats and went after them. Crossing a stone bridge that was quite narrow and precarious, the goats ran away. Gēn and his friend followed them across, thus heading toward a sheer cliff. The cliff stood up like a wall, straight and red, and was named "Scarlet Wall." Water flowed down from the top of it. Its width was like a length of cloth so the people of Shàn called it [this water] "Cascading Cloth."[8]

The goat trail passed a gate-like mountain cave and, it being wide open, they passed through it. Once inside, [they saw that] it was broad and level and there were grasses

---

3. *Jiāo lóng* 蛟龍 ('*jiāo* dragons') here means a mythical type of horned and scaly dragon. See Wáng Niànsūn 王念孫 (1744–1832), *Guǎngyǎ shūzhèng* 廣雅疏證 (*Jīfǔ cóngshū* 畿輔叢書 edn.), 10B.25a–26a.

4. Shǔ 蜀 had been a Hàn Commandery and refers to an area that generally corresponds to modern Sìchuān.

5. Zhāng Huá 張華 (232–300) was well known for his wide learning. He compiled the *Bówùzhì* 博物志 (Treatise on the Investigation of Things). For his biography, see *Jìn shū* 36.1068-77; and Richard Mather, *Shih-shuo Hsin-yü: A New Account of Tales of the World*, 2nd. ed. (Ann Arbor: Center for Chinese Studies of the University of Michigan, 2002), 534. Also see Anna Straughair, *Chang Hua: A Statesman-Poet of the Western Chin Dynasty*, Occasional Paper no. 15, The Australian National Univ., Faculty of Asian Studies (Canberra: Australian National Univ., 1973).

6. *Yù jiāng* 玉漿 ("jade elixir"), also known as *yù quán* 玉泉, was supposed to confer immortality, see Bernard E. Read and C. Pak, *A Compendium of Minerals and Stones Used in Chinese Medicine from the Pen T'sao Kang Mu, The Peking Society of Natural History Bulletin* 3.2 (1928): 20 no. 29b; and *Běncǎo gāngmù* 本草綱目, comp. Lǐ Shízhēn 李時珍 (1518–1593), 3 vols. (Beijing: Renmin weisheng chubanshe, 1975), 8.499–500. *Shí suí* 石髓 ("stone marrow") was a type of stalactite said to renew youth; see Read and Pak, *Compendium*, 48 no. 68, and *Běncǎo gāngmù*, 9.569. On *lóng xuè* 龍穴 ('Dragon Cavern'), see below, j.10, no. 112, n. 244.

7. Shàn 剡 Prefecture in Guìjī 會稽 commandery was located southwest of Shèng 嵊 *xiàn* of modern Zhèjiāng.

8. The scene described here and its two landmarks, Chìchéng 赤城 ('Scarlet Wall') and Pùbù 瀑布 ('Cascading Cloth') were very well known. See Richard Mather, "The Mystical Ascent of the T'ient'ai Mountains: Sun Chuo's *Yu-t'ien-t'ai-shan-fu*," *Monumenta Serica* 20 (1961): 226–45, esp. 238 n. 62.

and trees, all quite fragrant. There was a small hut with two young women living inside. They were about fifteen or sixteen and of very, very beautiful color and appearance. They wore dark green clothing. One was named Yíngzhū 瑩珠, and the other named [ ].[9]

"We have been looking forward to your coming for a long time," they happily said when they saw the two men had come.

Thereupon they married them.

Shortly after that the two women went out, saying, "some others have also found husbands, we are going to celebrate."

They walked along shuffling their clogs on the sheer cliff, making a tinkling noise.

The two men thought of returning and snuck away. On their way home, the two women, who had discovered [their escape], chased them back but then told them, "you may go of your own accord."[10] They gave Gēn and his friend a small handbag, instructing them to "be careful not to open it." With that, the two men headed home.

When later [Gēn] went out, those at home opened his bag to have a look. The bag was like a lotus flower. When they peeled away one layer, there was another underneath, until they had gone through five covers. Inside was a small teal-blue bird that flew away.[11] When Gēn returned and learned of this, he was only rather disappointed, nothing more. But after that, when Gēn was in the fields tilling, his family, as was the usual rule, brought his food out to him. They saw him standing motionless in the center of the field. When they went closer and looked, there was only a shell, like a locust's exuviae.[12]

---

9. *Tpyl* simply gives one name and does not have the phrase *yì míng* [ ] [ ] 一名□□ ("and the other named [ ]").

10. Here the *Tpyl* reading is preferable: *yǐ zhī zhuī huán* 已知追還.

11. The *chīng niǎo* 青鳥 ('teal-blue bird') was a figure in the mythological pantheon, a member of the entourage of *Xī wángmǔ* 西王母 (Goddess of the West), said to be responsible for procuring the Goddess' food. See the text and commentary in *Shān hǎi jīng jiàozhù* 山海經校住, ed. Yuán Kē 袁珂 (Shanghai: Guji chubanshe, 1980), 7.306–7, 11.399. See also Sīmǎ Xiāngrú's 司馬相如 (197–117 BCE) "Dàrén fù" 大人賦, together with Zhāng Shǒujié's 張守節 (fl. 725) commentary, in *Shǐ jì* 史記 (Beijing: Zhonghua shuju, 1975), 117.3060, 117.3062.

12. *Chán tuì* 蟬蛻 ('locust's exuviae') has also the verbal sense of 'a locust molting', which well before this time had already extended to mean something like 'escape (the mortal world)' or 'get free and away'. See, for example, *Shǐ jì,* 84.2482, "Qū Yuán zhuàn" 屈原傳, where Sīmǎ Qiān describes the protagonist's journey in "Lí sāo" 離騷: "蟬蛻於濁穢以浮游塵埃之外" ('[as a] locust molting amid dirt and filth, he thus rose to roam beyond the dust of the earth'). Hence, a double entendre results in this context which appears to be intentional.

4. The Sháo Dance: A Hidden Land of Fertility

A man from Xíngyáng surnamed Hé, whose first name has been forgotten, was a man of renown.[13] In Jīngzhōu he was appointed Aide-de-Camp.[14] But he did not take the position and instead retired from the world to cultivate his resolve.

He once visited a farm cottage. When the people were out harvesting in the fields, suddenly there was a man over ten feet in height, wearing coarse brown, unlined clothing and a cornered cap coming to greet him.[15] The man came dancing [toward him] with his hands spryly raised up in the air. He spoke with Hé.

"Have you ever seen the Sháo dance?" he asked.[16] "This is the Sháo dance."

Then he went dancing away and Hé followed after him. His trail headed toward a mountain. On the mountain there was a cave that could hold just one man. The fellow had already gone into the cave and Hé went in after him. At first it was quite tight, but he went on ahead and it soon broadened. The man then disappeared. Seeing there were about 10 *qǐng* of fine land, Hé cultivated it and established [farming] as a family occupation.[17] His descendants still rely on it today.

5. The Peach Blossom Wellsprings

During the Tàiyuán reign of the Jìn there was a fellow from Wǔlíng who caught fish for a living.[18] Once when following along a brook and paying no heed to how far he went,

---

13. I follow the *Tpyl*, which reads *xíng* 滎 here for *róng* 榮. Xíngyáng 滎陽 was a Hàn prefecture located in the southwest of what is modern Chénggāo 成皋 *xiàn* in Hénán.

14. Jīngzhōu 荊州 was a province that occupied the area of the Jiāng and the Hàn river valleys, including modern Húnán, Húbéi, and parts of Sìchuān.

15. *Tpyl* reads *huáng* 黄 for *xiāo* 蕭. *Shū* 疎 indicates loose spacing between the warp and woof in cloth that is woven of coarse silk, see Liú Xī 劉熙 (fl. 200), *Shì míng* 釋名, *Hàn Wèi cóngshū* 漢魏叢書 edn., 2.28b and 2.29b. Hence, this line is most successfully read as *huáng shū dān yī* 黄疎單衣 "coarse brown, unlined clothing."

16. The Sháo 韶 Dance, or "Succession Dance," was a dance done to Sháo music attributed to the legendary emperor Shùn. For further reference, see David R. Knechtges, *Wen xuan or Selections of Refined Literature*, vol. 1: *Rhapsodies on Metropolises and Capitals* (Princeton: Princeton Univ. Press, 1982), 166, l. 244 n.

17. 10 *qǐng* 頃 are approximately equivalent to one hundred acres.

18. This piece also appears in Táo Qián's collected works as a preface to his poem "Táohuā yuán" 桃花源 ("The Peach Blossom Wellsprings") and it may be this connection that finds the *Sshj* attributed to him. However, none of the *lèishū* citations ascribe it in any way to the *Sshj* or the *Xssj*, but rather attribute it directly to Táo Qián. See *Ywlj*, 86.2193; *Cxj*, 28.674; the commentary to the *Shì lèi fù* 事類賦 (n.p., n.d.) [hereafter *Slf*], 26.1b; also Lǐ Hàn 李翰 (fl. 746), *Méng Qiú jízhù* 蒙求集注 (*Xuéjīn tǎoyuán* 學津討源 edn.), B.14a. Chén Yínkè ("'Táohuā yuán jì' pángzhèng," 467–76) believes that this *Sshj* version may be a draft copy, which Táo later refined into the version found in his collection. Wáng Yáo dates its composition to 421, when Táo was 57 years old, see Wáng Yáo, ed. and comm., *Táo Yuānmíng jí* 陶淵明集 (Beijing: Zuojia chubanshe, 1956), 94. Tàiyuán 太元 was a reign title (376–396) of the Jìn emperor Xiàowǔ 孝武 (r. 373–396). Except for the *Slf* commentary, the *lèishū* citations all give the date as the Tàikāng 太康 reign (280–289) of the first Jìn emperor, Wǔdì 武帝 (r. 265–289). The *Slf* commentary erroneously reads "*tàiyuán*" 太原.

he came across some blossoming peach [trees] which lined the banks for several hundred paces without a single other type of tree. The fragrant flowers were brightly colored and delightful. Fallen blossoms scattered profusely everywhere. The fisherman found it quite unusual. (The fisherman's surname was Huáng 黄 and his name Dàozhēn 道真.)[19]

He continued on, hoping to find the limits of this [peach] grove. The grove came to an end right at the source of the brook. Then he found a hill that had a small entrance in which there seemed to be light. So he got out of his boat and went into the entrance.

At first it was extremely narrow, with only enough room to let one man through. He went on several dozen paces and it broadened out, becoming expansive and bright with land that was spacious and open. There were huts and houses in neat order, fertile fields, pleasant ponds, and mulberry trees, bamboo and the like. Paths criss-crossed through the fields and dogs and chickens could be heard among them. The clothes that the men and women wore were all like the people on the outside [of the cave]. The grey-haired and those with child's locks were happy together and self-content.

Seeing the fisherman, they were very much alarmed. When they asked him where he had come from, he answered them fully. Some then invited him to go home with them where they set out some wine and dressed a chicken to prepare a meal. The people in the village heard that this fellow had arrived and everyone came to inquire about news [of the outside world]. They told him that in a former age to escape from the tyranny of Qín, they led their wives, children, and fellow villagers to this isolated realm and had not gone out again, thus becoming cut-off from the outside.[20] They asked what year it was presently and had not even heard of the Hàn, not to mention the Wèi or the Jìn. This

---

Commentaries appear to agree that the Tàikāng date is a mistake that originated with Rèn (or Wǔ) Ānpín 任 (or 伍) 安貧 (n.d.; of the Liáng 梁, 502–557) in a version of this story in his *Wǔlíng jì* 武陵記, see Zhào Quánshān 趙泉山 (n.d.) cited in Lǐ Gōnghuàn 李公煥 (n.d.) ed., *Jiānzhù Táo Yuānmíng jí* 箋注陶淵明集 (*Sbck* ed.), 5.4b and Hóng Jūfù 洪駒父 (n.d.) cited in Wèi Zhòngjǔ 魏仲舉 (fl. 1195–1200) ed., *Wǔbǎi jiā zhù Chānglí wénjí* 五百家注昌黎文集 (*Sìkù quánshū zhēnběn* 四庫全書珍本 edn.), 3.8a–b. Wǔlíng 武陵 commandery was located in the West of Chángdé 常德 *xiàn* in modern Húnán.

19. According to the *Sìkù quánshū zǒngmù* notice for the *Sshj*, this additional note distinguishes the *Sshj* entry from that in Táo's collection. See the translation of the notice in the appendix. But at least one editor of Táo's collection also has included this note, though it is not found in the *lèishū* versions. See Lǐ Gōnghuàn, *Jiānzhù Táo Yuānmíng jí*, 5.1a. The name for the fisherman seems to have originated with Huáng Mǐn's 黄閔 (n.d.; of the Southern Qí 南齊, 479–501) mention of Táo's piece in his *Wǔlíng jì* 武陵記, where he says: "In earlier times, Huáng Dàozhēn of Línyuán 臨沅 was fishing beside this hill when he entered the Peach Blossom Wellsprings." See the citation preserved in Yuè Shǐ 樂史 (930–1007), *Yǐng Sòng běn tàipíng huányǔ jì bǔquè* 影宋本太平寰宇記補闕 (Taipei: Wenhai chubanshe, 1963), 118.6b.

20. Chén Yínkè argues that the Qín actually referred to here is not the Yíng Qín 嬴秦 of the Warring States period, but rather the Fú Qín 苻秦 or Former Qín (351–494), one of the sixteen kingdoms that existed in the North concurrently with the Eastern Jìn and which was founded by Fú Jiān 苻堅 (338–385); see Chén Yínkè, "'Táohuā yuán jì' pángzhèng," 467–76. A literal reading of this passage, however, tends to argue against Chén's opinion.

fellow told them in detail all that he knew and all sighed in wonderment. Others then each invited him to their home, all providing food and wine. He stayed for several days and then bid them good-bye. The people here told him there was no need to tell people on the outside [about this place].

Once he had gone out, he found his boat and went back the way he had come, marking all the places that he passed. When he got back to the commandery, he went to see the Grand Administrator and told him of this experience. The Grand Administrator Liú Xīn sent someone to go back with him.[21] They followed the marks he had left but did not find [the entrance] again.

6. Líu Línzhī: A Glimpse of Elixers for Immortality

Liú Línzhī, styled Zǐjì 子驥, of Nányáng enjoyed roaming the mountains and waters.[22] Once he went to Mt. Héng to pick medicinal herbs, going deeply [into the hills] and paying no heed to turning back.[23] He found a river there, south of which were two stone grain bins, one open and one closed. The river was very wide and he could not cross it. Once he was ready to go back, [he discovered] he had lost his way. He ran into a man cutting wood to make bows and asked him the way [out]. Only then was he able to return home.

There were people who said that the grain bins contained elixirs for immortality, divine medicines and every sort of unusual thing. Línzhī wanted to go search again for them, but he could not find that spot anymore.

7. World Within a Cave

In Lǐlíng prefecture, Chángshā, there is a small river.[24] Two men were there gathering firewood from a boat when they saw water flowing out from an earthen cave below the bank. There were newly cut lengths of wood floating out with the water. In the deep hills [beyond it] there were human footprints. The men found it strange.

"Should we try to go into the water to see where it is coming from?" they remarked to each other.[25]

---

21. It is unclear exactly who this Grand Administrator Liú Xīn 劉歆 is. The name may have slipped into this text from a secondary reference in the same way that the fisherman's name got included in this *Sshj* version. The Lǐ Gōnghuàn edition of the preface to the poem, 5.5a, also preserves the phrase *Tàishǒu* Liú Xīn 太守劉歆 ("Grand Administrator Liú Xīn") but only as a note.

22. Liú Línzhī 劉驎之 (fl. ca. 380) was a well-known recluse. His biography can be found in *Jìn shū*, 94.2447–48. See also Mather, *Shih-shuo Hsin-yü*, 584. Táo Qiān mentions him in a final line in the preface to his poem "The Peach Blossom Wellsprings," which is not included in the *Sshj* version (no. 5 above).

23. Mt. Héng 衡, the southern of the Five Peaks and also known as Mt. Huò 霍, is in Húnán.

24. Lǐlíng 醴陵 prefecture of Chángshā 長沙 commandery exists today as Lǐlíng *xiàn* southeast of Chángshā *xiàn* in Húnán.

25. Here following the *Tpyl*, 54.263, and *Btsc*, 158.7a, which reads *rù* 入 for *rú* 如.

After that one of the men, using his hat to shield himself, went into the cave. The cave would only hold one person; but he went about ten paces when it opened up bright as day, no different from the regular world.

8. Eye Crag
In Pínglè prefecture there is a mountain overlooking a river.[26] Between the crags, there are two eyes. They are like human eyes, but extremely large. The pupil, the dark and the white are clearly distinct. It is named "Eye Crag."

9. Musical Sounds in Stone Caverns
On the east of Mt. Jī 機 in Shǐxīng there are two crags that turn toward each other like sparrow hawks' tails.[27] [There are also] ten stone caverns from all of which, when passed by, can be heard the sounds of bells, chimes, harps and flutes.

10. Chaste Maiden Gorge
Chaste Maiden Gorge is in Zhōngsù prefecture.[28] At the western bank of the gorge, by the water's edge, there is a stone shaped like a person. Its form seems like that of a young woman. This is called the "Chaste Maiden." The elders maintain that in Qín times there were a number of women gathering snails here. Once when they encountered wind and rain that lasted from dawn to dusk, one of the women was transformed into this stone.

11. Spring of the Maiden Shū
Mt. Gài 蓋 is fourty *lǐ* south of Línchéng prefecture.[29] One hundred or so paces [up the mountain] there is the Spring of the Maiden Shū.[30] A long time ago a girl [named] Shū was splitting firewood with her father at this spring. She sat down and [her father] could not budge her even by pulling. He went home to tell the family. By the time they returned, all they saw was clean, clear spring water. "My daughter likes music," the girl's mother said and began to sing to a zither. The spring water spouted up in a whirling flow and there was a pair of crimson carp.[31] Today when people make music or sport in fun [here], the spring squirts up as it did then.

---

26. Pínglè 平樂 prefecture is in modern Guǎngxī.

27. Shǐxīng 始興 prefecture is southwest of Nánxióng 南雄 *xiàn* in modern Guǎngdōng. *Chī* 鴟 usually refers to *Milvus lineatus*, the sparrow hawk or black eared kite, see Bernard E. Read, *Chinese Materia Medica: Avian Drugs* (Peiping: French Bookstore, 1932), 85–86, no. 314.

28. Zhōngsù 中宿 prefecture was situated northwest of Qīngyuǎn 清遠 *xiàn* in modern Guǎngdōng.

29. Línchéng 臨城 prefecture is south of Qīngyáng 青陽 *xiàn* in modern Ānhuī.

30. *Gū shū quán* 姑舒泉 should read *Shū gū quán* ("Spring of the Maiden Shū"), as it is found in *Tpyl*, 70.331, and *Cxj*, 15.378.

31. *Lǐ* 鯉 is *Cyprinus carpio*, the common carp, see Read, *Chinese Materia Medica: Scaly and Scaleless Fish* (Peiping: French Bookstore, 1939), 5 no. 128.

Sōushén hòujì: Juàn 2

12. Chamberlain Wú: The Filial Daoist

Chamberlain Wú was named Měng and his sobriquet was Shìyún 世云. He was adept in the Daoist arts.[32] [Once] Zōu Huìzhèng of the same province came to meet Měng.[33] One evening they were burning incense in the middle hall of his home when suddenly a tiger came, grabbed Zhèng's son and jumped away over the fence.

"No need to worry," Měng said, "he'll return in a short time."

The tiger went about ten paces then suddenly brought the boy back. With that Zhèng became zealous and begged to become a good Daoist.

Měng was extremely filial by nature. When he was a child he would sleep by his parents' side. On summer days when there were lots of mosquitoes and bugs, he would not once wave his fan. When those living in the same place noticed this and asked why, Měng answered, "I fear the mosquitoes and gadflies will go bite my parents."

After his parents died, he camped by their grave during the mourning. In Shǔ the bandits were wilfully savage. They burned village houses and dug up graves. The people would all flee and hide. But Měng stood beside his parents' grave crying sorrowfully that he would not leave. The robbers were touched and saddened by this and so did not invade [the grave].

13. Xiè Yǔn: Conjuring a Carp

Xiè Yǔn returned from Mt. Wǔdāng and was seated with Huán of Xuānwǔ.[34] The conversation turned to the story of how Zuǒ Yuánfàng presented a perch to Duke Cáo.[35]

---

32. Though his origin is of some confusion, Wú Měng 吳猛 was probably from Yùzhāng 豫章 (in modern Jiāngxī). See his biography in *Jìn shū*, 95.2482–83; and in Zhào Dàoyī 趙道一 (n.d.; of the Yuán), *Lìshì zhēnxiān tǐdào tōngjiàn* 歷世真仙體道通鑑 (Shanghai: Guangcang xuejun, 1936), 27.1a–b. There is also information on him in *Shí'èr zhēn jūn zhuàn* 十二真君傳, cited in *Tpgj*, 14.123–24. For a discussion of his biography, see the notes to the piece on Wú Měng found in Wáng Shàoyíng, *Ssj*, 1.13–14, no. 26, nn. 1 and 2.

33. I can find no further information on Zōu Huìzhèng 鄒惠政.

34. Xiè Yǔn 謝允 (n.d.), *zì* 字 Dàotōng 道通, was from Lìyáng 歷陽 (Hé 和 *xiàn* in modern Ānhuī). See Dài Zuò 戴祚 (n.d.; of the Jìn) *Zhēn yì zhuàn* 甄異傳, in Lǔ Xùn, *Gǔ xiǎoshuō gōushěn*, 180. His name may have originally been Xiè Yìn 謝胤 and the *yìn* changed to *yǔn* because of a Sòng taboo. See Wāng Shàoyíng, *Ssj*, 2.23, no. 40, n. 1. Mt. Wǔdāng 武當 is in Jūn 均 *xian*, Húběi. Huán of Xuānwǔ 桓宣武 is the posthumous title of Huán Wēn 桓溫 (312–373), *zì* Yuánzǐ 元子, a powerful general in the Eastern Jìn court. For his biography, see *Jìn shū*, 98.2568–80; and Mather, *Shih-shuo Hsin-yü*, 570.

35. Yuánfàng 元放 is the sobriquet of Zuǒ Cí 左慈 (n.d.). His biography can be found in *Hòu Hàn shū* 後漢書 (Beijing: Zhonghua shuju, 1975), 82b.2747–48. For a translation see Kenneth J. DeWoskin, *Doctors, Diviners, and Magicians of Ancient China: Biographies of Fang-shih* (New York: Columbia Univ. Press, 1983), 83–86. The story concerning Zuǒ Cí's presentation of a perch to Cáo Cāo 曹操 (155–220) can be found in Zuǒ's biography as well as in *Ssj*, 1.9–10, no. 21. *Lú* 鱸 is *Lateolabrax japonicus*, commonly known as perch or sculpin. Minced sculpin was considered a delicacy. See Read, *Scaly and Scaleless Fish*, 42 no. 149.

"This can be achieved," Yǔn said.

He requested a large bowl filled with water into which he tossed a talisman written in vermilion ink. At once a carp appeared, waving its fins in the water.

14. Dù Zǐgōng: Fishing up a Knife

Dù Zǐgōng of Qiántáng was skilled in the art of magic.[36] Once he approached a man to borrow a melon knife. When the owner of the knife asked for it [back], Zǐgōng said, "it should be returned to you right away." Right after that the owner of the knife traveled to Jiāxīng and a fish jumped into his boat.[37] When he split open the belly of the fish, he found his melon knife.

15. The Mouse Market

During the Tàixīng reign [318–321] one Qū Chún of Héngyáng made a "mouse market."[38] Its four sides were over a *zhàng* [each], and it had four doors.[39] By [each] door there was a wooden man. When four or five rats were released inside, if they tried to go out the doors, the wooden man would immediately push them with his hands.

16. The Buddhist Nun: A Warning for Huán Wēn

The Commander-in-Chief Huán Wēn of the Jìn went by the sobriquet Yuánzǐ. In his later years, a Buddhist nun, whose name has been forgotten, came unexpectedly from some far off place and took refuge with Wēn as a Danapati nun. Her talent and bearing were quite extraordinary and Wēn treated her with great respect, allowing her to live inside the gate.

Whenever the nun bathed, she would inevitably take a great deal of time. Wēn was suspicious of this and spied upon her. He saw the nun naked and brandishing a knife. She split open her abdomen, removed her viscera, severed her head from her body, cut away her limbs and hacked them up. Wēn returned, shocked by the abnormality. But when the nun came out of the bathing hall, her body and form were normal. Wēn confronted her

---

36. Zǐgōng 子恭 is the sobriquet of Dù Jiǒng 杜炅. He is said to have been the teacher of Sūn Ēn's 孫恩 (d. 402) uncle, Sūn Tài 孫泰 (d. 395), who carried on Dù's arts as a well-known Daoist magician after Dù died. See *Jìn shū*, 100.2631–32; and *Nán shǐ* 南史 (Beijing: Zhonghua shuju, 1975), 57.1405 and 75.1882. Qiántáng 錢塘 was within the area of modern Zhèjiāng.

37. Jiāxīng 嘉興 still exists today as Jiāxīng *xiàn* in Zhèjiāng.

38. Tàixīng 太興 was a reign name of the Jìn emperor Yuándì 元帝 (r. 317–322). Héngyáng 衡陽 is in Húnán. I can find no other reference to the identity of Qū Chún 區純. This story is the only known reference to such a "mouse market." Outside of this collection the story is identified as part of Sūn Shèng's 孫盛 (ca. 302–373) *Jìn yáng qiū* 晉陽秋. See *Ywlj*, 95.2455; *Tpyl*, 752.3337 and 911.4036; *Tpgj*, 225.1645.

39. Though it may have been shorter in classical times, I translate one *zhàng* 丈 loosely as 'ten feet' were it occurs elsewhere in this collection.

with the facts, to which she replied, "If one overcomes and rises above one's lord, such is the form [that punishment will take]."[40]

At the time Wēn had been plotting to take over the empire, and when he heard this he was quite upset. He thus took it as a warning to fear and adhered to his position as minister until his death. Later on, the nun departed and it is not known where she went.

17. The Three Bur-Nuts

In the state of Pèi there was a gentleman surnamed Zhōu 周 who had triplets.[41] When they were approaching twenty they could make sounds but could not talk. Unexpectedly, a traveler passed by their gate and begged for something to drink. Hearing the [abnormal] sounds of the boys, [the traveler] asked Zhōu, "what sound is that?"

"My sons, none of them can talk," he answered.

"You may go inside and consider what you did wrong and how it has come to this," the traveler said.

The host [Zhōu] found what he said unusual and knew this was no ordinary man. After a good long time he came out and said, "I can't recall anything that I have done wrong."

"Try thinking of your childhood instead," the traveler instructed.

He went in and in a short time came out and told the traveler, "I remember when I was a young boy, there was a swallow's nest above my bed with three baby birds in it. Their mother would get food outside to feed the three babies and they would all stick out their mouths to accept it. This went on for many days. I tried sticking my finger into the nest and the swallow chicks stuck out their necks to accept it as well. So I collected three bur-nuts and fed one to each [chick].[42] They died immediately. The mother returned and, not seeing her chicks, let out a mournful cry and left. This happened long ago but I still truly regret it today."

When the traveler heard his story, he changed into the guise of a Daoist and said, "since you yourself know regret, your transgression is now expunged."

---

40. Xíng 形 (form) can be seen to be a pun on *xíng* 刑 (punishment), which is the graph found in the version of this story cited as Wáng Yǎn's 王琰 (fl. late fifth century) *Míng xiáng jì* 冥祥記. See *Fyzl*, 45.12a–b; and Lǔ Xùn, *Gǔ xiǎoshuō*, 396.

41. The state of Pèi 沛 was a Hàn and Jìn commandery located northwest of Sù 宿 *xiàn*, modern Ānhuī.

42. For *qiángcí* 薔茨 ('bur-nuts') all *lèishū* versions (except *Tpgj*, 131.923) read *jílí* 蒺藜; see *Tpyl*, 740.3284, 997.4414, *Bslt*, 29.1054; also see the same story in Liú Yìqìng, *Xuān yàn jì* 宣驗記 in Lǔ Xùn, *Gǔ xiǎoshuō*, 365. *Jílí*, often written simply *cí* 茨, is *Tribulus terrestris*, commonly known as calthrop, puncture-vine, or ground bur-nut. This plant is known for its thorny seeds which grow in five two-spined segments and are painfully sharp. Other Chinese common names reflect their nasty reputation: *qū rén* 屈人 ('bend-a-man') or *xíng zhǐ* 行止 ('stop-a-stroll'). *Qiángcí* is not a name found elsewhere in the literature, but *jílí* is undoubtedly what is meant here. See Read, *Chinese Medicinal Plants from the Pen Ts'ao Kang Mu* (Peking: Peking Natural History Bulletin, 1936), 108 no. 364; *Běncǎo gāngmù*, 16.1102–5.

When he was done speaking, [Zhōu] then heard his sons talking normally. Suddenly the Daoist was not to be seen.

18. Fótúdèng
The Indian Fótúdèng came to Luòyáng in the fourth year of the Yǒngjiā reign [310].[43] He was skilled at chanting divine spells and at manipulating ghosts and spirits.[44] At the side of his abdomen there was a hole, which he usually kept stuffed with silk wadding. Whenever he read at night, he would pull out the wadding and light would shine out of the hole, lighting up the whole room. At early dawn, he would go [to a spot] beside flowing water, pull out his five organs and six viscera from the hole, and wash them.[45] When he finished, he would put them back into his abdomen.

19. A Foreign Monk's Skill at Incantation
In Shí Hǔ's [capital], Yè, there was a foreign Monk who was versed in the techniques of spell casting.[46] He rode a donkey as a traveling merchant. While he was journeying abroad, in the deep mountains where a steep ravine formed a yawning abyss below, a nasty ghost unexpectedly snuck away with this Monk's donkey and went down into the ravine. The Monk followed the tracks, casting spells and making oaths that he yelled to the ghost king. In a short time the donkey and everything were as before.

20. Tán Yóu: Avoiding Sorcery
Tán Yóu, a man of the Dào, was a poverty-stricken Sramana.[47] In Shàn prefecture there was an establishment engaged in the business of venom sorcery.[48] Among those who partook of their food or drink, there were none who would not spit blood and die. Yóu once visited them, and when the host brought the food, Yóu recited his vows as he always

---

43. Fótúdèng 佛圖澄 (fl. 310–348) has biographies in *Gsz*, 10.240–54, and in *Jìn shū*, 95.2484–90. For a discussion of his life and a translation of the *Gsz* biography, see Arthur F. Wright, "Fo-t'u-teng: A Biography," *Harvard Journal of Asiatic Studies* 11 (1948): 321–71. See also Mather, *Shih-shuo Hsin-yü*, 553–54. Yǒngjiā 永嘉 was the reign name of Huáidì 懷帝 of the Jìn (r. 307–312).

44. For further reference to Fótúdèng's skills, see Chou Yi-liang, "Tantrism in China," *Harvard Journal of Asiatic Studies* 8 (1944–45): 242–45.

45. The *wǔ zàng* 五臟 ('five organs') are the heart, the liver, the spleen, the lungs, and the kidneys. The *liù fǔ* 六腑 ('six viscera') are the stomach, the gall, the bladder, the large intestine, the small intestine, and the three *jiāo* 焦 (the three visceral cavities that house the esophagus, the stomach and the intestines).

46. Shí Hǔ 石虎 (*zì* Jìlóng 季龍, d. 349), a Xiōngnú, was the ruler of the Later Zhào (r. 335–349) who moved the capital to Yè 鄴 (in the area of modern Línzhāng 臨漳 *xiàn* in Hénán). For his biography, see *Jìn shū*, 106.2761–107.2799; and Mather, *Shih-shuo Hsin-yü*, 597.

47. For a biography of Tán Yóu 曇遊, usually written 曇猷, see *Gsz*, 12.287–89.

48. For an examination of the term *gǔ* 蠱 ('venom sorcery') and a survey of the practice as it is revealed in Chinese literature, see H. Y. Feng and J. K. Shryock, "The Black Magic in China Known as *Ku*," *JAOS* 55 (1935): 1–30. Shàn 剡 prefecture was southwest of what is modern Shèngzhōu 嵊州 in Zhèjiāng.

did. A pair of centipedes over a foot long jumped out of his plate and crawled away. Yóu then ate his fill and returned home, healthy and without any problem.

21. Xìng Líng: Expelling Ghostly Trouble

Gāo Kuī's home was haunted with ghostly peculiarities:[49] Talking and conversation, screaming and scolding, and heaving and tossing inside and out, with no sign of human form. Sometimes things would move by themselves, or ignite on fire over and over. Shamans performed their exorcisms, yet were unable to stop it.

[Gāo Kuī] happened to run into Xìng Líng and so requested his aid.[50] When [Xìng Líng] got to the gate, he saw there were a large number of amulets and charms. He gathered them all together and burned them. Then he simply took over the porch, sat a bit, and then left. That evening, the ghostly trouble had already ceased.

22. Guō Pú Revives a Horse

Zhào Gù usually rode a certain sorrel horse on his military expeditions.[51] He loved it very much. He once tied it up in front of the office where he lived when suddenly its abdomen swelled up and it died in a short time. Guō Pú was passing by on his way from the North and so came to visit Zhào Gù.[52]

"The General's favorite horse, one he loved and cherished, is now dead and he is quite grieved and disappointed," the gatekeeper told him.

"You may go in and notify him that I am able to revive that horse, he will surely see me then," Pú told the gate keeper.

Hearing this, the gate keeper was surprised yet pleased and went right in to inform Gù. Gù was exuberant. He ordered the gate keeper to rush back out to welcome Pú. At first they just made simple conversation and then [Gù] asked, "Are you able revive my horse?"

"I can revive him," Pú said.

Gù was delighted and immediately asked, "What magical techniques does it require?"

Pú answered, "Find twenty or thirty healthy men of sympathetic disposition and order them all to carry bamboo poles and go thirty *lǐ* east of here where they should come to a group of tombs in a wooded area, situated rather like a temple to the Earth God. When they have found this place, they should then stir up a disturbance by beating and clapping

---

49. Gāo Kuī 高悝 (fl. early fourth century) was from Guǎnglíng 廣陵 (northeast of Jiāngdū 江都 *xiàn* in modern Jiāngsū) and served as governor (*yǐn* 尹) of Dānyáng 丹陽 (south of Zhènjiāng 鎮江 in Jiāngsū). See *Jìn shū*, 61.1671–72. Also see his son's biography, "Gāo Sōng zhuàn" 高崧傳, *Jìn shū*, 71.1894–95; and Mather, *Shih-shuo Hsin-yü*, 574.

50. Xìng Líng 幸靈 (n.d.) of Jiànchāng 建昌 prefecture, Yùzhāng 豫章 commandery (west of Fèngxīn 奉新 *xiàn* in modern Jiāngxī) has a short biography in *Jìn shū*, 95.2483.

51. Zhào Gù 趙固 (d. ca. 318) was general to Liú Cōng 劉聰 (d. 318), second ruler (310–318) of the Former Zhào. See *Jìn shū*, 63.1708, 104.2727.

52. Guō Pú's biography can be found in *Jìn shū*, 72.1899–1910; and Mather, *Shih-shuo Hsin-yü*, 579.

with their bamboo poles. Then, when they find a beast, they should quickly carry it back. Once you've obtained this beast, the horse will come back to life."

Thereupon [Gù] sent off fifty of his bravest aids. It turned out just as Pú had said. They found a large wooded thicket out of which a beast came running that seemed like a monkey, but was not. The men chased and caught it, then carried it back. When the beast saw the dead horse from a distance, it jumped about and wanted to go over [to it]. Pú ordered them to let it go and the beast ran off by itself toward the horse's head and breathed into its nose. After a fair length of time, the horse got up. Its whinny was energetic and its gallop was swift. The beast then disappeared.

Gù rewarded him generously, and Pú was able to cross the lower Yangtze.

23. The Mirror in the Vase

Wáng Wénxiàn once ordered Guō Pú to divine his fortune for a year.[53] Guō told him, "You are facing a bit of adverse luck. You can take two large Guǎngzhōu vases, fill them with water, and put them at two corners of your bed curtain.[54] Name them 'the mirror's depletion', and thus suppress your poor luck.[55] When a certain time comes, toss out the vases and discard the water. In this way its misfortune can be eliminated."

Yet when [he had done it and] the time came, [Wénxiàn] forgot [to throw out the vases]. Soon after that he was missing a copper mirror. He did not know where it was. Later, he [finally] threw out the water [in the vase] and only then discovered that the mirror he had lost was inside one of the vases. The mouth of the vase was only a few inches wide while the mirror was over a foot in size. Wáng ordered to call back Pú and have him divine the meaning of the mirror and the vase.

Pú told him, "Being remiss about the time for tossing out the vases has resulted in this weird occurrence. It was caused by nothing other than the work of a perverse demon."

He had an axle pin burnt and the mirror immediately came out.[56]

24. Guō Pú Makes an Advance Plea

At the beginning of the Zhōngxīng reign, each time Guō Pú would cast his own hexagram, he would learn of his cruel death.[57] Once when passing by a fenced pond near Jiànkāng, he encountered a young man walking along at a hurried pace who was very,

53. Wáng Wénxiàn 王文獻 is the posthumous name of Wáng Dǎo 王導 (276–339), whose sobriquet was Màohóng 茂弘. He was principal advisor to Sīmǎ Ruì 司馬睿 (276–322). See *Jìn shū*, 65.1745–61; and Mather, *Shih-shuo Hsin-yü,* 626.

54. *Zhāng* 張 should read *zhàng* 帳, as it does in *Tpyl*, 717.3179.

55. *Jìng hào* 鏡好 should read *jìng hào* 鏡耗, as found in the *Tpyl* version, the reading I follow here.

56. The significance of the burning of a *jū xiá* 車轄 ('axle pin') is unclear.

57. There was no Zhōngxīng 中興 reign in Guō Pú's lifetime. The Tàixīng reign (318–322) of Yuándì ended two years before Guō's death and may be what originally was meant here. However, none of the *lèishū* versions of this story gives any date at all. See *Btsc*, 129.10a; *Tpyl*, 693.3094, 728.3230.

very cold.[58] He stopped [the young man], then pulled off his silk gown and handed it to him. The fellow declined to accept it.

"Just take it," Guō Pú said, "later you will naturally know [why]."

The fellow accepted it and went off.

When [Guō Pú] was facing death, it turned out this man would be carrying out the execution.[59] Witnesses pleaded [for mercy] on his behalf, but Pú said, "I have made my plea with him for a long time now."

The man wept for Guō Pú, choking with sobs. But once the execution was finished, he was cheerful.

25. Dù Bùqiān: Divination by Pheasant

Chī Chāo of Gāopíng, who went by the sobriquet Jiābīn 嘉賓, contracted a serious illness when he was a little over twenty years old.[60] Dù Bùqiān of Lújiāng had studied divination using the *Book of Changes* with his maternal grandfather, Guō Pú, and frequently had positive results.[61] Chāo ordered [Dù] to try divining for him.

When the hexagram was complete, Bùqiān said: "According to what the hexagram says, your illness will shortly be followed by recovery. Still, it would be a good idea to go thirty miles northeast to a family named Shàngguān 上官 and ask them for the male pheasant that they keep.[62] Cage it, tie down its leg, and put it under your eastern eaves. Then nine days later on a *jǐngwǔ* day 景午日 at mid-day, a wild female pheasant should come flying by and mate with it.[63] When they are finished, they will fly off in a pair. If this is indeed how it turns out, your illness will be over in no more than twenty days. It would also be a propitious sign, [meaning that] you will live to be eighty years old and your status will reach that of a minister. If, however, only the female departs and the male remains, then your illness will last a full year's cycle before it is over, your age [will reach] only half of eighty, and your reputation and status will be lost as well."

At the time, Chāo was gravely ill and quite weak. He thought his life was nearing the end. So he smiled and answered [Bùqiān], "If I can make it to half of eighty, that

58. Jiànkāng 建康 is now modern Nánjīng.

59. Wáng Dūn 王敦 (266–324) had Guō Pú executed in 324.

60. Chī Chāo 郗超 (336–377) also went by the sobriquet Jǐngxīng 景興. See his biography in *Jìn shū*, 67.1802–5; and in Mather, *Shih-shuo Hsin-yü*, 543. The Gāopíng 高平 meant here is probably the prefecture established by the state of Wú (222–280) during the Three Kingdoms period and situated around the locality of Xīnhuà 新化 *xiàn* in modern Húnán.

61. On Dù Bùqiān 杜不愆 (n.d.; mid-third century) see *Jìn shū*, 95.2479–80. Lújiāng 廬江 was west of Huòqiū 霍丘 *xiàn* in modern Húnán.

62. The *zhì* 雉 is *Phasianus colchicus*, the ringed pheasant. See Read, *Avian Drugs*, no. 269.

63. This and the following date which read *jǐngwǔ* 景午 are rendered thus because of a Táng dynasty taboo on the graph *bǐng* 丙 during the reign of the Gāozǔ 高祖 emperor (618–626) imposed because the emperor's father's name was Lǐ Bǐng 李昞. The *Jìn shū* version of this story in Dù Bùqiān's biography (cited above) correctly gives both dates as *bǐngwǔ* 丙午. This would indicate that, one, this story was not copied from the *Jìn shū* and, two, the earliest source for the entry available to the *Sshj* editors could not be prior to Gāozǔ's reign.

would be more than enough. Even if it takes a year to get well, that would hardly be a long time." Thus Chāo still did not really believe him.

But someone urged him to seek out the pheasant following Bùqiān's instructions and they got it as predicted. When the *jǐngwǔ* day arrived, Chāo lay in his southern porch watching it. At late day a female pheasant did fly into the cage, mate with the male, and then fly off. But the male pheasant did not move.

Chāo let out a sigh and said, "How could the wonders of Guǎn Lù and Guō Pú have exceeded this!"[64]

Chāo was sick for over a year before [he was well enough to] get up. When he reached forty he died as clerk to the Palace Secretary.[65]

---

64. Guǎn Lù 管輅 (209–256) was well known for his prognostications based on the *Yì jīng*. See his biography in Mather, *Shih-shuo Hsin-yü*, 576; as well as in the *Sānguó zhì* 三國志 (Beijing: Zhonghua shuju, 1975), 29.811–29, a translation of which is found in DeWoskin, *Doctors, Diviners and Magicians*, 93–134.

65. Though the age given here for Chī Chāo's death conflicts with his dates, Dù Bùqiān's biography (*Jìn shū*, 95.2480) also gives forty as his age at death. Chī Chāo's dates are based on his biography in *Jìn shū*, 67.1804, which says he died at age forty-two. This latter age is confirmed by an entry from Hé Fǎshèng's 何法盛 (n.d.; fl. fifth century) *Jìn zhōngxīng shū* 晉中興書 cited in chapter 17 of Liú Yìqìng's *Shìshuō xīnyǔ* 世說新語, Wāng Zǎo 汪藻 (thirteenth century), ed. (Beijing: Zhonghua shuju, 1962) [hereafter *Ssxy*], C.11b and Mather, *Shih-shuo Hsin-yü*, 350.

Sōushén hòujì: Juàn 3

26. Chéng Xián: A Sign of Success

Chéng Xián (one version gives his name as Chéng Wǔ) went by the sobriquet Xiánxiū.[66] When his mother was first pregnant with Chéng, she dreamed her husband handed her some medicine [and told her], "If you take this, you should give birth to a noble son." By the time of emperor Wǔ of the Jìn [r. 265–290], his rank had attained that of Palace Attendant, and he was well known in the age.

27. A Shooting Star Falls into an Urn: Huán Xuán's Origins

When Yuán Zhēn was in Yùzhōu, he sent the courtesan Jì Líng 紀陵 to present Huán of Xuānwǔ with the three courtesans A-Xuē 阿薛, A-Guō 阿郭, and A-Mǎ 阿馬.[67] When they reached their menses, the three went out together to the front of the courtyard to look out and gaze beneath the moon. Beside them was a copper urn of water. Suddenly they saw a shooting star fall directly out of the night sky into the urn. Pleasantly startled, they watched together as it quickly sank to the bottom of the water like a two-inch pearl of fire, resplendently bright and clear.

"This means good luck," they then said to each other.

"Who should respond to it?"

With that, Xuē and Guō both tried to pick it up with a gourd dipper, but neither could get it. A-Mǎ tried last. The star went right into the dipper and she then drank it. No sooner had she done so when she seemed to have a feeling inside. Soon she was pregnant with Huán Xuán.[68]

Though Xuán's usurpation of power did not last, for a few years his glory and nobility did reach the extreme.

---

66. Chéng Xián 程咸 (n.d.; fl. late third century) is known by this name in the *Jìn shū*, which does not indicate his sobriquet. See *Jìn shū*, especially 30.926, 40.1170. I can find no reference to him by the name Chéng Wǔ 程武, which was probably a simple copy error resulting from the similarity of the graph *xián* to the graph *wǔ*. In the *lèishū* citations of this story, his sobriquet, which is given here as Xiánxiū 咸休, reads Yánxiū 延休. See *Tpyl*, 219.1044 and *Ywlj*, 48.1321. Reference to Chéng Xián in Wáng Yǐn's 王隱 (fl. fourth century) *Jìn shū* 晉書 and Zàng Róngxù's 臧榮緒 (fl. late fifth century) *Jìn shū* 晉書 both give his sobriquet as Yánzuò 延祚. See *Btsc*, 58.10a.

67. Yuán Zhēn 袁真 (d. 370), Duke of Xuānchéng 宣城 (now Xuānchéng xiàn in modern Ānhuī), was a general subordinate to Huán Wēn. He was sent to Yùzhōu 豫州 (in modern Ānhuī) around 362. See *Jìn shū*, 8.206, 98.2576–78.

68. Huán Xuán 桓玄 (369–404) was Huán Wēn's son. He carried on his father's ambition to establish a new dynasty but was killed after only three months as the self-proclaimed emperor of the Chǔ. See his biography in *Jìn shū*, 99.2585–2603; and Mather, *Shih-shuo Hsin-yü*, 568.

28. The Gondola: A Fisherman Forsees the Duke's Success

Xún Xù, the Duke of Línhuái, had the sobriquet Xiūxuán 休玄.[69] His mother, Lady Huá, had an unusual affection and love [for him]. He was ten years of age when they set out on a return from southern Lín and were passing by Lake Qīngcǎo.[70] At the time, their sail stood straight up as [the boat] sped along. When Xù left the border walls he suddenly fell into the water. By the time they were able to bring down the sail, the boat had already gone several dozen *lǐ*. The waves rose and swelled as [Xù's] mother clasped her breast and looked off into the distance. After a short time, she saw a gondola. A fisherman had taken up oars and rowed the gondola as if he were flying, carrying Xù back to her.

"I have brought his honor back," he said.

In later years, Xù's position reached Regular Executive and Minister to Chángshā.[71] Hence, [the fisherman] had called him 'his honor'.

29. The Grain Comes to Fullness: An Unexpected Cornucopia

Wén Cháo (one version reads Zhōu Miǎn), a man from Bāqiū, Lǘlíng, had inherited farming as his occupation.[72] He usually harvested several dozen *qǐng* of farmland each year and his family gradually became rich. During the Jìn, in the early Tàiyuán period [376–397], an autumn harvest had just passed and the cutting and reaping were completed. The next day [Cháo] went to his fields [and discovered] the grain had all returned to fullness, as plump as before. He immediately went ahead and harvested again and what he reaped overflowed the granary. After that they became tremendously wealthy.

30. Monetary Malevolence

Wèi Quán of Shàngyú had his home in the north of the prefecture.[73] Once unexpectedly a man wearing the clothing of a mourning son, a black hat, and a handkerchief covering his mouth, came to visit Quán's family.

---

69. Xún Xù 荀序 (n.d.; fl. early fourth century) was a great-great-grandson of Xún Yǐ's 荀顗 (205–274) brother. See *Jìn shū*, 39.1152. Línhuái 臨淮 was a commandery in the locale of modern Xūyí 盱眙 *xiàn* in Jiāngsū and Língbì 靈壁 *xiàn* in Ānhuī.

70. Lake Qīngcǎo 青草 is southeast of Lake Dòngtíng 洞庭 in Húnán. It is unclear to exactly where 'southern Lin' (*nán* Lín 南臨) refers.

71. The *cháng bó* 常伯 ('Regular Executive') was roughly the equivalent of the *shì zhōng* 侍中 ('Palace Attendant') during the Han. See David R. Knechtges, *The Han shu Biography of Yang Xiong (53 B.C.–A.D. 18)*, Occasional Paper no. 14 (Tempe: Center for Asian Studies, Arizona State Univ., 1982), 116 n. 317.

72. Bāqiū 巴丘 was a prefecture in Lǘlíng 廬陵 commandery occupying area north of Xiájiāng 峡江 *xiàn* in modern Jiāngxī. I can find no other information on Wén Cháo 文晁 or on the other name given in the note, Zhōu Miǎn 周冕.

73. Shàngyú 上虞 prefecture was east of Shàoxīng 紹興 in modern Zhèjiāng. I can find no other information on Wèi Chuán 魏全.

He spoke with them and said, "You, sir, have ten thousand cash and as much in copper utensils. The money is under a large willow tree.[74] If you go get it, you should be able to find it. But it would be highly inauspicious for your family. I'll soon [come again and] take it [away] for you."[75]

He then left.

From this time over thirty years passed and he did not come again, nor did Quán's family go to get the money.

31. Bees Sting the Bandits

In the first year of the Yuánjiā reign [424], in Jiàn'ān commandery, over a hundred mountain bandits laid havoc to the order of the commandery.[76] They seized the possessions and children of the common people. Then they went into a Buddhist monastery to forcibly gather the valuables and treasures there. Earlier the offering utensils had all been placed sealed in another room. When the bandits broke the door, suddenly tens of thousands of bees came out of a bamboo trunk biting and stinging the group of bandits all at once. Their heads and bodies swelled in pain and their eyes all shut in blindness. They dropped all of the things they had seized earlier and ran.

32. Dead Thieves: The Formidable Cài Yì

Cài Yì was courageous, and his voice was like the rumble of thunder.[77] Once two young thieves entered his chamber. Yì rapped on his bed, let out a shout, and the two bandits both dropped dead.

33. A Horse's Urine Relieves an Affliction

There was once a man who contracted an abdominal illness at the same time as his servant. Treatment was unable to cure it. When the servant died, the man cut open his abdomen to look at it. He found [there] a white turtle with red eyes that were extremely bright in color. He tried dousing it in every sort of poisonous agent as well as pouring chemicals into the turtle's mouth. [But] it did not stop wiggling in the least. So he tied it to the foot of the bed.

Unexpectedly he was visited by a guest who came riding a white horse. Shortly, some of the horse's urine splattered onto the turtle. The turtle, terrified, tried to quickly escape

---

74. *Liǔ* 柳 is *Salix babylonica*, the common willow. See Read, *Chinese Medicinal Plants*, 202, no. 624.

75. For *qǔ cǐ* 取此, *Tpyl*, 957.4248, reads *qǔ yú cǐ* 取於此.

76. Yuánjiā 元嘉 was the reign name of emperor Wén of the Southern Sòng (420–479), Liú Yìlóng 劉義隆 (r. 424–454). Jiàn'ān 建安 commandery was in modern Húběi.

77. Cài Yì 蔡裔 (n.d.; fl. fourth century), by the sobriquet Yuánzì 元子, was a nephew of Cài Bào 蔡豹 (269–320). He held both military and civilian offices and died in the military. See *Jìn shū*, 81.2112.

the urine. But because it had been tied up, it could not get away and so retracted its head, neck, and feet into its [shell].

The sick man had seen this [happen] and said to his son, "My illness can perhaps be cured,"

He tried taking some of the white horse's urine and sprinkling it onto the turtle. In a short time [the turtle] had dissolved into a few cups of water. The sick man then immediately drank a cup or so of the white horse urine and he recovered in an instant.

34. A Shoot of Fern Turns into a Snake

Grand Commandant Chī Jiàn, by the sobriquet Dàohuī 道徽, was garrisoned in Dāntú.[78] He once went hunting in the middle of the second month, when the ferns had begun to sprout.

One of his armorclad soldiers picked a shoot and ate it.[79] He immediately felt dizzy and was on the verge of vomiting. After that they returned and [his discomfort] turned into pains in his heart and abdomen. After about half a year, he suddenly vomited heavily, throwing up a crimson snake that was over a foot long and still alive and wiggling. He hung it at the front of the eaves to his quarters. Slowly oozing moisture, the snake gradually dried up and shrank. After a night had passed he looked at it [and found] it had become a shoot of fern just like he had eaten earlier. After that, he recovered from his illness.

35. Gallon-and-a-Half Nausea

During the time of Huán of Xuānwǔ, there was a Supervisory General who after [contracting] some prevalent illness was weak and feverish, but had become quite adept at drinking restorative tea. It inevitably would take a gallon and a half before he was full.[80] If he cut down only an ounce or two he would not be satisfied. This did not go on for just one day and his family became poor.

---

78. Chī Jiàn 郗鑒 (269–339) has a biography in *Jìn shū*, 67.1796–1801. Dāntú 丹徒 is now Dāntú *xiàn* in Jiāngsū.

79. *Jué* 蕨 commonly refers to a variety of ferns, usually *Pteridium aquilinum*, common braken or eagle fern. See Read, *Chinese Medicinal Plants*, 274, no. 811. What may be meant here is the fern known as *míjué* 迷蕨 or *zǐqí* 紫淇, probably *Osmunda japonica*, a plant that according to *Běncǎo gāngmù*, 27.1668, can be eaten when young. See also *Zhōngguó gāoděng zhíwù tújiàn* 中國高等植物圖鑑, edited by Zhōngguó kēxuéyuàn, zhíwù yánjiùsuǒ (Beijing: Kexue chubanshe, 1972), 1: 124.

80. *Fùmíng* 複茗 ('restorative tea') is unclear. *Míng* alone is *Thea sinensis*, Chinese tea, and was a local Wú 吳 term that later referred more specifically to "late-picked" tea. See Read, *Chinese Medicinal Plants*, 75, no. 267; *Běncǎo gāngmù*, 32.1870–74; and Mather, *Shih-shuo Hsin-yü*, 663. I find only one other reference to *fùmíng* in Pí Rìxiū's 皮日休 (ca. 834–ca. 883) "Chádǐng shī" 茶鼎詩, which gives no further clues as to what kind of tea it refers to. See Lù Guīméng 陸龜蒙 and Pí Rìxiū, *Sōng Lù jí* 松陸集 (*Sìkù quánshū zhēnběn* edn.), 4.24b–25a.

Later a guest came to visit and happened upon him just as he was drinking his restorative tea. [The guest] had heard before that this disease was going around at the time and had him take an additional cup. With that he vomited hard and something came out. It was as big as a pint measure and had a mouth. Its form was all wrinkled and it had a texture similar to tripe. The guest had him put the thing into a dish and sprinkle it with a gallon and a half of mixed tea. The thing completely absorbed [the tea] yet they only discerned it to be slightly swollen. They added another cup and then everything came spurting out of its mouth in a gush. Once he had thrown up this thing, he recovered from his illness.

"What disease was that?" someone asked him.

"Gallon-and-a-half nausea," he answered (Some read 'Gallon-of-tea [nausea]').[81]

36. Huán and Méi Share a Dream

Huán Zhé had the sobriquet Míngqí 明期 and was living in Yùzhāng.[82] At the time, Méi Yuánlóng was the Grand Administrator and had earlier become ill.[83] Zhé went to see how he was.

"Last night I unexpectedly dreamed I was a foot soldier and met you coming to be the Lord of Mt. Tài mansion," he told Méi.[84]

Méi was startled when he heard this and said, "I also dreamed you were a foot soldier coming to greet me dressed in funeral attire."

After several days had passed, they again had similar dreams just as before and were told, "You should be meeting formally on the twenty-eighth."

On the twenty-seventh in the late afternoon, Huán suddenly became terribly sick with a bloated abdomen. He approached Méi and requested some musk pills.[85] When Méi heard, he ordered coffins to be prepared. Huán died on the twenty-seventh and Méi passed away on the twenty-eighth.

37. Huá Xīn Will Be a Duke

Huá Xīn of Píngyuán had the sobriquet Zǐyú 子魚.[86] When he was a student he once spent the night outside someone's gate. The mistress of the house gave birth that night

---

81. For the reading given in this parenthetical note, see *Tpyl*, 867.3844 and *Slf*, 17.2a.

82. For Huán Zhé 桓哲, *Tpgj*, 276.2032, reads Huán Shì 桓誓. I can find no information on either name.

83. I can find nothing further on the name Méi Yuánlóng 梅元龍. However, Méi Yí 梅頤 (n.d.; fl. mid-fourth century), *zì* Zhòngzhēn 仲真, once served as Grand Administrator of Yùzhāng. See chapter 5 of *Ssxy*, B.17a; and Mather, *Shih-shuo Hsin-yü*, 179 n. 39, and 590. Perhaps this is the same man.

84. *Tàishān fǔjūn* 泰山府君 ('the Lord of Mt. Tài mansion') was a deity thought to be in charge of life and death. Tàishān 泰山 ('Mt. Tài') is the eastern of the Five Peaks, located in Shāndōng.

85. Musk was taken for pain and swelling of the abdomen. See Read, *Chinese Materia Medica: Animal Drugs* (Peiping: Peking Natural History Bulletin, 1931), no. 369.

86. Huá Xīn 華歆 (157–231) has a biography in *Sānguó zhì*, 13.401–6. Píngyuán 平原 commandery was south of modern Píngyuán *xiàn*, Shāndōng.

and soon after that two clerks came up to the gate. [Seeing Huá Xīn] they recoiled away from him and were about to turn back, saying to each other, "The Duke is here."

After that, they hesitated for a long time [before] one of the clerks said, "[Zǐyú's residence] registration should be stipulated, how is that he can stay [here by the gate]?"

With that they went forward to formally greet Zǐyú and then the two went in. When they came out, they were walking side by side and talking together.

"How many years should we give him?"

"We should give him three years," one said.

At daylight, Zǐyú left. Later on, he wanted to verify this matter and after three years had passed, he went to look for news about the child. As predicted, the child had died at three years of age. Delighted for himself, [Zǐyú] said, "I shall surely be a Duke." It did turn out that he later became a Grand Commandant.[87]

38. Image and Soul Strangely Apart

In Sòng times there was a man, his name has been forgotten, who slept together with his wife.[88] One morning soon after the wife had gotten up and gone out, her husband also went out. [Yet] the wife returned and saw her husband still asleep beneath the covers. Shortly, their servant came in from outside and said, "Your husband wants the mirror."

The wife took the servant to be deceiving her and pointed to the bed to let the servant know.

"I just came from where your husband is," the servant said, and with that ran out to explain to the husband.

The husband was quite shocked and went right in to check it out together with his wife. The person inside the covers was serenely and restfully sleeping. He was exactly the husband's image, without a single difference. They thought it was his soul and did not dare to budge or alarm it. So they steadily stroked the bed and it gradually went into the mattress and disappeared.

Husband and wife sighed ceaselessly with terror. In a short time, the husband got ill. His nature went perversely awry and, never recovering, he died.

39. Dǒng Shòuzhī: Visiting the Family after Death

Dǒng Shòuzhī had been executed and his family did not yet know.[89] His wife was sitting at night and suddenly saw Shòuzhī at her side, sighing endlessly. His wife asked him, "How have you been able to come back at night?"

---

87. *Tàiwèi* 太尉 ('Grand Commandant') was considered to be one of the *sān gong* 三公 or Three Dukes, a collective designation for offices at the upper echelon of court administration (see below j. 6, no. 67, n. 158). Hence, Huá Xīn did become a 'Duke'. Note, however, that this reference to rank is not in Huá's *Sānguó zhì* biography, though this story is cited there from Cáo Pī's 曹丕 (187–226) *Liè yì zhuàn* 列異傳.

88. *Sòng shí* 宋時 ('Sòng times') is the period of the Liú Sòng 劉宋 (420–279).

89. I can find nothing on Dǒng Shòuzhī 董壽之.

Shòuzhī did not answer at all. After a bit, he went out the door and walked around the chicken coop. The chickens in the coop squawked in alarm. The wife suspected something unusual and went out the door carrying a torch to check it out. She saw several pints of blood, but Shòuzhī was not to be found. After that she went in and told her mother-in-law about it, then joined with the young and old [of the family] in wailing and crying, knowing there had been trouble.

By morning they did end up receiving notification of his death.

40. A Spirit Cart

In Sòng times there was a scholar who went afar to study. His parents had lit a fire and were working at night when their son suddenly showed up in front of them. He sighed and said, "Today I am merely a spirit, not someone who has come back to life."

When his parents asked about it, he said, "I got sick at the beginning of this month, and died at a certain time today. Now I am at the home of Rén Zǐchéng in Lángyé, and tomorrow I will be placed in the coffin and greet you, my parents."[90]

His parents said, "As for going this thousand li, even if all were turned upside down, how could we reach you [there]?"

"There is a carriage outside. Just get in it and you will naturally be able to get there," the son said.

His parents did as he said and got in the carriage. Swiftly, as if they had slept, by [the time of] the rooster's crow, they had arrived at where he was. They inspected their conveyance [and found] it was just a spirit cart with wooden horses.[91] Then they met with the hosts and when they looked upon their son, they grieved, heartbroken. When they asked for information about his illness, it was just as he had said.

90. Lángyé 琅琊 commandery was in Shāndōng. I can find no information on Rén Zǐchéng 任子成.

91. A *hún jū* 魂車 ('spirit cart') was a cart used at a funeral in which the clothes of the deceased were placed to look as if he were riding in the cart.

Sōushén hòujì: Juàn 4

41. The Daughter of Xú Xuánfāng: A Dream Comes to Life

In Jìn times, Féng Xiàojiāng 馮孝將 of Dōngpíng was the Grand Administrator at Guǎngzhōu.[92] His son, named Mǎzǐ 馬子 and over twenty years old, was sleeping alone in the stables when he dreamed one night that he met a young woman. She was about eighteen or nineteen.

"I am the daughter of the former Grand Administrator Xú Xuánfāng 徐玄方 of Běihǎi," she said.[93] "Unfortunately I died early. It has been four years now since my death. I was killed by a ghost for nothing. According to the register of lives, I should live to over eighty. So I have been allowed to return to life. But I must rely on [you], Mǎzǐ, if I am to be able to live. Moreover, we must become husband and wife. Can you go along with this plea and save me?"

"I can," Mǎzǐ replied.

So she set a date with Mǎzǐ and went out. When the day they had agreed on arrived, there was some hair on the ground in front of [Mǎzǐ's] bed just level with the ground.[94] [Mǎzǐ] ordered someone to sweep it away, but it became more distinct and he realized it was the young woman he had seen in his dream. So he sent all those nearby away. Gradually her forehead came out, then her head and face, and then her neck, shoulders and body came out all at once. Mǎzǐ had her sit on the opposite bed. What she said and her conversation was unusually fantastic and intriguing. Then she slept with Mǎzǐ.

Whenever she admonished [Mǎzǐ], saying, "I am still only etherial," he immediately asked what time she could come out [from her grave].

"My coming out must be on my birthday for my original life, which has not yet arrived," she answered.

Then they went to the stables. Others could all hear the sound of her voice as she spoke. The young woman calculated when her birthday would arrive and explained to Mǎzǐ the method for getting her to come out and taking care of her. When she was done talking, she departed.

Mǎzǐ did as she said and when the day arrived, he took up one red rooster, one dish of cooked millet, and one pint of clear wine, offered them in front of her grave and then went ten paces away from the stables.[95] When the sacrifice was over, [Mǎzǐ] dug up the coffin. He opened it to look and found that the appearance of the young woman's body was entirely as it had been originally. He carefully lifted her out and placed her inside

---

92. Dōngpíng 東平 prefecture was in the area of modern Fújiàn. Guǎngzhōu 廣州 took up the area of modern Guǎngdōng and Guǎngxī. I can find no information on any of the names central to this story.

93. Běihǎi 北海 commandery took up an area largely west of Yìdū 益都 *xiàn* in modern Shāndōng.

94. For *tóufà* 頭髮, *Tpyl*, 887.3941, reads *fǎngfú rú rén* 彷彿如人, 'it seemed like a person'.

95. On *qīngjiǔ* 清酒 ('clear wine'), see Ying-shih Yü, in *Food in Chinese Culture*, ed. K. C. Chang (New Haven: Yale Univ. Press, 1977), 68.

a felt tent. She was faintly warm only beneath her heart, and there was breath upon her mouth. He had four maidservants stay by and nurse her. They frequently applied drops of black goat's milk to her two eyes which then were slowly able to open. She could take porridge with her mouth and soon she was able to talk. Within two hundred days, she could walk using a cane. After a year, her complexion, flesh, and energy had all returned to normal.

Then notification was sent to the Xú clan and they all came, seniors and minors. An auspicious day was picked to present the gifts and [Mǎzǐ and Miss Xú] were betrothed as husband and wife. She bore two sons and one girl. The eldest son was styled Yuánqìng and in the early Yǒngjiā period was an assistant in the palace library.[96] The younger son was styled Jìngdù 敬度 and was a clerk to the Grand Tutor. Their daughter was married to Liú Zǐyàn 劉子彥 of Jǐ'nán 濟南 who is said to be the grandson of Yánshì, the Recruit for Office.[97]

42. Gān Bǎo's Father's Concubine

Gān Bǎo went by the sobriquet Lìngshēng 令升 and his ancestors were from Xīncài.[98] His father, Yíng 瑩, had a favorite concubine of whom his mother was extremely jealous. When Bǎo's father died, she took the opportunity to push the concubine right into the tomb. Bǎo and his brothers were still young and did not know of this. After ten years had passed, their mother died and when they opened the grave they saw the concubine lying prostrate upon the coffin, her clothing as if she were alive. When they had a closer look, [they found] she was still warm. She gradually began to breathe.

They carted her home in a litter and by the end of the day she had recovered. She said that Bǎo's father had often given her things to eat and drink, that he had slept with her—his love and affection just as if he were living—and that he had always talked [with her] about the good and bad fortunes of the family. Checking them out [the concubine saw that] they were all as he had said. She recovered completely and lived a good many years before dying.

Bǎo's brother had once been so sick that he stopped breathing.[99] But for many days his body remained warm. Afterwards he woke up and said he had seen the affairs of

---

96. For Yuánqìng 元慶 *Tpyl* reads Yuándù 元度.

97. Yánshì 延世 was the sobriquet of Liú Zhào 劉兆 (n.d.; fl. third century) who has a biography in *Jìn shū*, 91.2394–50. See also Xí Zúochǐ 習鑿齒 (d. 384), *Hàn Jìn chūnqiū* 漢晉春秋, cited in the notes to "Wáng Xiū zhuàn" 王脩傳, *Jìn shū*, 11.349.

98. Gān Bǎo was the author of the *Sōu shén jì*. He has a biography in *Jìn shū*, 82.2149–51. Xīncài 新蔡 commandery is now modern Xīncài *xiàn* in Hénán.

99. There is speculation that this brother of Bǎo's (Bǎo *xiōng* 寶兄) was Gān Qìng 干慶 whose revival was achieved with the help of Wú Měng 吳猛 (cf. j. 2, no. 12). See *Shí'èr zhēn jūn zhuàn* 十二真君傳, cited in *Tpgj*, 14.123–24; *Xīshān Xǔ zhēnjūn bāshíwǔ huà lù* 西山許真君八十五化錄, in vol. 200 of the *Zhèngtǒng dàozàng* 正統道藏 (Taibei: Yiwen yinshuguan, 1962–64), C.1b; Liú Yìqìng's *Yōu míng lù*, in Lǔ Xùn, *Gǔ xiǎoshuō*, 217–18; Shěn Shìlóng's preface to *Ssj* (in the *Mìcè huìhán* and *Jìndài mìshū* editions); *Yùzhāng jì* 豫章記 by Kulapati Lei (Léi *jūshì* 雷居士,

the ghosts and spirits between heaven and earth. It had seemed like a dream; he did not know he had died.

43. Chén Liáng: Retribution after Death

In the Tàiyuán reign of the Jìn, Chén Liáng 陳良 of Běidì was good friends with Liú Shū 劉舒 of Pèiguó 沛國.[100] He also worked as a merchant together with Lǐ Yān 李焉 of his commandery. After a time they made a great profit so Yān killed Liáng and took the goods. When he had been dead a little over ten days, Liáng suddenly came back to life and was able to return to his family. He said that while he was dead, he saw his friend Liú Shū.

Shū had been dead for a long time. He told Liáng, "Last year on the day of the Spring festival, during the offerings, there was a quarrel within [my] family. I was really angry with them and made a gaur at the front of the room.[101] When you go back, can you tell my family about this for me?"

Liáng had agreed and so went to tell Shū's family. But the oddity had already ceased. After that he reported Lǐ Yān to the officials and [Lǐ] was brought to justice for his crime.

44. Lǐ Chú: Bribery in the Other World

Lǐ Chú of Xiāngyáng died after coming down with a prevalent illness.[102] His wife was staying with the corpse. When it got to be midnight, he sat up with a start and grabbed at the gold bracelet on his wife's arm in quite a panic. His wife helped him take it off and once he held it in his hands, he returned to death. His wife kept an eye on him and at dawn his heart got warm and he gradually was able to come back to life.

Once back alive, he said, "I was being taken away by an official and those accompanying me were quite numerous. I saw someone procure release through bribery, so I promised the official the gold bracelet. The official ordered me to return and thus I came back to get it to give to the official. When he had obtained the bracelet, the official set me free and ordered me to return. I saw the official take the bracelet and go."

---

i.e., Léi Cìzōng 雷次宗 [n.d.; of the Liú Sòng]) cited in the *Wén xuǎn chāo* 文選鈔 commentary to Jiāng Yān's 江淹 (444–505) imitation of Guō Pú's "Yóu xiān shī" 遊仙詩 preserved in *Táng xiě Wénxuǎn jìzhù cánběn* 唐寫文選記住殘本, ed. Luó Zhènyù 羅振玉 (1866–1940), *Jiācǎo Xuān cóngshū* 嘉草軒叢書 ed. (1918), j. 62 (no further pagination); Zhào Dàoyī, *Lìshì zhēnxiān*, 27.1a–b; and Wāng Shàoyíng, *Ssj*, 1.13–14, no. 26 and no. 26, n. 4. Concerning the *Yùzhāng jì* citation, see Yú Jiāxī's 余嘉錫 *Sìkù tíyào biànzhèng* 四庫提要辨證 notice for the *Ssj*, and Wāng Shàoyíng's accompanying note, found in the appendix to Wāng's *Ssj*, 261–63, n. 6.

100. Běidì 北地 was a commandery in an area now of southeastern Gānsù and southern Níngxià. I find no other information on the people mentioned in this story.

101. The *sì* 兕 ('guar') is a large horned bovine. See the discussion in Carl Whiting Bishop, "Rhinoceros and Wild Ox in Ancient China," *China Journal* 18 (1933): 322–30. Its significance here is unclear.

102. Xiāngyáng 襄陽 commandery occupied what is now Xiāngyáng *xiàn* in Húběi. Lǐ Chú 李除 appears to be unknown.

A few days later, they unexpectedly [found the bracelet] still inside his wife's clothes. But his wife did not dare to wear it again and, because of this business, buried it with appropriate incantations.

45. Zhèng Mào: Reviving a Corpse

Zhèng Mào 鄭茂 had passed away. His corpse had already been placed inside the coffin but he had not yet been interred when unexpectedly his wife and the others in his family dreamed Mào said, "I should not yet be dead, I just happened to run out of breath. You can open the coffin and take me out, then heat a pot and singe the top of [my] head with it." They did as he said and he came to life.

46. The Daughter of Lǐ Zhòngwén: A Chance to Come Back to Life

In Jìn times, the Grand Administrator of Wǔdū, Lǐ Zhòngwén 李仲文, lost his eighteen-year-old daughter while at the commandery. He took temporary leave to bury her north of the commandery walls.[103] Zhāng Shìzhī 張世之 took his place at the head of the commandery. Shìzhī's son, styled Zǐcháng 子長, was twenty and assisting at the office. One night he dreamed of a young woman about seventeen or eighteen and of extraordinary complexion. She said she was the daughter of the former governor and had unfortunately died early. But it happened that now she was about to come back to life; and since she was very fond [of Zǐcháng] she had thus come to be near to him. This happened for five or six nights. Then suddenly she appeared during the day. Her clothing and fragrance were uncommonly exquisite. Thereupon they became man and wife and slept together. Her clothing became soiled just as if she were a virgin.

Later on, Zhòngwén sent a maid to visit his daughter's grave. She went to visit Shìzhī's wife after that. When she entered the office, she saw one of the daughter's shoes beneath Zǐcháng's bed. The maid picked it up and began to sob, screaming that [Zǐcháng] had opened up the girl's grave. She took the shoe back to show to Zhòngwén and he was much alarmed. He sent [someone] to ask Shìzhī, "How did your son obtain my dead daughter's shoe?" Shìzhī called [his son] to ask him. His son explained everything from beginning to end. Lǐ and Zhāng both found it quite strange and dug up the coffin to examine it. The young woman's body had grown flesh and her appearance and complexion were as they had been originally. There was a shoe on her right foot but not on her left.

Zǐcháng dreamed that the young woman told him, "Just as I have regained my life, I have now been dug up. Following this I will die, my flesh will rot, and I will not come to life anymore.[104] My heart is filled with a thousand regrets. How can I ever speak [of them] again?" Shedding tears, she departed.

---

103. Wǔdū 武都 was a commandery in an area west of Chéng 成 *xiàn* in modern Gānsù. I can find no information on the persons named in this entry.

104. For this final paragraph up to this point, the *Mìcè huìhán* and *Fyzl*, 92.21a–b, read: "Following this she died, her flesh rotted, and she did not come to life [again]." The *Tpyl*, 887.3941, reads the same way and then adds: "The following evening, the young woman came and said, "Our

47. Tiger Talismans: A Southern Technique

During the Wèi [220–265], the Southerners in the mountains north of Xúnyáng prefecture had a technique whereby they could cause people to transform into tigers.[105] Their hair, color, claws, and fangs would all be like a real tiger. The villager Zhōu Zhěn 周眕 had a servant whom he sent into the hills to gather firewood.[106] The servant had a wife and sister who also went together with him. When they got to the hills, the servant spoke to the other two.

"Climb a tall tree for now, then watch what I do," he said.

They did as he said. He immediately went into the bushes. In a short while, they saw a large yellow striped tiger come out from the bushes fiercely bolting and roaring. It was extremely frightening. The two of them were terrified. After a fairly long time it returned to the bushes and then shortly returned as the man. He then told the two of them, "When we return home be careful not to say anything."

But later they told their peers about it. Zhōu eventually found out and he then treated the servant to some rich wine and got him good and drunk. He had someone go through his clothes and person, examining everything thoroughly.[107] There was nothing unusual. Only in his hair knot did they find a piece of paper upon which was drawn a large tiger. Beside the tiger was a talisman. Zhōu secretly kept and made record [of it]. When the servant had come around, [Zhōu] called him in to ask about it. Seeing that the affair had already been exposed, he then told all, from beginning to end:

"Earlier, I had been buying grain from the Southerners when a Southern master said he knew this technique. He taught me the method, making use of three feet of cloth, several cups of fine rice, one red rooster, and one pint of wine."[108]

48. Transforming into a Turtle

During the Wèi, the mother of Sòng Shìzōng of Qīnghé took a bath in the bathhouse on a summer's day in the Huángchū reign.[109] She had the children in the family close the door.

---

feelings as man and wife had achieved their ultimate and I thought we could grow old together. Yet I thoughtlessly left my shoe behind and ended up being exposed. I will not be able to live anew."

105. Xúnyáng 尋陽 prefecture occupied territory north of Huángméi 黃梅 *xiàn* in modern Húběi. I find nothing else on Zhōu Zhěn.

106. A note to this sentence says the graph *yú* 餘 appears above *xiāng rén* 鄉人 ('villager') in one version. Such a reading can be found in the *Fyzl*, 43.12a–b. There is no such a place as 'Yúxiāng', so this reading must be a copy error.

107. For *xī* 悉, *Tpyl*, 88.3946 and *Fyzl* read *shì* 視.

108. For *mǐ xǔ* 米糈, *Fyzl* reads *mǐ jīng* 米精 (the *Mìcè huìhán* edition reads 糈, which is a variant of *xǔ* 糈). Neither *mǐ xǔ* or *mǐ jīng* are very clear in meaning. The term *xǔ mǐ* 糈米 means 'rice for offering' and since that would likely be 'fine rice', or 'refined rice', the essential meaning of the graph *jīng* 精 or *jīng mǐ* 精米, I have translated it as such.

109. This entry is not found in the *Jìndài mìshū* or *Mìcè huìhán* editions of the *Sshj*. It is found, however, in an almost identical but slightly more detailed version in *Ssj*, 14.175–6, no. 356. This and the fact that *Ywlj*, 96.2472, cites this story as *Ssj* may be why the editors of the *Mìcè huìhán* did not include it even though *Fyzl*, 43.20b–21a, *Tpyl*, 888.3946, and *Tpgj*, 471.3545, cite it as

But the family peeked through a hole in the wall and saw a large turtle in the water.[110] They opened the door and young and old all went in. [The turtle] could not the least bit be compared to a person, [though] the silver hairpin that [their mother] had often worn before was still on her head.[111]

They stayed with her, watching over her and crying, yet there was nothing that could be done. [After a time] she went outside at [such] a fast pace they could not keep up with her. Then she went into the water. Several days later, she suddenly returned. She crawled all around the house, just like in her ordinary life, and then left without a word.

The people of his day said Shìzōng should observe mourning. Shìzōng felt that though his mother's body had changed she was still quite alive, and so in the end would not organize a mourning. This is similar to [the story of] the mother of Huáng 黃 of Jiāngxià.[112]

Xssj. It may have found its way from the *Xssj* into the *Ssj* via inclusion in a *Ssj-Xssj* conflation. The story of Sòng Shìzōng's 宋士宗 mother is also listed in the "Wǔ xíng zhì" 五行志 of the *Jìn shū*, 29.906, and of the *Sòng shū* (Beijing: Zhonghua shuju, 1975), 34.1004. Qīnghé 清河 commandery occupied an area that now forms part of Héběi and part of Shāndōng. Huángchū 黃初 was the Wèi reign name of Cáo Pī (r. 220–226).

110. For *yuán* 黿, the *Ssj* reads *biē* 鱉. *Yuán* is generally used to refer to larger turtles and often specifically to *Pelochelys cantorii*. See Read, *Chinese Materia Medica*: *Turtle and Shellfish Drugs* (Peiping: Peking Natural History Bulletin, 1937), no. 213.

111. The *Fyzl* and *Ssj* read *cháng* 嘗 for *dāng* 當. The latter is probably a copy error and the sentence should read, "*Cháng xiān zhuó yín chāi . . .*" 嘗先著銀釵 This is the reading I translate.

112. Jiāngxià 江夏 was located within the boundaries of modern Húběi.

Sōushén hòujì: Juàn 5

49. The Fair Maiden of Pure Waters

During the time of the Ān emperor of the Jìn, Xiè Duān of Hòuguān lost his parents at a young age.[113] Since he had no relatives, he was raised by his neighbors. When he reached seventeen or eighteen, he was respectful and prudent, took care of himself, and did not tread astray of the law. [Yet] by the time he first lived away [from home], he still did not have a wife. His neighbors, all feeling sorry for him, planned to help [Duān] find a wife, but had not yet succeeded.

Duān would go to bed at nightfall and rise early. When tilling the fields, [however], he worked with great effort, heedless of day or night.

After a time, he found a snail near his village which was rather like a three-pint teapot. He thought it to be an unusual creature and picked it up to take home with him, where he kept it in an urn. He stored it there for over ten days. Each time Duān returned after going to the fields in the morning, he would discover food, drink, hot water, and a fire, just as if someone had set it all up. Duān thought his neighbors were being kind to him. After several days like this, he went to thank them.

Yet his neighbors said, "We didn't do this to start with, why do you thank us?"

Duān figured that his neighbors didn't understand what he meant, but he got this [response] several times. So in the end he asked [outright], spelling out the facts.

"You've already taken a wife, and keep her secretly inside to tend to your hearth," his neighbors laughed and said, "Yet you say we're doing the cooking?"

Duān was silently suspicious and did not know the explanation. After that he went out at cockcrow and stole back at dawn to sneak a peek inside his house from outside the fence. He saw a young woman come out from the urn and go over to light a fire under the stove. Duān then went in the door and headed directly over to the place where the urn was to check out the snail. All he saw was the woman.[114]

He went over to the stove and asked her, "Where have you come from, young bride, that you do the cooking for me?"

The woman became flustered and was going to return to the urn but could not get there.

---

113. The Ān 安 emperor, Sīmǎ Dézōng 司馬德宗, reigned from 397 to 418. However, other fairly complete versions of this story identified as *Ssj* read *Jìn'ān Hòuguān* 晉安候官 without the intervening *dì shí* 帝時, identifying Hòuguān 候官 prefecture as belonging to *Jìn'ān* commandery (now Nán'ān 南安 *xiàn* in present day Fújiàn). Though this reading is quite valid, there is no reason to believe it is the preferable, or even the prior, reading. See *Ywlj*, 97.2477; *Tpgj*, 62.410; and Duàn Gōnglù 段公路 (of the Táng) *Běi hù lù* 北户錄, (Changsha: Shangwu yinshuguan, 1941), 2.20. I find nothing else on Xiè Duān 謝端.

114. According to both Wāng Shàoyíng (*Sshj*, 5.31, no. 49, n. 3) and Wáng Guóliáng (*Sōushén hòujì yánjiū*, 5.75, no. 9, n. 5), the Míng manuscript edition of the *Tàipíng guǎngjì* reads *ké* 殼 'shell' for *nǚ* 女 'woman'. This edition of the *Tàipíng guǎngjì* was not available to me, so I could not verify the reading. However, it would appear to be much more satisfactory.

"I am the Fair Maiden of Pure Waters from the Milky Way," she replied, "The Celestial King was moved that you were orphaned when young. Since you are respectful, prudent, and take care of yourself, he sent me to temporarily look after your house and do the cooking. I was to see that within ten years you came to live in prosperity and found a wife. Then I was to return. Yet you have unreasonably stolen up and peeked at me. Since you have already seen my form, I cannot stay any longer and must leave you and go. Though that be the case, things will naturally improve for you later on. Work hard in the fields, at fishing, and at tending your life. I will leave this shell when I go [for you] to keep grain in. It should never run out."

Duān requested that she stay, but to the end she was unwilling. At this time, it suddenly got windy and began to rain. Then she flew off like a phoenix. Duān set up a spirit altar for her and made offerings at festival times. He lived always in ample sufficiency; he just never became really wealthy, that's all. The villagers then married him to one of their daughters. It is said that his official career reached that of District Magistrate.

The Temple of the Fair Maiden [found] along the road today is this one [of hers].

50. The Qīngxī Temple Diety

During the Tàikāng reign of the Jìn, the Sramana Zhú Tánsuì of the Xiè 謝 family, twenty years of age or so, fair and white [of complexion], and straight and proper [of manner], traveled among common monks.[115] He would often walk by Qīngxī temple, going in to look around.[116] [One] evening when he returned home he dreamed a woman came.

"You should be coming to be our temple deity," she said, "It won't be long."

"Who are you madam?" Tán asked in his dream.

The woman said, "I am a lady of the Qīngxī temple."

About a month after this he became ill. Just before dying, he told the youths who studied together with him:

"I am without blessing, yet also have [done] no great wrong, so when I die I will become the Qīngxī temple deity. Whenever it is convenient for you, do come by to see it."

After he died, all the young devotees came to visit his temple. Once they had arrived, his soul spoke and inquired after their health. His voice was like it had been in earlier times.

"It has been a long time since I have heard the sound of your Patha," he said just as they were leaving. "I wish to hear it once."

So their companion Huìjìn then did a Patha for him.

When he was done his spirit seemed to sing in praise:

---

115. Jìn Tàikāng 晉太康 ('the Tàikāng reign of the Jìn') should read Jìn Tàiyuán 晉太元 ('the Tàiyuán reign of the Jìn'), i.e., 376–396. See *Tpgj*, 294.2168, *Fyzl*, 108.22a–b, and Gāo Chéng 高承 (fl. 1078–1085), *Shìwù jìyuán* 事物紀原, *Xīyīnxuān cóngshū* 惜陰軒叢書 edn., 7.29b. Compare the similar copy error in *Sshj*, j. 1, no. 5 above. I find no further information on Zhú Tánsuì 竺曇遂.

116. For *cháng* 長, *Fyzl* and *Tpgj* read *cháng* 嘗. Qīngxī temple 清溪廟 is in Jiāngníng 江寧 *xiàn*, Jiāngsū.

A parting at a fork in the road,
 is yet filled with melancholy.
How much more so is this departure,
 when spirit and body are scattered apart.
With a secluded and distant sigh,
 how can my feelings be expressed?

When he was finished, he sobbed unbearably and all the devotees shed tears for him.

51. Wáng Dǎo's Son Yuè: Sold in a Dream

Wáng Dǎo's son Yuè was Clerk to the Palace Writers.[117] Dǎo dreamed someone offered to buy Yuè for a million in cash. Dǎo secretly performed prayers to ward off [trouble]. But after a short time, when digging, he found a million in cash.[118] He thought it utterly detestable and buried it all away. Then Yuè became desperately ill. Dǎo's distress over him was especially extreme, and he did not eat for days.

Suddenly he saw a man, very imposing in stature, dressed in armor and brandishing a sword. He asked him who he was.

"I am Marquis Jiǎng," he said.[119] "Your son is not doing well. I am going to plead for his life for you. Hence, I have come. Please do not be distressed anymore."

After that Dǎo gave him something to eat and he partook of several helpings. When he was done eating, he addressed Dǎo with great agitation.

"The Palace Writer's life has run out, he cannot be saved," he said.

He finished speaking and disappeared. Yuè died at the same time.

---

117. A fragment of this entry is cited in Wāng Zǎo's (thirteenth century) "*Shìshuō xīnyǔ kǎoyì*" 世說新語考異 found in his edition of the *Ssxy*, 22b. He is probably citing *Tpgj*, 141.991, which gives the same fragment identified as *Ssxy*. A translation of this fragment can be found in Mather, *Shih-shuo Hsin-yü*, 15. Other *lèishū* cite the fragment version as *Yōumíng lù*, see Lǔ Xùn, *Gǔ xiǎoshuō*, 218. This *Sshj* version is the most detailed. Wáng Yuè 王悅 (n.d.; d. before 339) was Wang Dǎo's favorite son. On him see *Jìn shū*, 65.1754–55.

118. The *Yōumíng lù* and *Ssxy* versions (cited above) say he found the money when digging to build a house.

119. Jiǎng hóu 蔣侯 ('Marquis Jiǎng') is probably Jiǎng Zǐwén 子文 (n.d.) of the Eastern Hàn who was killed by bandits at the foot of Mt. Zhōng 鐘山 (northeast of Nánjīng in Jiāngsū). He was eventually deified and Sūn Quán 孫權 (182–252), as emperor of the state of Wú, posthumously enfeoffed him Zhōngdū *hóu* 中都侯 'Marquis of Zhōngdū' (Zhōngdū was a Hàn prefecture in an area northwest of Píngyáo 平遙 *xiàn* in modern Shānxī). At the same time, Sūn Quán built a temple for him and renamed Mt. Zhōng to Mt. Jiǎng 蔣山. See Wāng Shàoyíng, *Ssj*, 5.57–61, nos. 92–96, especially no. 92.

52. Wú Wàngzǐ: Meeting Marquis Jiǎng

In the eastern outskirts of Mào prefecture in Guìjī, there was a young lady surnamed Wú 吳, with the sobriquet Wàngzǐ 望子.[120] On the road she suddenly saw a person of nobility, sitting straight up in a dignified manner. It was the image of Marquis Jiǎng. Then he threw a tangerine to her.[121]

His form appeared over and over again [after that] and their affection grew quite affable. Whenever Wàngzǐ desired something, she would get it immediately out of thin air. Once she thought of minced fish and a pair of carp came out from mid-air.

53. A Wooden Image Draws His Bow

When Sūn Ēn was rebelling and Wúxìng was divided and chaotic, a fellow [once] burst into the temple to Marquis Jiǎng.[122] He had just gone through the door when a wooden image drew a bow and shot him. He died immediately. Everyone walking [past] and all in charge of the temple saw the whole thing.

54. The White-Haired Duke: A Diety Descends

During the Tàiyuán reign of the Jìn [376–396], Gāo Héng of Lèān was Grand Administrator of Wèijūn and garrisoned at Shítóu.[123] His grandson Yǎzhì had [once] been in the stables [where he] said a deity had descended.[124] Calling himself the White Haired Duke, [the deity] leaned on a staff and his brilliance lit up the room ('the White Haired Duke' is white jade).[125] He joined Yǎzhì to levitate and roam through the night, going to

---

120. An abridged version of this story is found in *Tpyl*, 936.4160, and in *Cxj*, 28.681, identified in the former as *Xssj* and in the latter as belonging to the *Sshj*. A more detailed version of the story is found in *Fyzl*, 78.3b–4a, and cited as from *Xssj*. This more complete *Fyzl* version, however, found its way into the *Ssj*, 5.60, no. 95, perhaps because it was identified as part of that collection in *Btsc*, 145.10a, or perhaps because the fuller version of this story is also incorporated into a long piece on Jiǎng Ziwén in *Tpgj*, 293.2157, which is also cited as *Ssj*. Mào 鄮 prefecture was in an area east of Yín 鄞 *xiàn* in present day Zhèjiāng.

121. *Jú* 橘 is *Citrus nobilis*, the tangerine. See Read, *Chinese Medicinal Plants*, 103, no. 347

122. Sūn Ēn 孫恩 (d. 402), *zì* Língxiù 靈秀, was a nephew of the Daoist magician Sūn Tài 孫泰. Beginning in 399, he led a peasant rebellion in the area of Jiāngsū and Zhèjiāng. See his biography in *Jìn shū*, 100.2631–34; and in Mather, *Shih-shuo Hsin-yü*, 605. For a discussion of some of the religious elements surrounding the rebellion, see Hisayuki Miyakawa 宮川尚志, "Local Cults around Mount Lu at the Time of Su En's Rebellion," in *Facets of Taoism*, ed. Holmes Welch and Anna Seidel (New Haven: Yale Univ. Press, 1979), 83–101. The area that was Wúxìng 吳興 commandery is now Wúxìng *xiàn* in Zhèjiāng.

123. On Gāo Héng 高衡 (n.d.; fl. fourth century) see *Jìn shū*, 79.2081, 84.2188, and 113.2901. Lèān 樂安 prefecture was in an area west of present Xiānjū 仙居 *xiàn* in Zhèjiāng. Wèijūn 魏君 was a Jìn commandery located within the are of Jiāngníng 江寧 *xiàn* in modern Jiāngsū. Shítóu 石頭 was a city located west of modern Nánjīng.

124. Information on Gāo Yǎzhì 高雅志 (n.d.; fl. ca. 400) can be found in *Jìn shū*, 10.253–54, 84.2186, 2191–92, 99.2592, 127.3171–72.

125. This note about 'the White Haired Duke' 白頭公 is in the original text. Its significance is not clear at present.

Jīngkǒu at dusk and returning [by dawn].[126] Later on, Yǎzhì and his father were killed by Huán Xuán.[127]

55. The Grand Administrator of Línhè: The Thunder Carriage

During the Yǒnghé reign, a man of Yìxīng, surnamed Zhōu 周, left the city riding a horse with two persons in attendance.[128] He had not yet arrived at a village when the sun set. Beside the road there was a new little grass hut. A woman of about sixteen or seventeen came out the door. Her appearance was neat and her clothing fresh and clean.

"The sun has just now already set and it is still far to the next village," she said, looking out and seeing Zhōu pass by. "How can you possibly make it to Línhè?"[129]

So Zhōu then requested lodging. This woman lit a fire and made a meal for him. When it was close to ten in the evening, he heard a child outside call out Ā-xiāng 阿香."[130] The woman responded, "Yes?!"

"The officer is calling you to push the thunder carriage," [the child] said shortly.

The woman then left, saying, "Today I've got some business and must go."

That evening there was a great thunder storm. When it was approaching dawn, the woman returned.

[Later], after Zhōu had mounted his horse, he looked at the spot where he had spent the night. All he saw was a fresh grave at the mouth of which was some horse urine and some leftover grass. Zhōu was very alarmed.

Five years after that, [Zhōu] ended up as Grand Administrator of Línhè.

56. The Daughter of Adjutant Hé: Sent by the Goddess of the West

Liú Guǎng of Yùzhāng ('Liú' sometimes reads 'Wáng'), was young and not yet married.[131] He went to the countryside where he saw a young girl.

"I am the daughter of Adjutant Hé 何," she told him. "I died young, at fourteen. I was raised by the Goddess of the West, and have now been sent to have relations with a person of the earth."

---

126. Jīngkǒu 京口 is now in Zhènjiāng 鎮江 *xiàn* in Jiāngsū. *Lái huán* 來還 ('returning') is preceded by the graphs *chén yǐ* 晨已 ('already by dawn') in a virtually identical version of this story cited as *Yōu míng lù* in *Tpgj*, 294.2166.

127. According to the *Jìn shū*, especially j. 99 and 127 as cited above, Gāo Yǎzhì was not executed but managed, rather, to escape.

128. Yǒnghé 永和 was one of the reign names (345–356) of Mùdì 穆帝 of the Eastern Jìn (r. 345–361). Yìxīng 義興 was a commandery in an area south of Yíxīng 宜興 *xiàn* in Jiāngsū.

129. Línhè 臨賀 was located within the boundaries of modern Hè 賀 *xiàn*, Guǎngxī.

130. The *Tpgj*, 319.2348, does not have the graph *zhōng* 中 in this line.

131. The *Tpyl*, 981.4346, reads Wáng Guǎng 王廣 for Liú Guǎng 劉廣, but I find nothing further on either name.

Guǎng became very intimate with her. On another day, he found cloves wrapped inside a handkerchief beneath his mat.[132] His mother took the handkerchief and burned it, but it was fire-retardant cloth.

57. A Divine Appearance: Huán Wēn Visits Emperor Jiǎnwén

When Commander-in-Chief Huán, on his way back from from Nánzhōu, paid his respects to the tomb of emperor Jiǎnwén, his attendants sensed there was something unusual about it.[133] Once he had mounted his carriage, he told those in attendance, "The former emperor made a divine appearance just now."

Yet he never outlined what the emperor said, so no one in the crowd knew. All they saw was that when he went to make his obeisance, he repeatedly said, "Your minister dares not." That was all.

Then he asked his attendants what Yīn Juān looked like.[134]

"He is short and fat, of dark [complexion] and extremely ugly," someone answered.

"[A person] also appeared by the emperor's side just now who looked like that," Huán said.

He had intended to harm Yīn. But he became ill and died shortly thereafter.

---

132. *Jīshéxiāng* 雞舌香, known more commonly today as *dīngxiāng* 丁香, is *Carophyllis aromaticus* (or *Eugenia aromatica*) of the myrtle family (Myrtaceae): cloves. See Edward H. Schafer, *The Golden Peaches of Samarkand* (Berkeley: Univ. of California Press, 1963), 171–72.

133. Huán *dàsīmǎ* 桓大司馬 ('Commander-in-Chief Huán') is Huán Wēn, who visited the tomb of emperor Jiǎnwén 簡文 (r. 371–372), located in Jiāngníng 江寧 *xiàn*, Jiāngsū, in early 373. See *Jìn shū*, 28.841, and *Sòng shū*, 31.910. Nánzhōu 南州 was at Gūshú 姑孰, now Dāngtú 當塗 *xiàn* in Ānhūi.

134. Yīn Juān 殷涓 (n.d.) was the son of Yīn Hào 殷浩 (306–356). In 371 Huán Wēn accused Yīn Juān of joining in a plot to rebel. See Yīn Hào's biography in *Jìn shū*, 77.2043–49.

Sōushén hòujì: Juàn 6

58. Chén Ā-Dēng: An Eerie Evening Song
In Hàn times a man of Jùzhāng, Guìjī had gone to the eastern countryside and was returning when the sun set before he could make it back home.[135] He saw a small hut by the side of the road where a fire had been lit, so he asked to spend the night there. [In it] there was a young woman who, not wishing to sleep with her husband, had called her neighbor's daughter over to keep her company. That night they were strumming together on the *kōnghoú*.[136] When he asked her name, the woman did not answer, but plucked at the strings and sang:

Continuous and sinuous the hemp climbs the vine,
  Now creeping, then extending;[137]
If you wish to know my name, last and given,
  My last name is Chén 陳, my given Ā-Dēng 阿登.

The next day he arrived outside the eastern walls to the city, where there was a shop in which a woman was selling victuals. The fellow took a seat and spoke [to her] of what he had seen the day before. When the woman heard [the name] "Ā-Dēng," she said with a shock, "That is my daughter. She died recently and was buried outside the city walls."

59. The Maiden Zhāng: Love in a Grave
In Hàn times, Wú Xiáng, a clerk in Zhūjì prefecture, fearing the oppressive fatigue of conscript service, was making an escape into the deep hills.[138] He had walked to a brook and the sun was about to set, when he spotted a young woman. Her colorful clothing was extremely neat and proper.[139]

"I live alone, with no neighbors besides a solitary old woman, only a dozen or so paces away from here," the woman said.

Hearing this, Xiáng was delighted and went right off following her. When they had walked about a *lǐ*, they immediately came upon the woman's house, an extremely humble house, where she set out some food for Xiáng. When it neared ten in the evening, they suddenly heard an old woman calling, "Miss Zhāng!"

"Yes!" The woman replied.

---

135. Jùzhāng 句章 was a prefecture (in an area now part of Zhèjiāng) of Guìjī commandery.

136. The *kōnghoú* 箜篌 was a seven stringed harp-like lute played either horizontally or vertically. For a further description, see "Yīnyuè zhì" 音樂志, *Jiù Táng shū* 舊唐書 (Beijing: Zhonghua shuju, 1975), 29.1076–77.

137. There is a note to this line that says the graph *suī* 綏 reads *huǎn* 緩 elsewhere. Such a reading can be found in the *Fyzl*, 59.17a. Though one of the readings may be a copy error resulting from the similarity of the two graphs, either can be interpreted here to mean 'moving along slowly' or 'creeping'.

138. Zhūjì 諸暨 prefecture was within the area of modern Zhèjiāng. I find no other information on Wú Xiáng 吳詳

139. Reading *cài* 菜 for *lái* 來 as found in the *Fyzl*, 59.17a.

Xiáng asked who it was and she answered, "The lonely old woman I spoke of earlier."

The two of them then slept together. In the early morning at cockcrow, Xiáng departed. The two had feelings of love for each other and the woman gave Xiáng a purple handkerchief, while Xiáng offered an ordinary cloth handkerchief in return. Xiáng went to the spot they had met the day before and [tried to] cross the brook. That night, however, there had been torrential flooding and it was too deep to ford. So he headed back toward the woman's house.

But he could not find the place from the day before. There was only a grave.

60. The Official's Boat at the Zither and Flute Confluence

At Zither and Flute Confluence in Lújiāng, there is a ship overturned in the waters' junction, which is said to be a great ship of Duke Cáo's.[140] Once a fisherman spent the night at its side, tying his boat up to it. [There,] he heard only the strings and rhythm of a zither and a flute, and [noticed] a heavy pervasive fragrance in the air. The fisherman then dreamed someone was chasing him away.

"Don't get near the official's boat!" they said. The man awoke with a start and moved his boat away. Legend has it that a boat of Duke Cáo's, which was carrying several singing girls, overturned here, where it still is today.

61. Privy Treasurer Cuī: Marriage for Lú Chōng

Lú Chōng was hunting and spotted a river deer.[141] He then shot and [his arrow] struck

---

140. Lújiāng 廬江 was a commandery within the boundaries of modern Ānhuī. Its precise territory, however, varied with the times. *Zhēngdí pǔ* 箏笛浦 ('Zither and Flute Confluence') is identified in Yuè Shǐ's *Tàipíng huányǔ jì* 太平寰宇記 (Nanjing: Jinling shuju, 1882), 126.4b–5a, as being in Héféi 合肥 prefecture (now Héféi *xiàn*, Ānhuī), Lújiāng commandery. Unfortunately, the *Tàipíng huányǔ jì* does not clarify what rivers form this confluence. *Lèishū* citations of this story read *Héféi kǒu* 合肥口 for the location, a place about which I can find no information. See *Fyzl*, 49.13b; *Tpyl*, 769.3411; and *Ywlj*, 44.11b. *Ssj* (16.196, no. 385) and Xún's 荀氏 (n.d.) *Líng guǐ zhì* 靈鬼志 (in Lǔ Xùn, *Gǔ xiǎoshuō*, 174) each have virtually duplicate versions of this story, except both read *Rúxū kǒu* 濡須口 ('Mouth of the Rúxū') for the location. The Rúxū River is now known as the Yùncáo River 运漕河, or the Yùxī River 裕溪河, and flows southeast out of Lake Cháo 巢湖 into the Yangtze. The 'Mouth of the Rúxū' is where this river flows out onto the Yangtze. Cáo Cāo was sometimes active at the mouth of this river and, hence, this appears to be the most satisfactory locale for the confluence named by this anecdote. The area was also called Héféi during the Wèi (220–265). See Wāng Shàoyíng, *Ssj*, 16.196, no. 385, n. 1.

141. This story is found in a more detailed version in *Fyzl*, 92.19a–20b, cited as from the *Xssj*. Though both this abridged version and the detailed version are found in *Tpyl*, 30.144, 884.3927 respectively, the detailed version is identified as being from the *Ssj*, as it is also identified in the *Tpgj*, 316.2325–26. Though perhaps based on a conflated *Ssj-Xssj* text, and thus erroneous in their identification, these latter two citations are probably the reason the detailed version found its way into the present *Ssj* (16.203–5, no. 397) For a translation of the *Ssj* entry, see Yang Hsien-yi and Gladys Yang, *The Man Who Sold a Ghost: Chinese Tales of the 3rd–6th Centuries* (Peking: Foreign Languages Press, 1958), 37–40. In addition, a fairly exact copy of the detailed version is also found in the commentary to the *Ssxy*, where it is identified as being from Kǒng Yuē's 孔約 (n.d.; of the

it. [Chōng] chased after it, not noticing the distance [he ended up covering]. Suddenly he saw a village gate which was rather like [that of] a mansion.[142]

"This is the home of the Privy Treasurer Cuī 崔," the steward replied when [Chōng] asked him.

He went in and met the Privy Treasurer.

"Your father, on your behalf, has requested my young daughter's hand in marriage. This is the reason I welcome you," the Privy Treasurer said to Chōng.

The marriage was concluded in three days and then Chōng was sent home in a carriage. When his mother asked about it, he answered her with a complete description. On the third day of the third month, four years after he had parted with Cuī, Chōng was amusing himself beside a stream. In the distance he saw an ox drawn coach beside the water. He went over, opened the door, and saw the young lady Cuī, and [his] three-year-old son riding inside. [Chōng and Cuī's] feelings were just like they had been from the start. She handed the boy to Chōng, then gave him a golden bowl and departed.

62. The Tomb of Lǔ Zǐjìng: Disturbing the Dead

Wáng Bóyáng's family [lived] at Jīngkoǔ 京口. East of their house was a large grave which was said to be the tomb of Lǔ Sù.[143] Bóyáng's wife, the niece of Xī Jiàn, had died and Wáng leveled the tomb for her burial.[144] Several years after that Bóyáng was spending the day in the office when he suddenly saw an aristocratic personage ride up in a shoulder-level palanquin. [The man] was accompanied by several hundred attendants, as well as horses, all armor-clad. He came straight in and sat down.

"I am Lǔ Zǐjìng who has been peacefully buried here for several hundred years," he told Bóyáng. "For what reason have you torn down my tomb?"

He then looked at those around him and said, "Why don't you attack?"

His attendants pulled Bóyáng off the couch, dealt him several hundred blows with the hilts of their swords, and left. He immediately passed out and only revived after quite some time. The places he had been hit were all ulcerated and festering. In a short time, he died.

One account maintains that after Bóyáng died, his son, while constructing his grave, found a lacquered coffin which he then moved to a southern hill. That night he dreamed Sù angrily told him, "I will kill your father!" Shortly after that, he then dreamed Bóyáng

---

Jìn) *Zhìguài* 志怪. See chapter 5 of *Ssxy*, B.9b–10a; and Lǔ Xùn, *Gǔ xiǎoshuō*, 181–83. A translation is found in Mather, *Shih-shuo Hsin-yü*, 167–69. Lú Chōng 盧充 (n.d.; of the Eastern Hàn) is presumed to be the great grandfather of Lú Zhí 盧植 (d. 192) who has a biography in the *Hòu Hàn shū*, 64.2113–20. See Kǒng Yuē's version of this story (cited above). The *zhāng* 獐, also written 麞, is *Hydropotes inermis*, the river deer, a small hornless deer. See Read, *Animal Drugs*, no. 368.

142. For *lǐ mén* 里門 ('village gate'), *Tpyl*, 30.144, reads *hēi mén* 黑門 'black gate'. The longer versions cited above read *gāo mén* 高門 'tall gate'.

143. Lǔ Sù 魯肅 (172–217), whose sobriquet was Zǐjìng 子敬, has a biography in *Sānguó zhì*, 54.1267–73. I find no information on Wáng Bóyáng 王伯陽.

144. Xī Jiàn 郗鑒 (269–339) has a biography in *Jìn shū*, 67.1796–1801.

told him, "Lǔ Sù is fighting with me about the grave. If I can't hold out against him, I will be unable to return."[145] Later, he saw several pints of blood on the pad at the altar to Bóyáng's spirit and suspected it to be because of Lǔ Sù.

The tomb today is one *lǐ* east of the Chángguǎng 長廣 bridge.

63. Chéng Jiǎn: Watching out for Grave Robbers

Chéng Jiǎn was from Dōngguǎn.[146] He died of illness and was buried within the borders of his native prefecture. Ten years later he suddenly spoke in a dream to the magistrate of the prefecture and said, "I, the deceased Chéng Jiǎn, am being robbed today. Magistrate, Sir, come to my aid quickly."

The magistrate instructed all inside and out to outfit themselves and raised a one-hundred-man armament. He then ordered them to race their horses to [Chéng Jiǎn's] grave. The sun was already about to rise, but the sky suddenly fogged over. They could not see ahead, and heard only the crunching sound of a coffin being broken open. There were two men on the lookout above the grave. Because of the fog and darkness, however, the men did not see anybody coming. Once the magistrate was upon them, his hundred men shouted all at once and caught three men inside the tomb. The two men above the grave were able to escape. The coffin was not yet [entirely] broken so the magistrate had someone fix it.

The next evening, the magistrate again dreamed of Jiǎn, who said, "Although the two men got away, people can all tell who they are: One has a dark birthmark on his face, like a bean leaf; the other has his two front teeth broken. Magistrate, Sir, [if you] just look for them by these [features], you will naturally be able to find them."

Guided by Jiǎn's words, the magistrate pursued and captured them both.

64. The Man from Shàngyú: Help for a Drifting Coffin

The Regional Inspector to Jīngzhōu, Yīn Zhòngkān, was still an ordinary commoner at Dāntú when he unexpectedly met a man in his dreams.[147] The man said he was from Shàngyú, that he had died, and was floating lost, drifting in the river, [adding that he] would probably be arriving [at Dāntú] the next day.[148]

---

145. According to Wāng Shàoyíng, for this line (若不如我不復得還 'If I can't hold out against him, I will be unable to return') the Míng manuscript copy of the *Tpgj* reads 吾日夜不得安 'I get no peace, day or night'. See Wāng Shàoyíng, *Sshj*, 6.39, no. 62, n. 2.

146. Dōngguǎn 東莞 prefecture is now Yíshuǐ 沂水 *xiàn* in present day Shāndōng. I find no information on Chéng Jiǎn 承儉.

147. Yīn Zhòngkān 殷仲堪 (d. 399/400) was an adherent of the *Tiānshīdào* 天師道 ('Way of the Heavenly Master') sect. He was forced to commit suicide by Huán Xuán. See his biography in *Jìn shū*, 84.2192–99. Also see Mather, *Shih-shuo Hsin-yü*, 634. Dāntú 丹徒 prefecture is now Dāntú *xiàn* southeast of Zhènjiāng *xiàn* in modern Jiāngsū.

148. Shàngyú 上虞 prefecture, now Shàngyú *xiàn* in Zhèjiāng, was a commandery in Guìjī.

"You have the humanity to aid [all] creatures. Could you possibly see to move me [to better circumstances]?" he said. "If you put me somewhere high and dry, your kindness will reach my long dead bones."

The next day Yīn went together with several others to the river to have a look. As expected, they saw a coffin. It floated down the river with the water and then drifted right to where Yīn was sitting. He had some people pull it out. The inscription coincided with what he had dreamed. He immediately took it to a hilltop and presented to it an offering of rice and wine. That night he dreamed the man came to thank him for his kindness.

65. The Man of the Hàn Tomb: An Ungrateful Traveler

In the Shēngpíng reign of the Jìn, the Regional Inspector of Xúzhōu 徐州, Suǒ Xùn, took boat and headed for Jìnlíng.[149] He left right at dusk and had wound along the river for several *lǐ* when a man requested that Suǒ give him a ride.

"My home is at the Hàn tomb," he said. "My foot hurts and I cannot walk. I hope to take your boat there."

In the early morning hours, they arrived at the Hàn tomb and the man left.[150] Xùn had someone pull the boat across a ford but he had quite a bit of trouble doing so.

"I gave you a ride for several miles," [Xùn] cursed after the man, "Yet you ran right off and didn't help us pull the boat. I'd like to give you a painful beating."

When the man then returned and joined in the pulling, they were able to cross without feeling that they had exerted any effort. The man then went straight into the tombs. Xùn suspected he was not a man and sent someone secretly to follow and watch him. But once the man had gone among the tombs, they did not see him again. In a short time he came out again, went to a tomb and called out, "Duke of Conveyance!"

There was a response, and the man [then] said, "I just got a ride in someone's boat, but didn't help him pull [his boat across the ford]. So the drudge wanted to beat me. Now I am going to go retaliate and want to borrow your *gānluó* for awhile."[151]

"If you harm my *gānluó*, you can't have it," the Duke of Conveyance said.

"Don't worry about it," the man said, "I just want to try it out."

---

149. The Shēngpíng 升平 reign (357–361) was one of the reign periods of the Jìn emperor Mù. Xúzhōu 徐州 occupied territory now divided between Jiāngsū, Shāndōng, and Ānhuī. Jìnlíng 晉陵 prefecture was located where Wǔjìn 武進 *xiàn* in Jiāngsū is today. I find no information on Suǒ Xùn 索遜.

150. Both Wāng Shàoyíng (*Sshj*, 6.41, no. 65, n. 1) and Wáng Guóliáng (*Sōushén hòujì yánjiū*, 6.84, no. 8, n. 1) say the Míng manuscript edition of *Sshj* reads *shí* 時 for *shǒu* 守.

151. Because of the description that follows in the text, Wáng Guóliáng (*Sōushén hòujì yánjiū*, 6.84, no. 8, n. 2) suspects *gānluó* 甘羅 may be an error for *dān luó* 丹籮, which would mean 'a red flat-bottomed round basket'. His argument makes sense.

When Xùn heard this, he turned his boat around. Soon something came from the bank. Coming straight for the boat, it was red and like a hundred-bushel bamboo bin, about twenty feet long.[152]

"You, drudge, took a ride in my boat," Xùn yelled, "but didn't help me pull. I didn't get the chance to beat you, [yet you] have just taken advantage of the Duke of Conveyance's *gānluó* and now come to attack me. Today, then, I shall forthwith smash your drudge's *gānluó*."

When he had finished speaking, it suddenly disappeared. With that, [Xùn] went on his way.

66. Four Men Seize a Horse: Unwanted Help to Cross a River

During the Jìn, in the Yuánxī reign, Féng Shù of Shàngdǎng was a clerk in the Prime Minister's office.[153] He was taking leave and on his way back to Hǔláo when he unexpectedly encountered four men.[154] They were coming toward Shù, each holding a rope and a staff. Shù whipped his horse to escape, but the horse refused to go on. The four men each seized one of the horse's legs and they swiftly arrived at a river.

"Do you wish to cross?" they asked Shù.

"The water is I don't know how deep," Shù said. "Moreover I have neither boat nor oars. How can I cross? You just want to kill me."

"We won't kill you," the four men said. "We are going to take you in to an official."

Thereupon, they again seized the horse's legs, entered the water, and headed north. Shù only heard the sound of the waves. He did not feel any water. When they were about to reach the bank, the four men said to each other, "This man is not clean, how can he [be let] go?"

At the time, Shù was dressed in mourning for his younger brother. He deeply feared that the demons would leave him and that he would be drowned in the water. So he whipped his horse and made a show of strength. He was thus able to land on the bank straightaway.

"Having received your beneficent favor, how would I dare to trouble you further?" Shù said, thanking them as he departed.

---

152. For *yuè* 籥 (a kind of three- or six-holed flute), *Tpgj*, 320.2357, reads *chuí* 篅 (a round woven-bamboo grain storage bin). Since the description given of the object in the text fits this *Tpgj* reading quite well, I have followed that reading here.

153. The Yuánxī 元熙 referred to here is the reign name (304–307) of the first ruler of the Former Zhào, Liú Yuān 劉淵 (r. 304–309). Shàngdǎng 上黨 commandery was in an area now part of southeast Shānxī. I find nothing on Féng Shù 馮述.

154. Hǔláo 虎牢 was in an area west of Xíngyáng 滎陽 *xiàn* of modern Hénán.

67. An Unusual Object Rather Like a Bird: Guidelines for Attending Funerals

Wáng Róng, Marquis of Ānfēng, went by the sobriquet Jùnchōng and was from Línyí in Lángyé.[155] He once went to someone's home for a funeral. The host had not yet finished preparing the coffin so the guests all went into his office [to wait]. [The Marquis of] Ānfēng lay in his coach [waiting] when he suddenly saw something unusual in the sky. It was like a bird and as he looked at it more closely, it became bigger. As it gradually got nearer, he saw [it was] a red four-horse carriage. Someone was in it, wearing a turban and red clothing and holding an axe in his hand. He landed on the ground, got out of his cart, and went straight into Wáng's coach.

He circled his cot, assessing his appearance, then told Wáng, "Your spirit and intelligence shine pure and bright. You have no secrets concerning anything. Still, because of a [certain] matter, I have come to be of service. Thus, for your sake, I say the following: Whenever anyone has a funeral and burial, if he is not an extremely close relative, you should not rush [to attend]. If you truly cannot find a way to keep from going, you should go in a red carriage.[156] Have a bearded servant drive it along with four white horses.[157] This way you will ritually avert the danger [that would otherwise result].

Then he told Róng, "You shall reach a position among the Three Dukes."[158]

He spoke for a long time. Then the host placed [the deceased] inside the coffin and was ready for the funeral so all of the guests went in. The ghost also went in. Once in the door, the ghost, carrying his axe, trod on to the bier canopy. A relative rushed toward the coffin and was about to say goodbye to the deceased when the ghost hit him right on the forehead with the axe. He immediately fell to the ground. The servants carried him out. The ghost looked at Róng from above the coffin and laughed. Everyone saw it. The ghost then left carrying his axe.

---

155. Wáng Róng 王戎 (234–305), *zì* Jùnchōng 濬沖, was the youngest of the *zhúlín qī xián* 竹林七賢 ('the seven worthies of the bamboo grove'). For his biography, see *Jìn shū*, 43.1231–35; and Mather, *Shih-shuo Hsin-yü*, 621. Ānfēng 安豐 prefecture was located east of Gushi 固始 *xiàn* in Hénán. Línyí 臨沂 Prefecture (northeast of Zǎozhuāng 棗莊 , Shāndōng) was in Lángyé commandery.

156. For *chì jū* 赤車 ('red cart'), *Tpgj*, 319.2353, reads *qīng niú* 青牛 'black ox'. The combination of black oxen and bearded servants were also thought to ward off ghosts and their attendant misfortune. See the story on Sòng Dài 宋岱 in Péi Qǐ's 裴啟 (n.d.; fl. ca. 362) *Yǔlín* 語林, in Lǔ Xùn, *Gǔ xiǎoshuō*, 18; and in *Xiǎo shuō* 小說 by Yīn Yún 殷芸 (n.d.; of the Liang, 471–529), in Lǔ Xùn *Gǔ xiǎoshuō*, 101–2. The *Tpgj* editors appear to have confused that legend with this *Sshj* story.

157. *Shèng* 乘 means the four horses of a team.

158. *Sān gōng* 三公 ('the Three Dukes') was a designation, often simply a generic term, for offices at the top echelon of court administration. The term usually included: (1) *sīkōng* 司空 'Minister of Works', (2) *sītú* 司徒 'Minister over the Masses', and (3) *tàiwèi* 太尉 'Grand Commandant'. However, the offices officially designated by the term varied over time. Wáng Róng was appointed Minister over the Masses around 303. For a discussion of the Three Dukes during Hàn times, see Hans Bielenstein, *The Bureaucracy of Han Times* (New York: Cambridge Univ. Press, 1980), 7–17; for the Jìn period, see Charles O. Hucker, *A Dictionary of Official Titles in Imperial China* (Stanford: Stanford Univ. Press, 1985), 18.

68. The Demon in his Abdomen

Lǐ Zǐyù was skilled in medicinal recipes when he was young and was praised for his thorough knowledge of the divine by [the people of] the time. Xǔ Yǒng was Regional Inspector of Yùzhōu and stationed at Lìyáng. [159] His brother had become ill and had pains in his heart and abdomen for over ten years. He was on the verge of death when suddenly one night they heard a ghost speak to the demon in his abdomen from behind a screen.

"Why don't you hurry up and kill him?" it said. "Otherwise, Lǐ Zǐyù will be passing by here. He will attack you with vermillion pills, and you will probably die."

"I'm not scared of him," the demon in his abdomen answered.

At sunrise, Xǔ Yǒng sent someone to wait for Zǐyù, who came just as expected. Before [Zǐyù] had gone in the door, the sick brother heard a moaning sound inside himself. When Zǐyù came in and had a look, he said, "This is a demon illness." Then he took some red octa-venom pills out of his satchel and gave them to him to take. [160] In a short time his abdomen roared like thunder and heaved in convulsions. He had several fits of copious diarrhea and then was cured. [161] This was the prescription for octa-venom pills [known] today.

69. Shèng Dàoér: Caring for His Family after Death

In the fourteenth year [437] of the Yuánjiā reign of the Sòng, Shèng Dàoér of Guǎnglíng died. [162] His orphaned daughter was entrusted to his wife's younger brother, Shēn Yìzhī. When the parental mourning period was over, Yìzhī married Shèng's daughter to the son of Yán Qí of Běixiāng. [163] They were a poor family, [yet Yán Qí] embellished the dowry gifts and thus the marriage was achieved.

"When I was gasping and short of breath," Dàoér said furiously out of mid-air, "I entrusted you with my entire family. How could you be so greedy for profit and so oblivious of what is right that you could and marry [my daughter] into an insignificant clan?"

At that Yìzhī became absolutely terrified.

---

159. Yùzhōu 豫州 occupied area now within Ānhuī. Lìyáng 歷陽 commandery is now Hé 和 *xiàn* in Ānhuī. I find nothing on either Lǐ Zǐyù 李子豫 or Xǔ Yǒng 許永.

160. *Bā dú* 八毒 ('octa-venom') was used to cure abdominal obstructions. See Gé Hóng 葛洪 (ca. 250–ca. 330), *Zhǒu hòubèi jífāng* 肘後備急方 (Shanghai: Shangwu yinshuguan, 1955), 4.102.

161. *Lì* 利 should be read as the word usually written *lì* 痢, 'diarrhea'.

162. Yuánjiā 元嘉 was the reign name of Wéndì 文帝 (r. 424–453) of the Southern Sòng. During the Southern Sòng, two prefectures called Guǎnglíng 廣陵 were established, one within the area of modern Jiāngsū, one within the area of modern Guǎngxī. Neither exists today. I can find no information on Shèng Dàoér 盛道兒 or the names Shēn Yìzhī 申翼之 and Yán Qí 嚴齊 mentioned in the following lines.

163. Běixiāng 北鄉 was in Shāndōng.

70. The Temple to the Spirits at Lìyáng

During the Jìn, Hú Màohuí of Huáinán was able to see ghosts.[164] Though he did not enjoy seeing them, he was unable to stop it. After a time, he went to Yángzhōu and returned to Lìyáng.[165] East of the city walls there was a temple to the spirits.[166] Just at the time, the people were bringing a shaman there to make offerings. Shortly after they arrived, a crowd of ghosts [began] yelling amongst themselves.

"The high officials are coming!" they said.

They all [then] burst forth and ran out of the temple.

[Màohuí] looked behind him and saw two *Sramana* coming, who then went into the temple. All of the ghosts huddled together in groups of two or three and observed from inside the bushes beside the temple. As they watched the *Sramana*, they were all petrified. In a while, after the *Sramana* had gone, the ghosts went back into the temple. From then on, Huí believed in the Buddha, and served with perfect sincerity.

71. A Ghost Sets up Snares

There was a savage little northern boy who herded cattle in the wilds.[167] He had [only] a few companions. He [once] saw a ghost crouching amongst the thickets of grass, setting up nets everywhere, preparing to trap people with them. After he had set some nets up, but was not yet finished, the savage little northern boy stole a net from the front. Likewise using it as a trap, he entangled and caught the ghost.

72. The Àonǎo Song

Dù Qiān of *Lújiāng* was prefect of Zhūjì.[168] Near the mountains in the West of the prefecture, there was a ghost. It was about thirty feet tall, wore earthen red cloth pant leg riding chaps, and [did the] 'pat and stretch' in the bushes.[169] [It would] also take off its

---

164. Huáinán 淮南, was the southern reaches of the Huái river, now generally within Jiāngsū and Ānhuī. I can find nothing on Hú Màohuí 胡茂回.

165. Yángzhōu 揚州 occupied area now included within Jiángsū, Ānhuī, Jiāngxī, Zhèjiāng, and Fújiàn.

166. For *Yǒu shén cí zhōng* 有神祠中, *Tpgj*, 319.2348 (citing *Fyzl*), lacks the graph 中. The present *Fyzl*, 59.18a, does include the graph here, however.

167. *Cāng* 傖 ('savage northerner') or *cāng xiǎo ér* 傖小兒 ('savage little northern boy') was a contemptuous term for northerners in the Six Dynasties period.

168. Zhūjì 諸暨 (composed of territory now within Zhèjiāng) was a prefecture in Guìjī commandery. I find nothing on Dù Qiān 杜謙.

169. For 著赭衣袴在褶, I follow Wāng Shàoyíng's (*Sshj*, 6.44, no. 72, n. 1) suggested revision and read it as 著赭布袴褶. The *Tpyl*, 573.2589, here reads 布袴布褶 The second *bù* in the *Tpyl* reading may be a copy error, because *kùxí* ('pant-leg riding chaps') is a term for a type of outfit worn for riding and shooting on horseback. See Wáng Guówéi 王國維, *Gǔ hú fú kǎo* 古胡服考. *Xuětáng cóngkè* 雪堂叢刻 edn. (n.p.: n.d.), 4b–15a. *Pāi zhāng* 拍張 ('the pat and stretch') was some kind of sword game. See "Wáng Jìngzé zhuàn" 王敬則傳 in *Nán Qí shū* 南齊書 (Beijing: Zhonghua shuju, 1975), 26.479.

riding chaps, toss them on to the bushes, and sing the "Àonăo song."[170] All the common people had seen it.

73. Zhū Bì: False Incrimination after Death

Zhū Bì of Guìjī was director of the Princedom Palace Gentlemen.[171] He was constructing an official mansion and had not completed it when he passed away. Xiè Zĭmù of the same commandery took over his affairs.[172] [Xiè] took advantage of Bì's death to greatly inflate the expenses and wages [reported] in the treasury record books. He increased them to over a million [cash] and then falsely incriminated Bì of graft while actually taking [the money] for himself.

[After that] Zĭmù was sleeping one night when all at once he heard someone call out Bì's name then suddenly arrive at the front of Zĭmù's main hall.

"You think because bones are dry and flesh rotten," he said to Zĭmù, "that you can then go all out in false incrimination.[173] I shall be coming on the evening of a certain day to put the books back into order and verify [them]."

When he had finished speaking, he suddenly disappeared.

74. Accidentally Hitting a Ghost's Foot

Xiàhóu Zōng was Military Assistant for the Pacification of the West.[174] He often saw ghosts riding horses all over the road, no different from people.[175] Once he was riding [a coach] with someone when he suddenly pulled at the person and spoke to him.

"This boy is soon to be quite sick," he said pointing to a boy on the road.

Soon the boy did end up sick and close to dying. His mother heard about what he had said and came to inquire of Zōng.

"There can be no other reason," Zōng said. "A while ago this boy was in the road throwing mud and accidentally hit a ghost's foot.[176] The ghost was angered and made

---

170. The "Àonăo gē" 懊惱歌, also known as "Ào nóng gē" 懊儂歌, was a song tune popular during the Liú Sòng. See the "Wŭ xíng zhì" in *Jìn shū*, 28.848, and in *Sòng shū*, 31.918. Further information and examples can be found in Guō Màoqiàn 郭茂倩 (n.d., twelfth century), *Yuèfŭ shījí* 樂府詩集 (Beijing: Zhonghua shuju, 1979), 46.667–68.

171. *Guó lángzhōng lìng* 國郎中令 should read *wángguó lángzhōng lìng* 王國, as found in *Tpyl*, 248.1171, and is the reading I follow. I find nothing else on Zhū Bì 朱弼.

172. I find no information on Xiè Zĭmù 謝子木.

173. *Kū gŭ fŭ* 枯骨腐, should read *kū gŭ fŭ ròu* 肉, as found in *Tpyl*.

174. For *ān xī cān jūn* 安西參軍, *Tpyl*, 755.3353, reads *yŭ ān xī cān jūn* 庾安西參軍. I cannot identify what *yŭ ān* would mean. However, Wáng Guóliáng (*Sōushén hòujì yánjiū*, 6.89, no. 17, n.1) suggests the *ān* is an error for *liàng* 亮, in which case the line would mean 'Western Military Assistant to Yŭ Liàng'. Yŭ Liàng (289–340), a powerful Jìn general, has a biography in *Jìn shū*, 73.1915–24. On him, also see Mather, *Shih-shuo Hsin-yü*, 638. I find nothing else concerning Xiàhóu Zōng 夏侯綜.

175. *Tpyl* reads *chéng jū* 乘車' riding in carts' above *qí mă* 騎馬 ('riding horses').

176. *Tpyl* has a note here that says *tú* 塗 ('mud') means *zhuān* 磚 'mud bricks'.

your son sick. You can leave some food and wine out for the ghost and he will get well right away."

The mother did as he said, and [her son] recovered.

75. Fàn Qǐ's Wife: Finding the Family Grave

The mother of Fàn Qǐ from Shùnyáng had died and was ready to be buried.[177] The grave of his father's previous wife was in Shùnyáng and he went to check it out. When he got there, [he found] the grave mounds were numerous and disorderly, very hard to tell apart. He did not know where [the right grave was]. Yuán Yànrén was governing Yùzhōu at the time.[178] [Fàn Qǐ] went to see him and he said, "I've heard there is someone who sees ghosts." Fàn, based on what [Yuán] had said, immediately ordered a search to find the man.

"In [such and such] a grave there is a person whose clothes and make-up are like such and so," [the man] said once he turned up.

They immediately opened the grave. The coffin and other things were all rotten. Inside the tomb, there was a layer of dust and grime over a foot deep. [Fàn Qǐ] was quite doubtful about it. He tried having someone knock away the dirt among the dust with his foot in hopes of finding something from before. They ended up finding a brick. The inscription on it read, "Wife of Fàn Jiān." Only after that did he believe it.

76. Dharma Master Zhú: Reporting from the Other World

Sramana Dharma Master Zhú was a man of Guìjī.[179] He was well acquainted with the Northern Gentleman-of-the-Household, Wáng Tǎnzhī.[180] Whenever they discussed together matters of life and death, punishment and blessing, reward and retribution, it was

---

177. Fàn Qǐ 范啟 (n.d.; fl. mid-fourth century), son of Fàn Jiān 范堅 (n.d.), has a short biographical notice in *Jìn shū*, 75.1990. Also see Mather, *Shih-shuo Hsin-yü*, 552. Shùnyáng 順陽 commandery, Jīngzhōu, was established during the Jìn and stood north of Guānghuà 光化 *xiàn* of modern Húběi.

178. Yuán Yànrén 袁彥仁 is probably Yuán Hóng 宏 (328–376), whose sobriquet was Yànbó 彥伯; the *rén* would be a copy error for *bó*. According to his biographical notice, Fàn Qǐ was a friend of Yuán's. Yuán served in Yùzhōu 豫州 (Anhui) under Xiè Xiàng 謝向 (308–357), who governed there between 350 and 354. See *Jìn shū*, 92.2391–98; Mather, *Shih-shuo Hsin-yü*, 562, 640.

179. Zhú Fǎshī 竺法師 ('Dharma Master Zhú') may be Zhú Qián 竺潛 (286–374), who had the sobriquet Fǎshēn 法深 and also went by the name Dàoqián 道潛. Zhú Qián was originally from Lángyé (Shāndōng) but later in his life he retired to Guìjī (Zhèjiāng). Of significance is that he did die about one year earlier than Wáng Tǎnzhī. See his biography in *Gsz*, 4.97–99; also Mather, *Shih-shuo Hsin-yü*, 547. The *Gsz*, 4.105, however, identifies one Zhú Fǎyǎng 竺法仰 as the monk who approached Wáng Tǎnzhī after death. *Fyzl*, 76.11a–b, in a version of this story it cites as *Gāo sēng zhuàn*, gives Zhú Fǎyìn 竺法印 as the name for the monk. *Fyzl* cites this *Sshj* version elsewhere (29.16a–b) (as *Xssj*), and the name reads as we find it here in the *Sshj*. I can find no further information on either of these two monks.

180. On Wáng Tǎnzhī 王坦之 (330–375), see his biography in *Jìn shū*, 75.1964–69; and in Mather, *Shih-shuo Hsin-yü*, 626.

vague and mysterious [and they found it] difficult to understand. So together they made a pact that if one of them should die first, he should report to the other. After that a year had gone by when Wáng, in a temple, suddenly saw the Dharma Master coming.

"This mendicant monk died on a certain month and day," [Zhú] said. "[In the next world,] neither punishment nor blessing are falsehoods, retribution comes as do shadows and echoes. [You, my patron] *dānapati* (*tányuè* 檀越) have only to diligently cultivate your morality to thereby rise to the divinity. Formerly I made a pact with you that the first to die would report to the other, thus I have come to speak to you."

When he finished speaking, he disappeared without notice. Tǎnzhī subsequently died as well.

77. The Ghost in the White Cloth Pants: Susceptible to Poison

Liú Chíjū of Lèān had his home at Xiàkǒu.[181] Unexpectedly [one day], a ghost came to stay with the Liú family. The first time, because of the darkness, they seemed to see a form similar to a man and wearing white cloth pants. After that it came once every few days and would no longer hide its form. Then it would not leave. It delighted in stealing food [and though the family] did not consider this to be a disaster, it was still a hardship for them. [Yet] from the outset, they did not dare curse it.

Jí Yìzǐ, an intrepid fellow who did not believe in ghosts, [once] went to the Liú home.[182]

"Where is the Liú family ghost?" he said to the master of the house. "Call him over. I will scold him for you [right] now."

They immediately heard a sound in the rafters. At the time they had quite a few guests and everyone looked up together. Then in a great confusion [the ghost] tossed something down and it landed right on Jí Yìzǐ's face. Upon inspection it turned out to be the host's wife's underclothing, filth still clinging to it. The crowd, entertained, laughed loudly together. Jí, greatly ashamed, washed his face and left.

"If this ghost steals food," someone said to Liú, "and the food is thus gone, it must be something that has a form. You can get it by means of poison."

Liú right away boiled some poison ivy at someone else's house.[183] He took up two pints of the broth and secretly carried it back home. When it was nearing evening, the whole family made porridge. They saved a cupful from their meal and then poured the poison ivy broth right into it. They set [the cup] on the table and covered it with a dish.

181. Liú Chíjū 劉池居 reads Liú Chígǒu 池苟 in *Cxj*, 26.638; Liú Tāgǒu 他苟 in *Tpyl*, 859.3815; Liú Tājū 他居 in *Btsc*, 144.12a; and Liú Tā 他 in *Tpgj*, 319.2353 (all readings are cited as *Xssj*). In addition, a version of this story cited in *Tpgj*, 322.2371, as from *Guǎng gǔjīn wǔxíng jì* 廣古今五行記, gives the name as Liú Dùn 遁. I find nothing on any of the names. Xiàkǒu 夏口 was a city west of modern Wǔchāng 武昌 *xiàn*, Húběi, on the Yangtze.

182. Jí Yìzǐ 吉翼子 appears to be unknown elsewhere.

183. *Yěgé* 野葛 is *Rhus toxicodendron*, common poison ivy. See Read, *Chinese Medicinal Plants*, 90, no. 37.

After everyone had settled down, they heard the ghost come in from outside, take off the [covering] dish and eat the porridge. Once it had finished, it tossed away the cup, breaking it, and ran away. In a short time, it vomited on top of the roof. Extremely enraged, it then beat [through] the windows and doors with a club. Earlier, Liú had already taken precautions and fought with it, so it did not dare come in. It was over by the early hours of the morning.

Sōushén hòujì: Juàn 7

78. A Man Transformed from a Rainbow

Chén Jì of Bāqiū, Lúlíng, was a regional official.[184] His wife, Qín 秦, was alone at home. A man once came to work for her who was over ten feet tall, of proper and upright appearance, and who wore a rich red and jade-green gown whose colors brightly dazzled. After that they often met in a mountain ravine. They would go to a place to lie down and before they knew it there would be lovemaking and a mutual meeting of feelings. It was like this for several years. The neighbors observed that wherever they went, a rainbow would suddenly appear.

Qín [once] went to the waterside. The man drew some water with a golden flask and drank with her. After this, she became pregnant. She gave birth and [the baby] was like a human, plump with flesh.

Jì returned on leave and Qín feared he would see the baby. So she put the child into a large urn. The man gave her the golden flask and told her to cover the child.

"This child is small and cannot yet be taken away," he said. "You don't need to make any clothes [for him]. I will clothe him myself."

He immediately gave her a red purse to wrap the baby up with. He instructed that she should take him out at certain times and give him some milk.

At [a later] time, when there was a storm and the sky grew dark and gloomy, the neighbors saw a rainbow come down into [Jì's] courtyard and transform into the man. A short time passed and he took the child and left. The sky again dark and gloomy from a storm, people saw two rainbows leave their house.

Several years [passed] and [the child] came to visit his mother. Later on, Qín went out to the fields and saw two rainbows in the ravine. She was afraid of them. Soon she saw the man.

"It was me," he said. "There is nothing to be afraid of."

After that, they never met again.

79. The Mountain Goblin

At the beginning of the Yuánjiā 元嘉 reign [424–453] in the [Southern] Sòng, a man from Fúyáng surnamed Wáng 王 set up a crab trap in a clogged up ditch.[185] At dawn, he went to check it out and saw a piece of wood about two feet long inside the trap while the trap [itself] was broken open and all the crabs were gone. He fixed the trap and took the wood out, [putting it] on to the bank. The next day he went to inspect it. The piece of wood was again inside the trap and the trap damaged as before. Wáng took out the wood and fixed the trap again. The next morning when he inspected it, what he saw was just like it had been the first time.

---

184. Bāqiū 巴丘 prefecture (north of Xiájiāng 峽江 *xiàn*, Jiāngxī) belonged to Lúlíng 廬陵 commandery during the Jìn. I find no information on Chén Jì 陳濟.

185. Fùyáng 富陽 prefecture is now Fùyáng *xiàn* in Zhèjiāng.

Wáng suspected the piece of wood to be [something] strange and bewitched. So he picked it up, put it into a crab basket, tied up one end, and carried it home over his shoulder.

"When I get home, I'll chop it up with an axe and burn it," he said.

Two or three *lǐ* before he got to his house, he heard a scuffling movement inside the basket. He turned his head and looked back to check it out. He saw that what had just been a piece of wood had become a creature with a human face and a monkey's body, with one torso and a single leg.

"By nature I enjoy [eating] crabs," it said. "It was I who went into the water everyday, broke your crab trap and went into the trap to eat the crabs. I will stop these transgressions against you and hope you will forgive me, open the basket, and let me out. I am a mountain spirit and will aid and assist you. Moreover, I will allow your trap to catch a large crab."

"From first to last," Wáng said, "it wasn't just once that you were cruel to someone in this way. Of course you should die for your wrongdoing."

The type of creature that this was knew only to plead to be set free.[186] Wáng turned his head back around and did not respond.

"What is your name?" the creature said. "I wish to know it."

It kept asking and would not stop, but Wáng never answered.

"Since you won't let me go," the creature said as they approached [Wáng's] house, "and you won't tell me your name, what recourse do I have? If you simply respond then you will die."

When Wáng arrived at home, he incinerated it in a roaring fire. After that it was silent and made no further sound.

Local custom refers to this [kind of creature] as a 'mountain goblin'. They say that if one learns a person's name, it will then be able to harm that person. Hence, it tried so hard to ask Wáng [his name], hoping to hurt the man and save itself.

80. The Flesh that Fell from the Sky in Píngyáng

In the first month of the first year of Liú Cōng's illegitimate Jiànyuán reign, there was an earthquake in Píngyáng and the Chóngmíng 崇明 monastery sank, becoming a pond.[187] Its water was red as blood, red vapor rose [from the pond] to the sky, and there was a red dragon that fiercely bolted [out and flew] away. A shooting star, with a dragon shape

186. Wáng Shàoyíng (*Sshj*, 7.49, no. 79, n. 1) and Wáng Guóliáng (*Sōushén hòujì yánjiū*, 7.95–6, no. 2, nn. 5–7) point out that the Míng manuscript edition for this line reads *cǐ wù kěn gào, kǔ qǐng qǐ fàng* 此物懇告 苦請乞放 'the creature earnestly requested and bitterly pleaded, begging to be let go'. This is a much more satisfactory reading.

187. Liú Cōng 劉聰 (d. 318) was the second ruler (r. 310–318) of the Former Zhào, a Xiōngnú dynasty. Jiànyuán 建元 was his reign name in the year 315. For his biography, see *Jìn shū*, 102.2657–77; and Mather, *Shih-shuo Hsin-yü*, 586. Concerning the events of this story, see also *Jìn shū*, 102.1665. Píngyáng 平陽 was the Xiōngnú capital and located south of present day Linfen 臨汾 *xiàn*, Shānxī.

and a snake at its tail, arose in Qiānniú and entered Zǐwéi.[188] Its brightness illuminating the earth, [the star then] fell ten *lǐ* north of Píngyuán.

Upon examination, the star proved to be flesh and its odor could be detected in Píngyuán. It was thirty paces long and twenty-seven paces wide. There was a crying sound beside the flesh that would not cease, day or night. Several days [passed] and Cōng's empress, Lady Liú, gave birth to a snake and a beast. Each attacked people and then ran away. They searched for them but did not find them. Soon, they appeared beside the fallen flesh. [Then] suddenly Lady Liú died and the crying sound ceased of its own accord.

81. Zhōu Zǐwén is Stupefied: A Giant Bow

After the restoration of the Jìn, Zhōu Zǐwén of Qiáo commandery had his home at Jìnlíng.[189] When he was young, he liked bow hunting. He once went into the hills and unexpectedly [came across] a man in a mountain cavern who was fifty or sixty feet tall. He held a bow and arrow in his hands. The arrowhead was about two feet wide or so and white as frost and snow. He suddenly made a sound, and yelled, "Ā-shǔ." (Ā-shǔ 阿鼠 was Zǐwén's childhood name.) Zǐwén, without knowing it, answered, "Yes!" The man then, with the arrowhead pointing toward Zǐwén, pulled tight his bowstring. Zǐwén, stupefied, submitted.

82. The Hairy Man: A Hidden Forest of Tea

During the period of [emperor] Xiàowǔ of the Jìn, Qín Jīng, of Xuānchéng once went to Mt. Wǔchāng to pick tea.[190] He suddenly encountered a person over ten feet tall, with hair over his entire body, coming from north of the mountain. When Jīng saw him, he was scared and thought to himself that he would surely die. The hairy man pulled directly at his arm and took him to a hidden corner in the hills. They entered a place with great thickets of tea. He let Jīng go and then left. Jīng then [continued] picking tea. After a while, [the man] returned, pulled twenty tangerines out of his breast [pocket], and handed them to Jīng. They were extraordinarily sweet. Jīng, quite amazed, shouldered his tea and left.

---

188. Qiānniú 牽牛 is a name for the constellation known as Altair in the West. See Knechtges, *Wen xuan*, 140, ll. 400–402 n. Zǐwéi 紫微, also known as Zǐwéi *yuán* 垣 'enclosure of purple elusiveness', was a group of fifteen stars that were seen to form a circle around the celestial north pole. For a description, see Knechtges, *Wen xuan*, 116, l. 143 n.

189. The 'restoration (*zhōngxīng* 中興) of the Jìn' refers to the Eastern Jìn. Qiáo 譙 commandery was established at the end of the Eastern Jìn in an area northwest of present Méngchéng 蒙城 *xiàn* in Ānhuī. Jìnlíng 晉陵 prefecture is now Wǔjìn 武進 *xiàn* in modern Jiāngxī. I find no information on Zhōu Zǐwén 周子文.

190. Emperor Xiàowǔ 孝武 reigned from 373–396. Xuānchéng 宣城 commandery is now Xuānchéng *xiàn* in Ānhuī. Mt. Wǔchāng 武昌山 is in Húběi. I find no information on Qín Jīng 秦精.

83. The Man in the Vermillion Gown
Shèng Yì of Guìjī once arose early in the morning, when no one was yet about on the road, and saw a person on the willow tree outside [his] gate.[191] [The person], about two feet tall, wearing a vermillion gown, and donning a hat, was crouched over licking the dew off the leaves with his tongue. After a good while, he suddenly saw Yì. He gave a startled, frightened expression, and immediately hid out of sight.

84. The Two-Headed Man
In the third year of the Yǒngchū reign during the Sòng, a maidservant to the family of Xiè of Nánkāng went for a walk and came across a black dog.[192]

"Look behind me," [the dog] said, speaking to her.

She raised her head and saw a man three feet tall that had two heads. Shocked and frightened, the maidservant ran back. [But] the man and the dog followed after her. When she reached the family's central courtyard, the whole family ran away to hide.

"What have you [two] come to do?" the maidservant asked the dog.

"Only to ask for some food," the dog said.

Thereupon, the maidservant set out some food for them. They ate together and when they were finished, the two-headed man went out.

"The man has already left," the maidservant then said to the dog.

"He'll be back right at ten o'clock," the dog said.

A long time passed and then [the dog] vanished. No one knew where he was. After that, almost all the members of the family died.

85. Something in the Walls: A Deadly House
During the Sòng, the father of Lǐ Yí of Xiāngchéng did not believe in evil spirits and demons.[193] There was a house that had always been haunted and could not be lived in.

Those who did live there always died. [Yet Lǐ Yí's] father bought it and lived there. For many years they lived there in safe good-fortune and the sons and grandsons prospered. [Lǐ Yí's father] held [a rank that earned] a two-thousand-bushel salary and was [eventually] appointed to an office that [required that he] move his family. Just before they left, he requested to meet with all of the relatives, his wife's and his own. Once the eating and drinking were underway, the father addressed them.

---

191. *Liǔ* 柳 is *Salix babylonica*, the weeping willow. See Read, *Chinese Medicinal Plants*, 202, no. 624. I find nothing on Shèng Yì 盛逸.

192. Yǒngchū 永初 was the reign name of the Liú Sòng emperor Wǔ (r. 420–422). Xiè of Nánkāng 謝南康 was a title that began with Xiè Shí 謝石 (327–388) when he was enfeoffed Duke of Nánkāng 南康 commandery (in southwest Jiāngxī). It was subsequently handed down within the family through the end of the Jìn. By the time this story takes place, the title probably belonged to Xiè Hào 謝暠 (n.d.), its last holder. See *Jìn shū*, 79.2088–89.

193. Xiāngchéng 襄城 commandery is now Xiāngchéng *xiàn* in Hénán. The name Lǐ Yí 李頤 reads Suǒ Yí 索頤 in *Tpgj*, 324.2388–89 (cited as *Fyzl*; *Fyzl*, 59.20a–b, cites this entry as *Xssj*). I find nothing on either name.

"After all," he said, "is there or is there not good luck and misfortune in the world? This house has always been said to be haunted. Yet since we have lived in it, we have had many years of safe good-fortune. Now that I have earned a change of office, where are the ghosts? From now on, this will be a house of good-fortune. When residents dwell here, they should have no apprehensions."

When he was finished speaking, he went to the toilet. Shortly, [all the relatives] saw something inside the wall. It was as big as a rolled-up mat, about five feet tall, and pure white. When [the father] returned, he took a knife and hacked at it.[194] It was severed in the middle and turned into two people. He hacked at them again from side to side and they became four people. Then they grabbed the knife and hacked back at Lǐ and killed him. Carrying [the knife], they went over to where [everyone] was sitting and hacked his brothers and sons to death. All [there] who had the surname Lǐ inevitably died and only those with a different name were safe.

Yí was still a baby-in-arms. When his family experienced this disaster, his wet nurse carried him out the back gate and hid in another home. Thus only he alone got away.

Yí's sobriquet was Jǐngzhēn 景真 and his position reached that of Grand Administrator to Xiāngdōng.[195]

86. A Dog Changes Form

In the Sòng, Wáng Zhòngwén was Master of Records in Hénán commandery and lived north of Gōushì prefecture.[196] He obtained leave and [on his way home] was heading through a marsh in the evening when he saw a white dog behind his coach.[197] Zhòngwén was quite fond of it and was going to pick it up when it changed into a human-like form. It had a physique similar to an exorcist: eyes as red as fire, ragged teeth, and a protruding tongue.[198] It was absolutely detestable. Zhòngwén was quite frightened and attacked it together with his servant. But they [had to] run away when they could not defeat it. He told his family about it and got together about ten people who, carrying knives and clutching torches, went back to check it out. They could not find where it had gone, [however]. In a little over a month, Zhòngwén suddenly saw it again. He and his servant ran away [from it] together. Yet before they reached home, both fell flat to the ground and died.

---

194. For *zhōng* 中 in this line, *Fyzl*, and *Tpgj* read *zhuó* 斫, the reading I follow here.

195. Xiāngdōng 湘東 commandery was in an area east of Héngyáng 衡陽 *xiàn*, Húnán.

196. Hénán 河南 commandery was northeast of modern Xīnyě 新野 *xiàn* in Húnán. Gōushì 緱氏 prefecture occupied an area in the south of Yǎnshī 偃師 *xiàn* of present day Hénán. I find no information on Wáng Zhòngwén 王仲文.

197. *Dé xiū* 得休 is followed in *Tpgj*, 319.2354, by *yīng guī* 應歸 'forthwith headed home'.

198. The *fāngxiàng* 方相 ('exorcist') was a demon impersonator dressed in bearskin and wearing a four eyed mask who was called on to expel evil influence and demon spirits at various occasions. For a description and discussion, see Derk Bodde, *Festivals in Classical China: New Year and Other Annual Observances During the Han Dynasty, 206 B.C.–A.D. 220* (Princeton: Princeton Univ. Press, 1975), 77–84; and William G. Boltz, "Philological Footnotes to the Han New Year Rites," *JAOS* 99 (1979): 431.

Sōushén hòujì: Juàn 8

87. Two Men Wearing Raven Black Clothing

Wáng Jī was Regional Inspector to Guǎngzhōu.[199] Jī [once] entered the toilet and suddenly saw two men wearing raven black clothing who were blocking his way. After a while, [Jī] caught them and ended up with two things similar to crows.[200]

He asked Bào Jìng about it.[201]

"These things are not auspicious," Jìng said.

Jī burned them but they flew straight up into the sky. Soon [after that] he was killed.[202]

88. Torches Become Butterflies

During the Yìxī reign of the Jìn, Gě Huīfū of Wūshāng was spending the night with his wife's family.[203] After midnight two people bearing torches arrived at the front of the steps. He suspected they were evil men and went over to beat them. Just as he was about to bring down his club, they both turned into butterflies and flew apart in confusion. [Something then] rushed at Huīfū's armpits and he fell to the ground.[204] In a short time, he died.

89. Zhūgě Chángmín: Haunted by Demons

After Zhūgě Chángmín became rich, he would frequently awaken suddenly in fright over ten [different] evenings in the course of one month, jumping all about as if fighting with someone.[205] Máo Xiūzhī, when he once spent the night with Chángmín, was startled and scared to see him [jumping about thus], and asked why he did it.[206]

---

199. Wáng Jī 王機 (n.d.; fl. early fourth century) has a short biography in *Jìn shū*, 100.2624–25.

200. The *wūyā* 烏鴉 is *Corvus macrorhynehus*, the common crow. See Read, *Avian Drugs*, no. 32.

201. Bào Jìng 鮑靚 (n.d.) studied Daoist techniques and is reputed to be a transcended personage (*xiān rén* 仙人) who lived to be over one-hundred years old. See his short biographical passage in *Jìn shū*, 95.2482. Concerning Bào Jìng also see Táo Hóngjǐng 陶弘景 (452–536), *Zhēn gào* 真誥 (*Xuéjīn tǎoyuán* edn.), 14.14b.

202. According to his biography, Wáng Jī died on the run, after an unsuccessful attempt at rebellion, when pursued by Xǔ Gāo 許高 (n.d.) who had been sent after him by Táo Kǎn 陶侃 (259–334).

203. Yixi 義熙 was the last reign period (405–418) of the Jìn emperor Ān (r. 397–418). Wūshāng 烏傷 prefecture (now Yìwū 義烏 *xiàn* in Zhèjiāng) was in Guìjī commandery. I find nothing further on Gě Huīfū 葛輝夫.

204. A virtually identical version of this entry, found in the *Tpyl*, 885.3932, cited as from *Yì yuàn* 異苑 by Liú Jìngshū 劉敬叔 (n.d.; of the Liú Sòng), follows *yǒu* 有 in this line with *yī wù* 一物 'something'. My translation reflects this reading.

205. On Zhūgě Chángmín 諸葛常民 (d. 413), see his biography in *Jìn shū*, 85.2212–13.

206. Máo Xiūzhī 毛修之 (ca. 375–446) has biographies in *Sòng shū*, 48.1426–30; *Nán shǐ*, 16.459–61; *Wèi shū* (Beijing: Zhonghua shuju, 1975), 43.960–61; and *Běi shǐ* (Beijing: Zhonghua shuju, 1975), 27.987–88.

"I just saw something," he answered, "which was very black with hair and indistinct feet. It was fantastically powerful and if it weren't for me, there would be no way to control it."

After that [such episodes] became even more frequent:

Among the posts and rafters in his house he would see snakes everywhere. He would have someone hack in the air [at them] with a knife but they hid in response to the blade. They would go away, then immediately come out again.

The batons for pounding and washing clothes would talk to him in what seemed like human sounds, but he could not understand them.

He would see huge hands on the wall, seven or eight feet long, with arms several times bigger than [a normal man's] arm span. When he ordered them chopped away, they would suddenly disappear.

In not too long a time, he was killed.[207]

90. A Dead Person's Head

The mother of Yǔ Jǐn of Xīnyě was sick and Yǔ Jǐn and his two brothers were all looking after her illness.[208] During the day they once lit a fire and suddenly saw her bed curtain strap rolling and unrolling itself. It did this four times. Shortly, there was an unusual dog sound at the front of the bed. The whole family looked together, but they did not end up seeing a dog. [Instead], they saw the head of a dead person on the ground. The head was still bleeding and its two eyes were still moving. It was really horrible and the family was terrified. [Yet] they did not then take it outside the gate, but buried it in the back garden. The next day when they went to look, it had come out and was on the ground, its two eyes still as they had been. They buried it again and the following day it came out once more. So they then buried it together with a brick and it did not come out again. On a later day, their mother died.

91. A Head Falls from Above

Wáng Suí went by the sobriquet Yànyú.[209] One night at his home a human head, through no apparent cause, fell out of the rafters on to the bed. It was bleeding profusely. Soon he was appointed Regional Inspector to Jīngzhōu, but was then tried [in connection with] his father's schemes and executed along with his brother Nà 納.

---

207. According to his biography, Zhūgě Chángmín was killed by Liú Yù 劉裕 (352–422), founder of the Liú Sòng.

208. Xīnyě 新野 commandery is now Xīnyě *xiàn* in Hénán. I find nothing on Yǔ Jǐn 庾謹.

209. Wáng Suí 王綏 (d. 404), *zì* Yànyú 彥猷, was the third son of Wáng Yú 王愉 (d. 404). He was killed along with the other members of his family by Liú Yù when Liú overthrew Huán Xuán, for whom Wáng Yú had been working. On Wáng Suí and Wáng Yú, see *Jìn shū*, 75.1973–74 and 75.1970; and Mather, *Shih-shuo Hsin-yü*, 625 and 628, respectively.

92. A Hundred Skulls

During the Jìn, in the fifth year of the Yǒngjiā reign [311], Zhāng (one reads 'Gāo') Róng was commander of the border patrol at Gāopíng.[210] At the time, Cáo Yí and [his] brigands were causing great disorder and the people had all taken to fortifications to safeguard themselves.[211]

[Róng] saw a fire arise in the mountains. Flying ashes and severe flames [shot up] over ten feet, the tops of the trees were aflame, and the roar [of the fire] resounded throughout the mountains and valleys. Then he heard the sound of people, horses, and armor, and thought Yí's brigands were coming. Everyone was panic stricken. [Róng] brought together a precautionary [force] and went out, ready to attack Cáo Yí. He led the cavalry to the mountains. But all they saw [there] was the scattered remnants of the fire shining hot upon them, scorching their horses' hair as well as their gowns and armor. Thereupon, the soldiers raced back. The next day when [Róng] went to check it out, [he found] no place that had been burned. He only saw a hundred skulls strewn over the hills.

93. The Shallots Shrink Away

The family of Zhào Zhēn of Xīnyě were growing shallots in their garden and had not yet pulled them up when suddenly one day [the shallots] all withdrew back into the ground.[212]

After that a little over a year passed and Zhēn's brothers one after another went their separate ways.

94. Mr. Wú's Catalpa

Niè Yǒu of Wú, who went by the sobriquet Wéntì 文悌, was from Xīn'gàn, Yùzhāng.[213] When he was young, he was very poor and often liked to go bow hunting. [Once] in the evening light, he saw a white deer. He shot and hit it. At daylight, having followed its tracks and blood to their end, he [still] had not found where [the animal itself] was. Moreover he was already quite hungry. So he lay down [to rest] beneath a catalpa tree.[214] Looking up, he saw an arrow stuck right into a branch of the tree. He took a closer look

---

210. The reading Gāo Róng 高榮 for Zhāng Róng 張榮 is found in *Tpyl*, 374.1727. I find nothing on either name. Gāopíng 高平 was a region in Yǎnzhōu 兗州 (now within Shāndōng province).

211. Cáo Yí 曹嶷 (n.d.; fl. early fourth century) was a rebel commander working under Wáng Mǐ 王彌 (n.d.). In 311 he defeated government troops led by general-in-chief Gǒu Xī 苟晞 (n.d.). See *Jìn shū*, 5.116, 61.1668.

212. *Cōng* 蔥 is *Allium fistulosum*, the welsh onion or shallot. See Read, *Chinese Medicinal Plants*, 217, no. 666. I find no information of Zhào Zhēn 趙貞 (*Tpyl*, 977.4328, reads Zhào Zhēn 真).

213. Niè Yǒu 聶友 (n.d.; fl. ca. 242–253) served as Grand Administrator to Dānyáng 丹陽 (near modern Nánjīng) and was good friends with Zhūgě Kè 諸葛恪 (203–253). See *Sānguó zhì*, 47.1145, 65.1437, 1442–43. Xīn'gàn 新淦 prefecture stood northeast of Qīngjiāng 清江 *xiàn* of present day Jiāngxī.

214. The *zǐ* 梓 tree is *Catalpa bungei*, the catalpa. See Read, *Chinese Medicinal Plants*, 25, no. 98.

[and saw] it was the arrow he had shot the night before. He found it quite strange that it was [here] like this.

Thereupon he went home and, taking some grain, he led his brothers to cut it down with an axe. The tree seemed to bleed [real blood] just slightly. Then they cut it up into two boards which they pulled back and stuck into their pond. The boards would often sink and then come back up again after a time. When they came up, the family always had good luck. Often when he greeted his guests, he would ride on the boards. They would suddenly sink and the guests would take fright. [But] Yǒu would [just] call them and [he and the boards] would come floating back out again.

His official career was very satisfactory and his position reached that of Grand Administrator to Dānyáng. A year had passed since he had been at the commandery when the boards suddenly came after him at Shítóu 石頭.

"The boards have come to Shítóu on the tide [of the river]," the outer officer reported.

"The coming of the boards," Yǒu said, shaken, "surely has a significance."

He immediately resigned his post and headed for home. When he got on to the boat, he closed the door, and the two boards took the boat between them, one one each side. [This way] he arrived [back] at Yùzhāng in just a day.

After this, when the boards would come out [of the water], that meant misfortune and disaster. The family [thus] hit upon hard times.

Today, twenty miles or so north of Xīngàn [at a place called] Fēngxī 封溪, there is a spot with bore tide mooring posts [made from] the boards Niè Yǒu cut from the catalpa tree.[215] There is [also] a catalpa tree [there] which still exists today. It is the one Niè Yǒu cut up in the past. Its leaves and branches all grow drooping downward.

---

215. *Zāngkē* 牂柯 are posts for mooring boats. See Yán Shāgǔ's 顏師古 (583–645) note concerning Zāngkē commandery in *Hàn shū* (Beijing: Zhonghua shuju, 1975), 28A.1602.

Sōushén hòujì: Juàn 9

95. The White Clothed Woman

A man from Qiántáng surnamed Dù 杜 was traveling in a boat, when at sunset during a heavy snow a woman in white clothing came to the bank.[216]

"Why don't you come on [my] boat?" Dù said.

Then they began to flirt with each other. Dù stopped the boat and took her on.[217] Later, she turned into a white egret.[218] Dù detested her [for it] and then got sick and died.

96. Tigers Divine for Fortune

Shěn Zōng from Dānyáng 丹陽 undertook divination as his occupation near the prefectural capital. During the Yìxī reign [405–418], the Left General Marquis Tán was stationed at Gūshú.[219] He enjoyed hunting and made it his business to stalk tigers.

[Once] unexpectedly a man wearing leather pants and riding a horse, who was accompanied by someone also wearing leather pants, came to see Zōng for a divination bearing over ten cash wrapped in paper.

"Is it best to go west in search of food?" he asked. "Or is it best to go east in search of food?"

Zōng cast a hexagram for him.

"To head east is auspicious," he prognosticated when the hexagram was complete.[220] "To head west is not advantageous."

Then [the man] approached Zōng and asked for a drink. He put his mouth into the bowl and drank in a manner much like that of an ox. Once they went out, they headed east for about a hundred paces. The horse and the servant then suddenly turned into tigers.

From this time on, tigers were extremely fierce.

97. The Bear Cave

During the Shēngpíng reign of the Jìn there was a man who had gone into the mountains stalking deer with a bow when he suddenly fell into an abysmally cavernous pit.[221] Inside it were several bear cubs. In a while, a bigger bear came and glared at the man. He figured he would surely be mauled. After quite a long time, [the bigger bear] took out some fruit that had been stored away and apportioned it among the cubs. It set down the last portion it made in front of the man. The man was very hungry and so, risking death, picked it up and ate it.

---

216. Qiántáng 錢塘 was within the area of modern Zhèjiāng.

217. *Gé* 閣 here is the word usually written *gē* 擱.

218. *Bái lù* 白鷺 is *Egretta garzetta*, the white egret. See Read, *Avian drugs*, no. 262.

219. Gūshú 姑孰 was located in the area of modern Dāngtú *xiàn* in Ānhuī. Tán *hóu* 侯 ('Marquis Tán') would be Tán Sháo 檀韶 (ca. 366–421), elder brother of Tán Dàojì 檀道濟 (d. 421). He has a short biography in *Sòng shū* 宋書, 45.1372–73. I find nothing further on Shěn Zōng 沈宗.

220. *Zhān* 占 ('prognosticated') in *Tpyl*, 892.3961, reads *gào* 告 'reported'.

221. Shēngpíng 升平 was a reign name (357–361) of emperor Mù 穆 of the Jìn.

Soon [the man and the bears] became more familiar with each other. The bear mother would go out every morning to search for food. When she returned she would always share some with the man, who stayed alive this way.

Afterwards the cubs grew big and their mother carried them out of the pit one by one. Once the cubs were all out, the man figured he would die in the pit, stuck there with no way out. [But] the bear mother soon returned and sat beside the man. The man figured out what she meant and grabbed hold of her foot. Thereupon [the bear] jumped out [with the man]. [Hence] in the end he was able to avoid any harm.

98. Deer Woman Jerky

A Mr. Chén from Huáinán was in the field planting beans when he suddenly saw two women.[222] They were of quite beautiful bearing and complexion and wore short violet jackets with dark skirts. It was raining, but their clothes did not get wet. [Chén] had hung a mirror on his wall earlier and in the mirror he saw [the women reflected as] two deer. So, stabbing them with a knife, he captured them to make venison jerky.

99. Monkeys Violate the Palace Singing Girls

During the Tàiyuán reign [376–396] of the Jìn, the Dīnglíng king Zhái Zhāo raised macaques in his rear palace, in front of the singing-girls room.[223] [Once] the forward and rear singing-girls became pregnant at the same time. Each gave birth to a child with three heads which leapt about when they came out. Only then did Zhāo realize [the pregnancies] were the monkeys doing and so he killed both the monkeys and the babies. [Then] both singing girls [began to] wail and cry at the same time.

"We met a young fellow," they said when Zhāo asked them about it, "wearing an unlined yellow silken shirt and a white cap of light silk. He was quite loveable and laughed just like a human."

100. Black Dragon: A Man's Closest Ally

Zhāng Rán, a man from Jùzhāng 句章 in Guìjī, had been retained in service at the capital. A year had gone by and he had not been able to go home. At home he had a young wife with no children and only a servant to watch over the house with her. The wife eventually had an affair with the servant. Rán raised a dog at the capital. It was quite quick and [Rán] named it 'Black Dragon'. He would usually take it along with him [wherever he went]. Later on [Rán] got leave to go home and Rán's wife and servant plotted to kill him.

---

222. Huáinán 淮南 during the Jìn, was south of present day Dāngtú *xiàn*, Ānhuī.

223. The Dīnglíng 丁零 (also written 丁令 or 丁靈) were a Tungusic tribe who roamed the north and northwest of China occupying essentially the area south of Lake Baikal to slightly beyond the Yenissei. See Otto Maenchen-Helfen, "The Tingling," *HJAS* 4 (1939): 77–86. Zhái Zhāo 翟昭, usually written 翟釗, (n.d.) was the son of the northern barbarian leader Zhái Liáo 翟遼 (d. 391). See *Jìn shū*, 9.236, 81.2133–34. Also see Sīmă Guāng 司馬光 (1019–1086), *Zīzhì tōngjiàn* 資治通鑑 (Beijing: Guji chubanshe, 1956), 107.3402. *Mí hóu* 獼猴 is *Macaca mulatta*, the macaque.

When Rán and his wife had prepared dinner and sat down together to eat, his wife told him, "I am about to say a big good-bye to you. You should eat heartily."

[Yet] before Rán had even begun to eat, the servant was already standing in front of the door with his bow and arrow drawn, waiting for Rán to finish eating. Rán, sobbing, did not eat, but instead tossed the meat and rice that were in his dish to the dog.

"I've been raising you for several years," he implored [of the dog], "and now I'm about to die. Can you save me?"

The dog got the food, but did not eat it. It just stood staring at the servant licking its lips. Rán understood what it meant. The servant got more impatient in urging him to eat when Rán, having settled on his plan, slapped his knee and yelled, "Black Dragon, Kill!"[224]

The dog attacked the servant in response to [Rán's] voice. The servant dropped his weapon and fell to the ground. The dog then bit him in the groin. After that, Rán grabbed his knife and killed the servant. [He then] turned his wife in to the prefect, who executed her.

101. Yáng Shēng's Dog: A Faithful Friend

During the Tàihé reign of the Jìn, Yáng Shēng of Guǎnglíng raised a dog that he was very fond of and would take wherever he went.[225] After a time, he got drunk on some wine and wandered to a large [area of] marsh grasses where he slept, quite immobile. It happened to be just the time when the open fields were being burnt off for the winter months. [Also] the winds were extremely heavy. The dog ran around [him] howling and in fear, but Shēng was too drunk to wake up. There was a puddle of water in front of him. So the dog ran into the water, then came back and shook water from his body onto the grass around Shēng. He did this several times, going around Shēng by half steps [until] all the grass was soaking wet. When the fire reached them, they escaped being burned. Shēng woke up and only then saw what had happened.

[Then] after this, Shēng was walking in the dark and fell into an empty well. The dog moaned and whined [by the well] until morning. [Then] someone passed by who found it strange that this dog was yowling into a well. He went to check it out and saw Shēng.

"If you help me out, there will be a generous reward," Shēng said.

"Give this dog to me and I will get you out," the man said.

"This dog once saved me from certain death." Shēng said. "I can't give it to you. Beyond the dog, there is nothing that I will begrudge."

"If such is the case," the man said, "I won't get you out."

224. On the term *yǔ shǒu* 與手 as an order to kill, see Hú Sānxǐng's 胡三省 (1230–1287) note in Sīmǎ Guāng's *Zīzhì tōngjiàn*, 185.5781. I find nothing on Zhāng Rán 張然.

225. Tàihé 太和 was the reign of the Duke of Hǎixī 海西公, Sīmǎ Yì 司馬奕 (r. 366–370). Guǎnglíng 廣陵 commandery was northeast of Jiāngdū 江都 *xiàn* of modern Jiāngsū. I find no further information on Yáng Shēng 揚生.

The dog then dropped its head and looked into the well. Shēng understood what it meant.

"I'll give you the dog," he said to the man on the road.

The man immediately helped him get out, then leashed the dog and left. But five days later, the dog ran away at night and returned [to Shēng].

102. The Cài Yǒng Family Dogs

During the period of [emperors] Mù and Āi of the Jìn, the dogs [belonging to] the family of the Intendant Major of the Army, Cài Yǒng, would always bark among themselves at night in a great pack.[226] When [Cài's family] went to check them out they would always hide. On a later day, they had a person stand watch at night. [He] saw a dog wearing yellow clothes with a white cap and about five or six feet long, which all the dogs barked at together. When he followed its tracks, he determined it was an old yellow dog of the Cài family's. He killed it immediately. The barking stopped after that.

103. Zhāng Píng's Dog

During the time of Fú Jiān, Zhāng Píng of Dàijùn was a brigand general who called himself Regional Inspector to Bìngzhōu.[227] He raised a dog named 'Flying Swallow' that was built rather like a small donkey. Suddenly one night it got on the roof of [Zhāng Píng's] office and walked around. The noise it made walking [there on the roof] was [no more quiet or careful than, but rather] just like [the sounds it made in] normal [walking]. Before a year had passed [after that], [Zhāng Píng] ended up being pursued by the Xiānbēi.[228] Defeated, he took flight and submitted to Fú Jiān.[229] He died soon thereafter.

104. The Old Yellow Dog: Impersonating Old Mr. Wáng

The imperial uncle from the Wáng 王 clan [in his] later [years] took the daughter of Mr. Yǔ 庾 as his wife.[230] She was young and beautiful while he was sixty years old and usu-

---

226. Emperors Mù 穆 and Āi 哀 ruled 345–361 and 362–365, respectively. Jìyáng 濟陽 commandery was northwest of Dìngtáo 定陶 *xiàn* of modern Shāndōng. I can find nothing on Cài Yǒng 蔡詠.

227. Zhāng Píng 張平 (n.d.; fl. mid-fourth century) was a powerful general of the Former Zhào who retained local power after the Zhào fell. See *Jìn shū*, 8.202–3, 113.2885 (translated in M. C. Rogers, *The Chronicle of Fu Chien* [Berkeley: Univ. of California Press, 1968)] 114–15), 122.3053; also see 7 and 203 n. 70. On Fú Jiān 苻堅 (338–385), early ruler of the Former Qín, see *Jìn shū*, 113.1883–114.2937. See also the translation and study of this biography in Rogers, *Chronicle of Fu Chien*, as well as Mather, *Shih-shuo Hsin-yü*, 554. Dàijùn 代郡 commandery occupied areas now a part of northeast Shānxī and Yù 蔚 *xiàn* of Hébĕi. Bìngzhōu 並州 occupied territory covering Shānxī and parts of Hébĕi and inner Mongolia.

228. The Xiānbēi 鮮卑 were a semi-agricultural Altaic people living in the area that is now Southern Manchuria after about the third century CE.

229. Zhāng Píng submitted to Fú Jiān around 359. See *Jìn shū*, 8.203.

230. Wáng Guóliáng (*Sōushén hòujì yánjiū*, 9.112, no. 10, n. 1) believes the term *tàishú* 太叔 ('imperial uncle') here is an error for *tàimò* 太末, a place name. Tàimò was a prefecture in Guìjī

ally slept outside, leaving his [young] wife deeply displeased. One evening she discovered Wáng had come back [inside] and that he was far more loving that usual. In the morning they sat and ate together. The servant came in from outside and was shocked to see this. [He ran out] to let [the real] Wáng know. Wáng came right in as the impersonator went out. The two met in the central courtyard. Both were wearing white caps and their clothing and appearance seemed to be one and the same. The real Wáng raised his staff first and beat the impersonator. Then the impersonator hit him back. The two both enjoined the sons and nephews [of the Wáng clan] and ordered an attack [on the other]. Wáng's son rushed forward and gave [the impersonator] a severe beating. It [turned out] to be a yellow dog and so he beat it to death. At the time, Wáng was an assistant in the Guìjī garrison.

"I have often seen an old yellow dog come by [here] from the north," the gatekeeper said.

Wáng's wife was deeply ashamed and died of illness.

105. The Dogs at the Traveler's Hut in the Mountains of Línlǜ

Near the mountains of Línlǜ there is a traveler's hut.[231] Those who spent the night when passing there always died of [some] illness. It is said that there were ten or so people, a motley mix of men and women, some wearing white and some yellow, who were always playing dice [there].[232] One time one Zhì Bóyí spent the night at this hut. Lighting a candle, he sat down to chant the classics.[233] At midnight suddenly ten or so people came and sat next to Bóyí to play dice. Bóyí secretly peered at them with a mirror [and found that] they were a pack of dogs. So he stood up with the candle in his hand and, feigning an accident, set their clothes afire with it. There was the steam of burning hair. Bóyí had a knife hidden in his bosom and he grabbed one of the people and stabbed him. At first the man screamed like a human, but after that he died and turned into a dog. The rest all ran away.

106. Roast Mutton

Gù Pèi was a man of outstanding talent from the state of Wú [222–280].[234] He once escorted a guest to Shēngpíng hut. At the time there was a Sramana sitting [in the hut].

---

commandery during the Hàn, and a prefecture in Dōngyáng 東陽 commandery during the Jìn, in an area that is now a part of Zhèjiāng. Beyond Wáng's speculation, there is no evidence to support the claim that *tàishū* is a copy error and a literal reading of the term as it stands is quite acceptable.

231. Línlǜ 林慮 prefecture is now Lín 林 *xiàn* in Hénán.

232. *Púbó* 蒱博 ('dice'), is probably akin to the term *púxì* 蒱戲 which Hú Sānxǐng, in Sīmǎ Guāng's *Zīzhì tóngjiàn*, 129.4067, glosses as "a dice game" 摴蒱之戲 (*shū* 摴 being a dice-like trinket used for gambling).

233. Zhì Bóyí 郅伯夷 (n.d.) was the grandson of Zhì Yùn 郅惲 (n.d.) and, hence, probably the son of Zhì Shòu 郅壽 (d. 89). See Yìng Shào 應劭 (ca. 140–ca. 206), *Fēngsú tōngyì* 風俗通義 (Peking: French Bookstore, 1943), 9.74; and Wang Shaoying, *Ssj*, 18.224, no. 427, n. 1. On Zhì Yùn and Zhì Shòu, see *Hòu Hàn shū*, 29.1023–32.

234. I find no other information on Gù Pèi 顧霈.

This [monk] was a devotee who wandered among the vulgar.[235] The host was about to kill a sheep when the sheep snapped its tether and ran. It took refuge between the knees of the devotee, pushing its head beneath [the folds of] his cassock. The devotee was not able to save it, and they immediately took it away to butcher.

Once they had roasted its meat, the host first cut [a piece] to give to the devotee to eat. The devotee ate the roast mutton and, when he swallowed it, felt the roast meat moving about under his skin. The poisonous pain was unbearable. They called a doctor to treat him with needles. [The doctor] pierced the roast mutton [beneath the monk's skin] with several needles, but it still wiggled about. So [the doctor] split open [his skin] and took [the thing] out to inspect it. It turned out to simply be a [plain] slice of meat. After that, the devotee became ill and began to bleat like a sheep and spit foam. He returned to his temple and within a short time had passed away.

107. The Old Fox in an Ancient Grave

Gù Zhān of Wújùn 吳郡 was hunting and came to a hill when he suddenly heard the sound of someone talking.[236]

"Tut, tut, you are well along in years now," [the voice] said.

At that, Gù went with his [hunting] party to find [where the voice was coming from]. There was a pit at the top of the hill. It was an old grave. [They] saw an old fox crouching inside the grave.[237] In front of it was a set of record books and the old fox was looking at the books and counting with its paws. It was calculating something. They let the dogs bite and kill it, then picked up the record books to have a look [and found] the names of people's ravished daughters [listed inside]. Those who had already been ravished were checked off at the top in red. There were over one hundred names enumerated and Zhān's daughter was listed among them.

108. The Fox Wearing a Fragrant Pouch

Xí Zuóchǐ, of the sobriquet Yànwēi 彥威, who was Master of Records in Jīngzhōu, accompanied Huán of Xuānwǔ on a hunt.[238] It was snowing heavily at the time. They saw vapor emanating from the snow on the brush west of the Jiānglíng city wall.[239] They went to investigate and saw a brownish creature. They shot it and it died when hit by their arrow. They went to pick it up [and found] it was an old male fox. There was a fragrant pouch of thin red silk brocade strapped to its leg.

---

235. I translate *dào rén* 道人 as 'devotee' here in order to maintain the generic quality it has in this context.

236. I find nothing else on Gù Zhān 顧旃.

237. The hú 狐 is *Canis vulgaris*, the fox. See Read, *Animal Drugs*, no. 374.

238. Xí Zuóchǐ 習鑿齒 (d. 384) served Huán Wēn around 371. See his biography in *Jìn shū*, 82.2152–58; and Mather, *Shih-shuo Hsin-yü*, 558.

239. Jiānglíng 江陵 (now in Jiānglíng *xiàn*, Húběi) was in Nánjùn 南郡 commandery, Jīngzhōu.

109. "Let Bóqiú go!"
During the Sòng, every time a Grand Administrator came to office in Jiǔquán commandery, he would always die within a short time.[240] After a time Chén Fěi of Bóhǎi was appointed to this commandery.[241] Anxious and unhappy [about it], he approached a diviner to prognosticate the fortunes, adverse and favorable, [of the appointment].

"Distance yourself from the nobles and let Bóqiú 伯裘 go," the diviner said. "If you can figure this out, you will have no troubles."

Fěi could not figure out what he said.

"Go, sir," [the diviner] responded, "and you will figure it out as a matter of course."

When Fěi arrived at the post, [he discovered that] the Attending Physician was Marquis Zhāng 張, the Physician on Duty was Marquis Wáng 王, and among the soldiers there was a Marquis Shǐ 史, and a Marquis Dǒng 董.

"This is what is meant by 'the nobles'," Fěi realized.

Thereupon he distanced himself from them.

Once he had gone to bed, he thought about what 'let Bóqiú go' might mean, but he did not know what it referred to. After midnight, something came onto Fěi's covers. Fěi woke up and caught it under his blanket. The thing then began to jump about and raised a clamorous din. People outside heard and came in carrying torches ready to kill it. The demon then spoke.

"I really do not have any malevolent intentions," it said. "I simply wish to test you. If you can release me this once, I will deeply repay your kindness."

"What [kind of] thing are you," Fěi asked, "that would suddenly assault the Grand Administrator?"

"I was originally a one-thousand-year-old fox," the demon said. "Now I have become a demon and was just about to transform into a spirit when I touched off your lordship's potent temper, [and thus] ran into this adversity. My sobriquet is Bóqiú. If you ever have any urgent difficulty, simply call out my sobriquet and things will be solved of their own course."

"[This] is the true meaning of 'let Bóqiú go'," Fěi said delighted.

He immediately let the demon go. He opened his covers a little bit and suddenly a ray of light, red and like lightning, went out the window.

The next evening someone knocked on his gate. Fěi asked who it was.

"Bóqiú," was the answer.

"What have you come to do?" [Fěi] asked.

"To report something."

"What?"

---

240. Jiǔquán 酒泉 commandery is now Jiǔquán *xiàn* in Gānsù. Established first in the Hàn, Jiǔquán commandery was not part of Southern Sòng territory but was occupied by the Northern Wèi (386–534).

241. Bóhǎi 渤海 commandery was within the area of present day Shāndōng. I find no information on Chén Fěi 陳斐.

"At the northern border there is a bandit," he replied. "It is the drudge Fā 發."

Fěi investigated Fā and [the report] was verified.

Whenever there was any trouble, [Bóqiú] would tell Fěi about it first. From then on there was no longer the slightest bit of illicit activity along the border. Thus everywhere they called [Fěi] "the Sagely Lord of the Manor."

A little over a month after this, the Master of Records, Lǐ Yīn 李音, had a secret affair with Fěi's maidservant.

Soon after, fearing Bóqiú would report it, he plotted with the various servants to kill Fěi.[242] When [Yīn] spied that there was no one beside [Fěi], he and the various servants went straight into [Fěi's chambers], carrying clubs, ready to attack and kill him. Fěi was terrified.

"Bóqiú, come save me!" he called out immediately.

At once something [appeared] that made cracking sounds and seemed as if it were whipping about a bolt of red silk. The various servants fell to the ground scared out of their wits. Then, one by one, [they were] tied up.

Upon interrogation, the servants all admitted their guilt.

"[Even] before Fěi had arrived in office," they said, "Yīn already feared he would lose his power and plotted with all of the servants to kill Fěi. [But at that time] it was rejected by the various servants when he met with them and so it didn't come off."

Fěi immediately killed Yīn and the others. Then Bóqiú apologized to Fěi.

"I had not yet [had the chance] to report Yīn's licentious passions before you summoned me," he said. "Though I put forth a slight effort [in the end], I am still quite ashamed about it."

A little over a month after that, he came to bid farewell to Fěi.

"After today, I will be on my way up to the heavens," [Bóqiú] said. "I will not be able to have any contact with you again."

Then he disappeared.

---

242. Here and in the following lines, *Tpgj*, 447.3342, and *Fyzl*, 63.13a–14a, read *zhū hóu* 諸侯 ('nobles') for *zhū pú* 諸僕 ('various servants'). This is the more appropriate reading.

Sōushén hòujì: Juàn 10

110. The Baby Crocodile

In Chángshā there was a man, his name is now forgotten, whose family lived beside a river. They had a daughter who once camped by the water's edge to wash some clothes when she felt something unusual inside her body, but never figured it was something to worry about.[243] She ended up pregnant and gave birth to three creatures, all rather like mudfish.[244]

Because she had given birth to them, the woman loved them dearly and thought them quite special. She raised them in water held inside a washbasin. After three months, the creatures grew big and [turned out to be] baby crocodiles.[245] Each had a name. The largest was Facing the Flood; the second largest was Breaking Barriers; and the smallest was Pounding the Shore.

[Then one day] the Heavens erupted in rain and the three crocodiles left all at once. After that she could not find them. Later, when it was about to rain again, the creatures suddenly came [back]. The young woman knew they would be coming and went out to look at them. The little crocodiles raised their heads to look back at their mother and did not leave for quite some time.

A year after that, the young woman died.

The three little crocodiles all came at the same time to her grave and cried over her. They did not go away for a [whole] day. If one listened to the sound of their crying, it seemed like the whine of a dog.

111. The Crocodile Protects the Cottage

Mr. Yǐn 尹 of Píngdū prefecture in Ānchéng lived in Rìhuáng village, ten *lǐ* east of the commandery, where he rented a plot of land and a cottage.[246] In the sixth month of the twenty-third year of the Yǒngjiā reign [446] Yǐn's son, who was thirteen years old, was keeping watch over the cottage when he saw a man of about twenty or so coming from the east. He was riding a white horse with a parasol opened out [above him] and, together with four servants, was dressed all in yellow. When they got to the door, he called Yǐn's son.

"I have come to temporarily take lodging and rest."

---

243. *Hòu* 後 in *Tpgj*, 425.3175, and *Tpyl*, 930.4135, reads *fù* 復.

244. *Tǐ yú* 鮧魚 is *Parasilurus asotus*, a catfish-like fish with a flat forehead and an anal fin extending the whole length of the tail. Common names for it include sheat-fish, Chinese wels and mudfish. See Read, *Scaly and Scaleless Fish*, 73, no. 171.

245. *Jiāo* 蛟 is the crocodile. See Bernard E. Read, *Chinese Materia Medica: Dragons and Snakes* (Peiping: Peking Natural History Bulletin, 1934), 18–19, no. 104. Also see j. 1, no. 2, n. 3 above.

246. Píngdū 平都 prefecture (southwest of what is now Ānfú 安福 *xiàn* in Jiāngxī) of Ānchéng 安城 (usually reads 成) commandery was in Jīngzhōu.

He then went into the central room of the cottage and sat on the couch. A man held the parasol over him. Yǐn's son looked closely at his clothing [and saw] that it had no seams. The horse had stripes in five colors, which seemed like scaly armor, and was hairless.

Shortly, a rainy pall descended and the men and horse left.

"I'll come again tomorrow," he looked back at Yǐn's son and said.

Yǐn's son watched them go. They headed west and mounting thin air, gradually rose upward. Soon a cloudy pall was all around, turning the bright daylight to gloomy darkness.

The next day, a great flood burst [from the sky] and the mountain valleys gushed swollen with water. The deepest valleys overflowed in a torrential deluge. [The flood] was about to inundate Yǐn's cottage when suddenly a great crocodile over thirty feet long appeared and coiled up around the cottage, shielding it from the flood.

112. The Qiú Dragon Dyke

At Mt. Qiú in Wǔchāng there is a Dragon Cavern.[247] The people who lived there often saw a divine *qiú* flying and soaring in and out.[248] If there was a drought during the year, [the people] would pray to it and it would rain immediately. In later times, people constructed a dyke at its foot which [they] called Qiú dyke.[249]

113. Chopping at the Duke of Thunder

Zhāng Gǒu, a man from Wúxīng, was tilling in the fields during the fifth month and would keep his food inside a wine-cup.[250] [But] every evening when he picked it up to eat, the rice was already all gone. This did not happen just once. Later he kept watch over it and

---

247. Mt. Qiú 虯山 was said to be 150 *lǐ* south of Wǔchāng prefecture (which stood where Wǔchāng stands today). See Lǐ Xián 李賢 (1408–1466), *Míng yītǒng zhì* 明一統志 (*Sìkù quánshū zhēnběn* edn., 1977), 59.8b. A more widely cited *lóngxué* 龍穴 ('Dragon Cavern') is a subterranean cavern said to be located within Xīnpíng 新平 prefecture (east of Héngyáng 衡陽 *xiàn* in modern Húnán), in Xiāngdōng 湘東 commandery of the State of Wú. This would be only a few hundred more *lǐ* south of the Wǔchāng cavern of this anecdote. See Knechtges, *Wen xuan*, 392, ll. 281–82 n.

248. *Qiú* 虬, also written 虯, was a kind of mythical dragon, usually said to be without horns (cf. *jiǎo lóng,* j. 1, no. 2, n. 3 above), but descriptions vary widely. See Wáng Niànsūn, *Guǎngyǎ shūzhèng*, 10B.25a–26a.

249. This story is strikingly similar to the one about the Dragon Cavern in Xīnpíng which brought rain when soaked with water (see Knechtges, *Wen xuan*, as cited in n. 5 above). The two stories appear to be drawn from a similar piece of local folklore.

250. Zhāng Gǒu 章苟 reads Zhāng Xún 荀 in *Tpyl*, 13.67 and Zhāng Gǒu 狗 in Qútán Xīdá 瞿曇悉達 (fl. early eighth century) *Táng Kāiyuán zhànjīng* 唐開元占經 (*Sìkù quánshū zhēnběn* edn., 1973), 102.7a–b. I can find no information on any of the names. *Gū* 菰 is *Zizania aquatica*, commonly known as water bamboo or Indian rice. The shoots of the young plant can be eaten as a bamboo shoot-like vegetable and the fruit of the plant is a grain that can be cooked and eaten like rice. See *Běncǎo gāngmù*, 19.1364–66; and Read, *Chinese Medicinal Plants*, 258, no. 766. However, it is much more likely that this graph represents here a homophonous word usually written 觚 or 柧 meaning 'goblet' or 'wine-cup'.

saw a large snake steal the food. Gǒu chopped at it with a dagger and the snake slithered away. Gǒu chased after it. It went to a slope on which there was a small hole. The snake went in the hole and all [Gǒu] could hear was the sound of sobbing.

"[He] has chopped at me and hurt me," it said.[251]

"What should he do?" another snake asked.

"Report him to the Duke of Thunder," another said. "Tell him to strike and kill the drudge with thunder and lightning."

Soon clouds and rain gathered darkly, while thunder and lightning [crashed] above Gǒu. Gǒu then wildly leapt about and loudly cursed.

"Celestial servant," he said, "I am poor and exert my effort in tilling and cultivation.[252] When the snake came and stole my food, the crime should have been with the snake. Yet why do you instead strike at me with thunder and lightning? You must be [quite] a brainless Duke of Thunder. If you come, I'll chop at your belly with my dagger."

In a short time, the wind and rain gradually dissipated and the thunder and lightning turned toward the snake hole. Several dozen snakes died.

114. The Men in Black Clothing: A Battle Between Snakes

At the end of the Wú, a man from Línhǎi went into the hills to go bow hunting and built a hut there to live in.[253] At night a man about ten feet tall and wearing brown clothing with a white belt came right in and spoke to the bowman.

"I have an enemy," he said. "[We] have agreed to fight tomorrow. If you could help me, I will generously reward you."

"Naturally I can help you," the bowman said. "What need will there be for gratitude?"

"Tomorrow, at mealtime," he replied, "you should go out beside the river. My opponent will come from the north and I will meet him out of the south. I will be the white sash and he the brown sash."

The bowman agreed to the task. The next day he went out and as expected heard a noise north up the bank. It sounded like wind and rain. The trees and vegetation were being blown in all directions. He looked south where it was also like this. All he saw were two great snakes, over one hundred feet in length, which met in the middle of the river then wrapped and coiled around each other. The white snake was losing. So the bowman drew his crossbow and shot. The brown snake died immediately.

The sun was about to set when he again met the man from the day before.

"Stay here and hunt for a year," he said thanking him as he parted. "Leave next year and take care that you do not come back again. Your return would mean disaster for sure."

---

251. *Wǒ mǒujiǎ* 我某甲 is redundant. *Tpyl* and *Táng Kāiyuán zhànjīng* read *mǒujiǎ* alone, while *Tpgj*, 456.3424, reads *wǒ yǐ* 我矣 and omits *mǒujiǎ*.

252. *Tiān shǐ* 天使 ('celestial servant') reads *tiān gōng* 天公 ('celestial duke') in *Tpyl* and *Táng Kāiyuán zhànjīng*. This is probably the correct reading for the context.

253. Línhǎi 臨海 commandery is now Línhǎi *xiàn* in Zhèjiāng.

"Fine," the bowman said.

He stayed and hunted for a year after that. He bagged a huge catch and his family became immensely wealthy. Several years later he suddenly remembered how great his catch had been [there]. Forgetting what he had been told before, he went back to hunt. [When he got there], he met the white belted man from before.

"I told you not to come again," he said to [the bowman] "Yet you could not see to doing as I said. My enemy's sons are now grown and will come today to revenge you for sure. I shall pay it no heed."

When the bowman heard this, he was quite frightened. He was about to run when he saw three people in black clothing, all eight feet long, coming toward him with their mouths open.

The bowman died immediately.

115. A Snake Snatches up the Eggs in its Mouth

During the Yuánjiā reign [424–453], there were three men in Guǎngzhōu who went into the hills together to chop some wood. They unexpectedly found a rocky burrow in which there were two eggs as big as a pint measure. They gathered them up and boiled them. Just as the broth began to get hot, they heard a sound in the woods like wind and rain. Shortly, a snake several arm spans thick and forty or fifty feet long came straight [toward them]. It picked the eggs out of the broth with its mouth and left. The three men all soon died.

116. A Woman Marries a Snake

During the Tàiyuán reign [376–396] of the Jìn, a man was marrying his daughter into a nearby village. When the time came, the groom's family sent someone to receive her. The bride's family gave her a fine send off and also had the girl's wet nurse escort her.

When they arrived [at the groom's house, they found] an overlapping succession of gateways and chambers, which seemed modeled after [the home of] a king or a marquis. There were lamps at the foot of the posts in the corridors, where a neatly dressed and made-up maidservant stood on watch duty. The bed curtain in the rear chamber was quite beautiful.

When evening came, the young girl hugged her wet nurse and sobbed but was unable to speak. [A little later], the wet nurse secretly used her hand quietly to stroke the girl inside the bed curtain. She discovered a snake [as thick] as a post wrapped around the girl, from head to foot. The wet nurse ran outside in shock. The maidservants watching the lamps beside the posts were all little snakes and the flames in the lamps were snake eyes.

117. Letting a Turtle Go

In the Jìn, during the Xiánkāng reign, the Regional Inspector to Yùzhōu, Máo Bǎo, was garrisoned at Zhūchéng.[254] A soldier [there] saw someone selling a white baby turtle at

254. Xiánkāng 咸康 was a reign title (335–342) of the Jìn emperor Chéng 成 (r. 325–342). Máo Bǎo 毛寶 (n.d.; fl. mid-fourth century) has a biography in *Jìn shū*, 81.2122–24. Yùzhōu 豫

the Wǔchāng market. It was four or five inches long, pure white and quite cute. So he bought it, carried it home, and put it into a crock to raise it.

Over the course of seven days it gradually got bigger, getting close to about a foot. The man, feeling a compassion for it, carried it to the side of the river, let it go in the river water, and watched it [swim] away.

Later on, Zhūchéng came up against attack and siege by Shí Jìlóng and Máo Bǎo abandoned Yùzhōu.[255] Everyone drowned who [attempted to escape by] crossing the river.

At this time, the man who had raised the turtle put on his armor, took up his sword, and went along to take refuge [via the river]. Once in the water, he felt as if he had fallen onto a boulder. The water came only up to his waist. Shortly he floated up and out and saw [the boulder] from [there in] the central current: It was the white turtle that he had released earlier, its shell [now] six or seven feet in diameter.

When they reached the eastern shore, it stuck out its head to look at the man, then slowly swam away. From the middle of the river [the turtle] seemed to turn its head around and look at this man before it submerged.

洲 during the Jìn, occupied territory within modern Hénán and parts of Húběi. Zhūchéng 邾城 (in an area northwest of Huánggāng 黃岡 *xiàn*, Húběi) was in Yìyáng 弋陽 commandery, Yùzhōu.

255. Jìlóng is the sobriquet of Shí Hǔ, third ruler of the Later Zhào (r. 335–349). He attacked Zhūchéng in 339. See *Jìn shū*, 7.182. For further reference, see j. 2, no. 19, n. 46 above.

The Twelve Passages Added by Lǐ Jiànguó from Xīnjí Sōushén jì, juàn 1–10

X7. The Hemp Frocked Monk (*Xjsshj* j. 1, no. 7)[256]
No one knows who Shǐ Zōng 史宗 is. He usually wears hemp clothing, often treasuring it as if it were a monk's frock. So people call him the Hemp Frocked Daoist. He has numerous ulcerated patches of skin on his body, and his temperament is ever-changing. He can be frequently seen by the White Clay Dam at Guǎnglíng, leaning against the dam and crooning in song, while pulling at his waist-cord in self-delighted joy. If he gets what he needs, he'll give it as alms to others. He has no regular place of rest. Sometimes he's in seclusion other times out in the open. [257]

When Tán Qí of Gāopíng was Magistrate of Jiāngdū, he heard about Shǐ Zōng and summoned him for a visit.[258] Witty in conversation and entirely uninhibited, erudite and well versed in ancient studies, Zōng could expound and debate upon profundities and Confucianism. He took the opportunity to compose a poem, as follows:

Where one has desire, bitterness is unceasing.
Lacking desire, one is also without worry.
Nothing surpasses the pure and unburdened,
  with rope belt at one's waist and black leather cape across one's shoulders,
Wandering freely at will in the world, foraging widely without docking one's boat.
Only then will one be done with the burdens of the dusty mortal world,
  and perch one's aspirations there upon the hill.

Tán Qí could tell this was no ordinary person, and sent him back with a gift of ten bolts of cloth, all of which Shǐ Zōng gave away to beggars.

Sometime later, a Daoist, whose name is unknown, would follow him carrying a cane and a chest. Once, nearing dusk, the Daoist paid a visit to the Magistrate of Hǎiyán and said to him "I wish to travel for a few days, and need to have an assistant for a short time, can one be provided?"[259] "Take along whomever you wish," the Minister replied. So he selected a young boy who looked after the geese and ducks, the ugliest and most wretchedly dressed to take with him. In no time they reached a mountain with a dwelling on it. There were three Daoists in the dwelling. They were all delighted to see him and chatted eagerly, though the boy did not understand it all. Around noontime, the Daoist approached the host of the dwelling to ask for some food for the boy. He got a small

256. Lǐ Jiànguó (*Xjsshj*, 477–78) incorporated this passage from *Gāo sēng zhuàn*, j. 10, where it is attributed to Táo Yuānmíng.

257. *Nà* 納 indicates the word normally written 衲 'monk's vestment'. Guǎnglíng 廣陵 commandery was northeast of Jiāngdū 江都 *xiàn* of modern Jiāngsū.

258. Tán Qí 檀祇 (369–419), who had the sobriquet Gōngshū, was from Gāopíng 高平 in Yǎnzhōu 兗州 (now within Shāndōng province).

259. Hǎiyán 海鹽 corresponds to modern Hǎiyán in Zhèjiāng 浙江.

cup of food for him that seemed to be rather like mugwort. But the boy's hunger ceased upon eating it. Toward dusk, the Daoist was about to take leave, intending to go back, when he heard someone in the room inquire, "Do you happen to know the whereabouts of Shǐ Zōng?" The Daoist answered, "He's north of the Yangtze in Xúzhōu 徐州 at the White Clay Dam of Guǎnglíng, it's likely his faults have come to an end." The person in the room made a book, which he handed to the boy, saying "Seek out the Magistrate gentleman and give this to him." They got back to the county seat near dawn, and the Daoist met with the Magistrate, telling him "I'd like to stay here a few days." To which the Magistrate replied, "Wonderful." When the Magistrate asked what was in the chest, the Daoist said, "just a few books and things."

As was his habit, the Daoist prepared to go to sleep after the Magistrate finished holding court, and placed the chest and cane near his bed. Wishing to have a look [at what was in the chest] the Magistrate sent a watchman who was on duty to sneak away with it. The Daoist had anticipated this, and [earlier] at dusk used a pully to lift the chest and cane above [his bed] and slept under them, leaving the [watchman] unable to reach them. Later, he took his leave from the Magistrate, saying "I wanted to stay a short while, while you Sir have an insatiable desire to steal things. That is precisely the reason that I am leaving." The Magistrate called for the boy [who had traveled with the Daoist] and asked him where they had traveled. The boy said the Daoist had told him to grasp onto the cane and they had then floated swiftly away; all that he heard was like waves beneath his feet. The boy added that someone in the mountain had entrusted him with a book that was still in his coat. The Magistrate opened it and had a look, yet understood nothing. But he copied it out and then sealed the book the boy had, after which he had someone take the boy to the White Clay Dam and give the book to Shǐ Zōng. Shǐ Zōng opened the book and exclaimed with great surprise, "Where did you get this Daoist book of Pénglái immortality?"

Later Zōng traveled south to Wúhuì and happened to pass a fishing weir where he saw fishermen making a huge catch. At that, Zōng took a swim in the upper section of the river and all the fish dispersed. Thus was the way that he saved the creatures by his diving. Afterwards he rested at the Grand Lóngshān Temple in Shàngyú.[260] He was brilliant at discussing Zhuāngzǐ and Lǎozǐ, seeking out deeper understanding through penetrating investigation. But he concealed all trace of his talents and nobody new about them. Xiè Shào, Wèi Màizhī, and [Wèi] Fàngzhī, all serious scholars of deep learning, had studied under him.[261] Sometime later, other monks who had also stopped [at the temple] heard about Zōng's evening conversations, and his rather extensive and serious discussions of Pénglái. But come daybreak, none knew where Zōng had gone.

---

260. Wúhuì 吳會 was a district in Guìjī 會稽 commandery in the area of Shàoxīng 紹興 in modern Zhèjiāng and Shàngyú 上虞 prefecture was to the east of it.

261. I find no details on the lives of these three, Xiè Shào 謝邵, Wèi Màizhī 魏邁之, and (Wèi) Fàngzhī 魏放之.

X11. The Shaman Dài Yáng (*Xjsshj* j. 2, no. 11)[262]
Early on, when Yǔ Liàng was ill [339], Dài Yáng the shaman said, "During the Sū Jùn Incident, you prayed for blessing at the White Stone Temple, and promised to make an offering of the ox that was hitched to your carriage, but the offering was not made. This has been confirmed by the ghosts, and you cannot be saved." The next year Liàng died as predicted.[263]

X22. Gāo Xún: Repentance (*Xjsshj* j. 2, no. 22)[264]
Gāo Xún of Xíngyáng at the age of 50 was arrested for murder and was locked in a dungeon.[265] He figured he was sure to die. A cellmate said to him, "Diligently chant to the Boddhisatva Guānshìyīn with me." Xún replied, "My crime is too serious. I am willing to accept death. What reason is there to avoid it?" His cellmate continued his effort to persuade him, and Xún began to accept the idea. He swore that he would give up criminal activity and only do good. He devotedly chanted to Guānshìyīn without cease, affirming that if he was released he would raise a five story Buddha mural, give his life to servitude and caring for the Buddhist Sangha. When he had continued his efforts for ten months, the lock on his cell opened of its own accord. The prison warden was startled by this and found it unusual. He said to Xún, "The Buddha's spirit has taken pity on you, you will not die at the executioner's hand." On the day he was about to be put to death, the executioner raised his sword but before it came down the sword split in half and the blade was rendered useless. Xún thus obtained exemption from death.

X37. Xiè Fèng: The Danger of Anger (*Xjsshj* j. 4, no. 37)[266]
Xiè Fèng of Guìjī was on good terms with Guō Bóyóu, the Grand Administrator of Yǒngjiā Prefecture. He dreamed once that was Guō was arguing over money bet on a

---

262. Lǐ Jiànguó incorporated this anecdote from the *Shìshuō xīnyǔ*, where it is found in a note attributed to the *Sōushén jì* (*Xjsshj*, 483–84). Also see Mather, *Shih-shuo Hsin-yü*, 348. Lǐ notes that this passage could not have been collected by the *Ssj* author Gān Bǎo before he died in 336, since the anecdote's protagonist Yǔ Liàng died after that in 340.

263. Yǔ Liàng 庾亮 (289–340) was a powerful Eastern Jìn statesman and writer. See Knechtges and Chang, *Ancient and Early Medieval Chinese Literature*, 3–4: 1994–97. I find no information on Dài Yáng 戴洋. The Sū Jùn Incident refers to Sū Jùn's 蘇峻 (d. 328) revolt and battle with Yǔliàng, who eventually prevailed after initial defeat.

264. Lǐ Jiànguó (*Xjsshj*, 479) incorporated this passage from the *Tàipíng guǎngjì*, j. 111, based on an attribution to the *Sshj* given in the *Biànzhènglùn* 辯正論, compiled by Fǎlín 法琳 (572–640).

265. Xíngyáng 滎陽 is within modern Hénán. I find nothing on Gāo Xún 高荀.

266. Lǐ Jiànguó (*Xjsshj*, 515) incorporated this anecdote from the *Tàipíng yùlǎn*, j. 400, where it is attributed to *Xù Sōushén jì*. It had been in the *Sōushén jì*, and as thus is summarized in Campany, "Two Religious Thinkers." But Lǐ Jiànguó points out that it could not have been in the *Sōushén jì* as it recounts matters that happened after Gān Bǎo's death. Xiè Fèng 謝奉 (fl. ca. 340–360) had been an important military commander in the far south; see Mather, *Shih-shuo Hsin-yü*, 560. I find nothing further on Guō Bóyóu 郭伯猷.

game of dice with some people along the Zhè River.[267] The water spirits censured Guō over it, causing him to fall into the river and drown as a way to set Guō straight from his malign behavior. When Xiè Fèng awoke, he went to Guō's place and played a game of encirclement chess with him. After some time had passed, Xiè asked, "Do you know why I came?" And then he told him all about the dream. Hearing about it, Guō was extremely angered and said, "If you believe that I had quarreled with someone, as was the case in your dream, how could you expect that to be the real thing!" Shortly afterwards Guō went to use the toilet, where he collapsed and died. Xiè considered the logic of the matter and found it to indeed correspond to what he had dreamed

X38. Zōng Yuān: Frees the Turtles (*Xjsshj* j. 4, no. 38)[268]
Zōng Yuān had the sobriquet Shúlín 叔林 and was from Nányáng.[269] During the Tàiyuán reign of the Jìn [376–396] he served as Grand Administrator of Xúnyáng Prefecture. He once obtained ten turtles which he brought to the chef, and instructed him to make turtle chowder with two of them in the morning. The others were to be kept and raised in a vat full of rice washing water. That evening Zōng dreamed that ten men in black pants and their hands tied up came to him and kowtowed, apparently begging for mercy. The next morning the chef killed two of the turtles; and that evening he dreamed of eight men in black entreating him as they had previously. At that point Zōng Yuān realized what it all meant and instructed the chef not to kill anymore turtles. The following night he dreamed of the eight men again, this time kneeling and thanking him for his compassion, which startled him awake. The next morning he took them to Mt. Lú and set them free and never ate turtle again.

X39. Wáng Méng: Saving the Turtle (*Xjsshj* j. 4, no. 39)[270]
Minister of the Masses Cài Mó had an orphaned relative named Wáng Méng 王蒙 that he had adopted.[271] Méng was only three feet tall and appeared to have no bones. He had to ask for a boost from others when getting in to bed and into carriages. Cài told him to go fishing one day and he caught a turtle the size of a carriage wheel. Cài took it to the chef who [unknown to Cài] hung it upside down under a canopy and the turtle reached

267. Yǒngjiā 永嘉 Prefecture was in the area of modern Wēnzhōu 溫州. The Zhè 浙 River is the Qiántáng 錢塘 River.

268. This passage appears in the *Tàipíng yùlǎn*, j. 399, where it is attributed to *Xù Sōushén jì*, and in *Tàipíng guǎngjì*, j. 276, where it is attributed to *Sōushén jì*. Lǐ Jiànguó (*Xjsshj*, 516) judges it belongs to the *Sshj* based on the dates of the events recounted. I find nothing further on Zōng Yuān 宗淵.

269. Nányáng 南陽 was within the region of modern Hénán 河南. Xúnyáng 尋陽 Prefecture corresponds in location to modern Jiǔjiāng 九江 in Jiāngxī 江西.

270. Lǐ Jiànguó (*Xjsshj*, 516) incorporated this anecdote from the *Tàipíng yùlǎn*, j. 931, where it is attributed to *Xù Sōushén jì*.

271. Cài Mó 蔡謨 (281–356) has a biography in *Jìn shū*, 77.2033-41; also see Mather, *Shih-shuo Hsin-yü*, 609–10. I find no information on Wáng Méng 王蒙.

the roof. That evening Méng had difficulty sleeping and staying asleep. This went on for several evenings. Cài asked him why he could not stay asleep and Méng replied, "I dreamt I was sleeping in a carriage and there was a person hanging upside down." Cài's thoughts turned to the turtle and he had someone go see where the turtle was. It was indeed hanging upside down reaching all the way to the roof. Cài let out a sigh and said, "It is indeed just as I thought." He ordered the turtle to be brought to the ground. After that, Méng was able to sleep at ease again and the turtle wandered away.

X40. Zhū Gōng: Crime Does Not Pay (*Xjsshj* j. 4, no. 40)[272]
There was a vile person names Zhū Gōng who made his living through murder and banditry. One evening he went to the Lotus Temple and killed a nun and stole things. In the night he slipped out around the temple buildings and ran off; it was not known where he had gone. But he ended up falling into an open-air latrine and dying, with the stolen goods still on his back.

X42. The Monkey Mother (*Xjsshj* j. 4, no. 42)[273]
A fellow went into the hills in Dōngxīng of Línchuān and found a baby monkey that he took home.[274] The monkey's mother followed it to the fellow's house, where the fellow had tied the baby monkey to a tree in the yard to display it. The monkey's mother slapped at her cheeks facing the fellow, as if begging in grief, but without the ability to talk. The fellow would not let the baby monkey go, and ended up beating it to death. The monkey's mother cried out mournfully and cast herself down, dying. When the fellow opened up the mother monkey's belly, her intestines were split all asunder. Before half a year had passed, the fellow's family was struck by some plague and in a very short time the entire family had perished.

X43. Huáng Zhě: Ungrateful (*Xjsshj* j. 4, no.43)[275]
Huáng Zhě of Póyáng 鄱陽 county [Jiāngxī 江西], went into the hills to gather poplar seeds and got lost, unable to remember the way back. After a few days, he had grown quite hungry when he happened to see a large turtle. Zhě cursed at it, saying, "As you are a sentient creature and I have lost my way, now I am going to have a ride on your back so you can show me the road out." The turtle turned and pointed its right front leg

272. Lǐ Jiànguó (*Xjsshj*, 517) incorporated this passage from the *Bìanzhènglùn*, where it is attributed to the *Sōushén lù*. I find no information on Zhū Gōng 朱恭.

273. Lǐ Jiànguó (*Xjsshj*, 519) incorporated this passage from the *Tàipíng guǎngjì*, j. 131. Though it had originally been collected in *Sōushén jì*, Lǐ assigns it to *Sōushén hòujì* on the basis of a note in Xiāo Shìbīn's 蕭士贇 (n.d., Yuán) *Fēnlèi bǔzhù Lǐ Tàibái shī* 分類補注李太白試, j. 11.4a, where it is attributed to the *Sōushén hòujì*.

274. Dōngxīng 東興 county of Línchuān 臨川 commandery was in the area of modern Guǎngxī 廣西.

275. Lǐ Jiànguó (*Xjsshj*, 520) incorporated this anecdote from the *Tàipíng yùlǎn*, j. 931, where it is attributed to *Xù Sōushén jì*. I find no information on Huáng Zhě 黄赭.

and Zhě went in the direction he indicated. After going several *lǐ*, arriving at a brook, he saw a peddler on a boat. Zhě went and begged the peddler for some food, and told him, "a while ago I saw a turtle beside the creek, it was really big. We can go together to get it." As soon as he finished speaking his face broke out in boils. They went forth, but did not see the turtle again. A few days after he had returned home, Zhě grew ill from the boils and died.

X69. *Zǐlù*: Bears in Trees (*Xjsshj* j. 7, no. 69)[276]
Bears have no caves and some live inside holes in big trees. In the eastern regions they call bears *zǐlù* 子路 and toss things at the tree, saying, "You can get up now *zǐlù*." At that they will come down. They will not move if one does not call out to them.

X81. The Wife of Mǎ Shì (*Xjsshj* j. 8, no. 81)[277]
The wife of Mǎ Shì 馬勢 of Fùyáng in the State of Wú was surnamed Jiǎng 蔣. When a local villager was ill and about to die, Jiǎng became dizzy and confused and slept for several days. She awaked after the person had finally passed away. But when she related everything to her family they did not believe her. She told them, "When a certain person was ill, I wished to kill that person, but I was frustrated by the strength of their soul and they did not die. When I went into their home, there was cooked white rice on the cabinet with several different prepared dishes of food. I went briefly over to the stove to play, and the servant girl attacked me for no reason. I hit her hard on her spine, causing her to faint away. She came to only after quite some time." When her elder brother was ill, a person dressed in black instructed her to kill him, imploring her to do so. But she could not bring herself to do it. When he awoke she said to him, "You are supposed to live."

X99. Gù Kǎizhī: The Life in Paintings (*Xjsshj* j. 10, no. 99)[278]
Gù Kǎizhī had the sobriquet Chángkāng 長康. He had a fondness for a young lady who was his neighbor and drew a picture of her on his wall, putting a tack in the middle of

276. Lǐ Jiànguó (*Xjsshj*, 547) incorporated this anecdote from the *Tàipíng yùlǎn*, j. 908, where it is attributed to *Xù Sōushén jì*.

277. Lǐ Jiànguó (*Xjsshj*, 567) incorporated this anecdote from the *Tàipíng guǎngjì*, j. 358, where it is attributed to *Sōushén jì*. Lǐ judges it must actually be from the *Sshj* because the location of the story, Fùyáng 富陽 (now essentially Fùyáng district in modern Hángzhōu 杭州), had originally been Fùchūn 富春 until it was changed during the reign of the Jìn Emperor Xiàowǔ 孝武, Sīmǎ Yào 司馬曜 (362–396), well after Gān Bǎo had passed away.

278. Lǐ Jiànguó (*Xjsshj*, 599) incorporated this anecdote from j. 5 of the *Lìdài mínghuà jì* 歷代名畫記 by Zhāng Yànyuǎn 張彥遠 (ca. 811–ca. 877), which attributes it to both *Yōumínglù* and *Sōushén jì*. The *Tàipíng yùlǎn*, j. 741, cites a version it attributes to the *Yōumínglù* which is slightly different. Lǐ judges that the *Lìdài mínghuà jì* version must be from the *Xù Sōushén jì* because Gù Kǎizhī was born after Gān Bǎo had passed away. Gù Kǎizhī 顧愷之 (349?–410?) was a painter and poet of the Eastern Jìn. He has a biography in *Jìn shū* 92: 2404–06. Also see Knechtges and Chang, *Ancient and Early Medieval Chinese Literature*, 1: 284–88; and Mather, *Shih-shuo Hsin-yü*, 575.

her chest. The young lady came down with a pain in her heart and told Chángkāng about it. He pulled out the tack and she got better.

TRANSLATOR'S POSTFACE

I have had many requests for a copy of this translation over the years since 1986 when I completed it for my Master's thesis under the direction of David Knechtges in the Department of Asian Languages and Literatures at the University of Washington in Seattle. I had only been able to supply a clunky multi-part copy of the original, first as a thick photocopy and later as a multi-file pdf version when that technology became possible. So when Antje Richter raised the possibility of publishing it in the AOS Monograph series, I was quick and happy to accept the idea. I want to thank her here for that suggestion and for working with me to make it into a reality.

In the migration from the old Master's thesis format to a modern form, I was fortunate to still have the original WordStar files of the thesis manuscript, which I had fairly scrupulously migrated from format to format as the years went by, from larger to smaller floppy disks, to files saved on computers and backed up to USB drives of various sorts, and finally to the cloud. But if I was going to be able to use those files and avoid completely retyping the text to produce a publishable copy I would need to convert the WordStar version to a current format. After a bit of research, I was happy to discover that that it would be possible to convert them to text (.txt) files, which I did fairly easily. But the text version, still in multiple files, had to be integrated into a single modern word-processing document. For example, hard carriage returns after every line in each paragraph had to be converted to soft returns, and footnotes had to be restored to footnotes and removed from the middle of the running text. In addition, Chinese characters in the original thesis had all been written in by hand. So these also had to be typed back in one-by-one.

The present text is the result of all of these conversion steps and processes, following which I added a brief new introduction and update regarding newer scholarship from the decades since I first rendered the translation. Aside from that introduction, the content remains essentially as it was in my original Master's thesis, with the exception of errata that were discovered and fixed (though others surely remain). I did not attempt to do any deep revision of the text, or to update and supplement the many references in the footnotes. But as I worked through the conversion and read through the text with, original in hand, I found that I am still generally quite happy with my original translations, which were intended to closely reflect the structure and tone of the original, and still do. The annotations also remain quite serviceable. I hope that readers will find the text and translation still to be of use despite the admittedly sparse attention to the wealth of fine scholarship on the Six Dynasties period that has accumulated over the many years since I first made this translation and wrote the annotations.

I was fortunate to have the assistance of three Rutgers undergraduate research assistants in my effort to convert the text to a modern format. Two of the assistants were undergraduate students in the Rutgers Aresty Undergraduate Research Program working with me in 2018–19, Anny Lu and Emili Yiu, and the third was a student who worked with me as part of an independent study project in Fall 2018, Christina Gaudino. The three of them helped with converting the WordStar-cum-text documents to modern versions, and added in the Chinese characters, as well as tones on the *pīnyīn*. In Spring 2019, Anny Lu and Emili Yiu also helped with proofreading of the clean, updated copy. I am grateful for the assistance of these three, without whose help this text would still be limited to a single copy in the University of Washington Library. Of course, all remaining errors and textual issues are entirely my own responsibility.

Richard VanNess Simmons
Hong Kong, January 2020

APPENDIX 1

The *Sìkù quánshū zǒngmù* Notice for the *Sōushén hòujì*

Old editions list Táo Qián 陶潛 as the author. Inside is recorded the "Táohuā yuán" affair in one entry, which copies entirely the preface to the poem [of the same name] in *Táo Yuānmíng jí* and only adds 7 characters of commentary: "The fisherman's surname was Huáng, his name was Dàozhēn."[1] It also records an affair concerning the concubine to Gān Bǎo's father, which is copied entirely from the *Jìn shū* as well.[2] Hence, evidence of plagiarism is evidently quite apparent. The preface by Shěn Shìlóng 沈士龍 says:

> Yuánliàng [ie. Tao Qian] died in the fourth year of the [Liú Sòng] Yuánjiā reign [427], but herein are affairs of the fourteenth and sixteenth years [437 and 439]. Táo's collection rarely names reign titles, using the *gānzhī* 干支 instead. But this book mentions the Yǒngchū [420–422] and Yuánjiā [424–453] reigns.[3]

That it has been falsely attributed is definitely not in need of debate. Yet while this is the case, the diction and style of this book are anciently elegant, not something that a person of the post-Táng could have done. In the "Monograph on Literature" of the *Suí shū*, it is already referred to as Táo Qián's. So the highly dubious false attribution of the authorship and name has existed a long time.

Lù Yǔ's 陸羽 (d. 804*) Chá jīng* 茶經 cites a line similar to what is recorded in this edition [of the *Sshj*]: "In the Wǔdì reign of the Jìn [265–289[, Qín Jīng of Xuānchéng [in Ānhuī] went into the Wǔchāng hills [in Húběi] to gather tea . . . ."[4]

---

1. See the translation and accompanying notes to *Sshj* j. 1, no. 5 for a further discussion.

2. See the translation for *Sshj* j. 4, no. 42 and see *Jìn shū*, 82.2149–50. It is very unlikely that the entry was copied from the *Jìn shū*. The similarity between *Sshj* and *Jìn shū* here results from the fact that this entry (cited as *Xssj* in *Tpyl*, 556.2514) was probably among the sources that the *Jìn shū* editors used when compiling their history, not because the editors of the *Sshj* found the story originally in the *Jìn shū*. The *Jìn shū* is well known to have been sloppy with its sources and was especially wont to copy strange stories form many Jìn and Liú Sòng period works. For discussions of the drawbacks of the *Jìn shū*, see the entry for it in *Sìkù quánshū zǒngmù tíyào*, I, 45.990. See also Liú Zhījǐ 劉知幾 (661–721), *Shǐ tōng* 史通 (*Sbck* ed.), 12.10a–11b, 17.1b–3b; and Zhào Yì 趙翼 (1727–1814), *Niànèr shǐ zhájì* 廿二史劄記 (*Sbby* edn.), 8.2b–3a. I suspect the story of the concubine may have been originally found in Xiāo Jí's 蕭吉 (d. 614) *Wǔxíng jì* 五行紀. It is cited as such in *Tpgj*, 375.2764.

3. See Shěn Shìlóng's preface to the *Ssj*, 2, found in the *Jìndài mìshū* edition. As my discussion on the history of the *Sshj* makes clear, the contents of the collection were for the most part transmitted in fragments and also consist of material from disparate sources. So discrepancies like this are to be expected and Shěn's doubts over the attribution of authorship to Táo are quite justified for the text as a whole. Shěn Shìlóng and Hú Zhènhēng's prefaces say little else of significance concerning the *Sshj*.

4. See the translation for *Sshj* j. 7, no. 82 and Lù Yǔ, *Chá jīng* (*Xuéjīn tǎoyuán* edn.), C.8a, citing *Xssj*.

Fēng Yǎn's 封演 [*jìnshì* 756] *Wénjiàn jì* 聞見紀 cites the line: "There was a man who, because he was sick, could drink a gallon and a half, and then spit out a creature . . . ." Except that between this citation and the *Sshj* entry "The Supervisory General [at the time of] Huán of Xuānwǔ" there are some discrepancies, such as *niúfèi* 牛肺 reads *tǔdù* 土肚 and *míngjiǎ* 茗瘕 reads *hú èr jiǎ* 斛二瘕, the affair is comparable to what is recorded in this edition [of the *Sshj*].[5]

We know, [from the above examples], that the presently circulating printed edition is similar to the ancient text.[6] The "Dīng Lìngwēi Transformed into a Crane" story and the "Ā-Xiāng Thunder Cart" story were both circulated, quoted and cited among the Táng and Sòng *cí* 詞 writers, and [thus] used up to the present.[7] [Hence, while] those that list Táo Qián as the author, are definitely incorrect, the crux of the matter is that this work cannot be said not to be a text transmitted from the Six Dynasties period.[8]

---

5. See the translation for *Sshj* j. 3, no. 35 and Fēng Yǎn, *Wénjiàn jì* (*Xuéjīn tǎoyuán* edn.), 6.2a, citing *Xssj*. The *Sìkù* editors appear to have erred here in that the *Wénjiàn jì* reads *niúyí* 牛胰 ('ox pancreas') where the *Sshj* reads *niúdù* 牛肚 ('tripe'), not *niúfèi* and *tǔdù*.

6. Both the *Chá jīng* and the *Wénjiàn jì* citations are identified as from the *Xssj*, a reminder that the so-called ancient text (*gǔběn* 古本) was not the *Sshj* at all, but rather the *Xù sōushén jì*. The *Sìkù* editors fail to explicitly identify this fact.

7. See *Sshj* j. 1, no. 1, and j. 5, no. 55.

8. See Jì Yún 紀昀 (1724–1805) et al., eds., *Sìkù quánshū zǒngmù tíyào* 四庫全書總目提要 (Shanghai: Shangwu yinshuguan, 1933), 139.2946.

APPENDIX 2

List of Entries by Title and Collation of Lǐ Jiànguó's Redaction

Traditionally the stories were not given a title but convention now assigns a title to each entry. The following are translations of the conventional titles as found in the Wāng Shàoyíng and Wáng Guóliáng editions. Subtitles are added for this translation to further characterize the nature or content of the story where it seemed useful. In addition, each entry indicates Lǐ Jiànguó's collation decisions, indicating what he includes in his *Xīnjí Sōushén hòujì* (*Xjsshj*), which he rejects for inclusion, and which he reassigns to *Sōushén jì*.

Sshj juàn 1

1. Dīng Lìngwēi: The Transcended One	*Xjsshj* assigns to *Ssj*
2. An Immortal's Abode and Jade Elixer	*Xjsshj* rejects
3. Scarlet Wall in Shān Prefecture	*Xjsshj* assigns to j. 1, no. 1
4. The Sháo Dance: A Hidden Land of Fertility	*Xjsshj* assigns to j. 1, no. 2
5. The Peach Blossom Wellsprings	*Xjsshj* rejects
6. Liú Línzhī: A Glimpse of Elixers for Immortality	*Xjsshj* rejects
7. World Within a Cave	*Xjsshj* assigns to j. 1, no. 3
8. Eye Crag	*Xjsshj* rejects
9. Musical Sounds in Stone Caverns	*Xjsshj* rejects
10. Chaste Maiden Gorge	*Xjsshj* rejects
11. Spring of the Maiden Shū	*Xjsshj* rejects

Sshj juàn 2

12. Chamberlain Wú: The Filial Daoist	*Xjsshj* assigns to j. 1, no. 5
13. Xiè Yǔn: Conjuring a Carp	*Xjsshj* assigns to j. 1, no. 6
14. Dù Zǐgōng: Fishing up a Knife	*Xjsshj* rejects
15. The Mouse Market	*Xjsshj* rejects
16. The Buddhist Nun: A Warning for Huán Wēn	*Xjsshj* rejects
17. The Three Bur-Nuts	*Xjsshj* assigns to j. 4, no. 41
18. Fótúdèng	*Xjsshj* rejects
19. A Foreign Monk's Skill at Incantation	*Xjsshj* assigns to j. 2, no. 19
20. Tán Yóu: Avoiding Sorcery	*Xjsshj* assigns to j. 2, no. 20
21. Xìng Líng: Expelling Ghostly Trouble	*Xjsshj* rejects
22. Guō Pú Revives a Horse	*Xjsshj* assigns to *Ssj*
23. The Mirror in the Vase Sorcery	*Xjsshj* assigns to j. 2, no. 8
24. Guō Pú Makes an Advance Plea	*Xjsshj* assigns to j. 2, no. 9
25. Dù Bùqiān: Divination by Pheasant	*Xjsshj* assigns to j. 2, no. 10

Sshj juàn 3

26. Chéng Xián: A Sign of Success — *Xjsshj* assigns to j. 4, no. 35
27. A Shooting Star Falls into an Urn: Huán Xuán's Origins — *Xjsshj* assigns to j. 4, no. 30
28. The Gondola: A Fisherman Foresees the Duke's Success — *Xjsshj* assigns to j. 3, no. 29
29. The Grain Comes to Fullness: An Unexpected Cornucopia — *Xjsshj* assigns to j. 4, no. 31
30. Monetary Malevolence — *Xjsshj* assigns to j. 4, no. 33
31. Bees Sting the Bandits — *Xjsshj* rejects
32. Dead Thieves: The Formidable Cài Yì — *Xjsshj* rejects
33. A Horse's Urine Relieves an Affliction — *Xjsshj* assigns to j. 2, no. 16
34. A Shoot of Fern Turns into a Snake — *Xjsshj* assigns to j. 2, no. 17
35. Gallon-and-a-Half Nausea — *Xjsshj* assigns to j. 2, no. 15
36. Huán and Méi Share a Dream — *Xjsshj* assigns to j. 4, no. 36
37. Huá Xīn will be a Duke — *Xjsshj* assigns to j. 4, no. 32
38. Image and Soul Strangely Apart — *Xjsshj* assigns to j. 10, no. 98
39. Dǒng Shòuzhī: Visiting the Family after Death — *Xjsshj* does not discuss
40. A Spirit Cart — *Xjsshj* assigns to j. 9, no. 89

Sshj juàn 4

41. The Daughter of Xú Xuánfāng: A Dream Comes to Life — *Xjsshj* assigns to j. 8, no. 80
42. Gān Bǎo's Father's Concubine — *Xjsshj* assigns to j. 8, no. 75
43. Chén Liáng: Retribution after Death — *Xjsshj* assigns to j. 8, no. 78
44. Lǐ Chú: Bribery in the Other World — *Xjsshj* assigns to j. 8, no. 76
45. Zhèng Mào: Reviving a Corpse — *Xjsshj* assigns to j. 8, no. 77
46. The Daughter of Lǐ Zhòngwén: Chance to Come Back to Life — *Xjsshj* assigns to j. 8, no. 79
47. Tiger Talismans: A Southern Technique — *Xjsshj* assigns to j. 2, no. 18
48. Transforming into a Turtle — *Xjsshj* assigns to j. 7, no. 68

Sshj juàn 5

49. The Fair Maiden of Pure Waters — *Xjsshj* assigns to *Ssj*
50. The Qīngxī Temple Deity — *Xjsshj* assigns to j. 3, no. 27
51. Wáng Dǎo's Son Yuè: Sold in A Dream — *Xjsshj* rejects
52. Wú Wàngzǐ: Meeting Marquis Jiǎng — *Xjsshj* assigns to j. 3, no. 28
53. A Wooden Image Draws His Bow — *Xjsshj* rejects
54. The White-Haired Duke: A Diety Descends — *Xjsshj* assigns to j. 5, no. 49
55. The Grand Administrator of Línhè: The Thunder Carriage — *Xjsshj* assigns to j. 3, no. 24
56. The Daughter of Adjutant Hé: Sent by the Goddess of the West — *Xjsshj* assigns to j. 3, no. 26
57. A Divine Appearance: Huán Wēn Visits Emperor Jiǎnwén — *Xjsshj* assigns to j. 5, no. 50

Sshj juàn 6

58. Chén Ā-Dēng: An Eerie Evening Song	*Xjsshj* assigns to j. 10, no. 95
59. The Maiden Zhāng: Love in a Grave	*Xjsshj* assigns to j. 10, no. 96
60. The Official's Boat at Zither and Flute Confluence	*Xjsshj* assigns to j. 9, no. 82
61. Privy Treasurer Cuī: Marriage for Lú Chōng	*Xjsshj* assigns to j. 10, no. 97
62. The Tomb of Lǔ Zǐjìng: Disturbing the Dead	*Xjsshj* assigns to j. 9, no. 83
63. Chéng Jiǎn: Watching Out for Grave Robbers	*Xjsshj* assigns to j. 9, no. 92
64. The Man from Shàngyú: Help for a Drifting Coffin	*Xjsshj* assigns to j. 9, no. 93
65. The Man of the Hàn Tomb: An Ungrateful Traveler	*Xjsshj* assigns to j. 9, no. 86
66. Four Men Seize a Horse: Unwanted Help to Cross a River	*Xjsshj* assigns to j. 9, no. 87
67. An Unusual Object Rather Like a Bird: Guidelines for Attending Funerals	*Xjsshj* assigns to j. 9, no. 85
68. The Demon in His Abdomen	*Xjsshj* assigns to j. 2, no. 14
69. Shèng Dàoér: Caring for His Family after Death	*Xjsshj* rejects
70. The Temple to the Spirits at Lìyáng	*Xjsshj* assigns to j. 2, no. 21
71. A Ghost Sets Up Snares	*Xjsshj* rejects
72. The Àonǎo Song	*Xjsshj* assigns to j. 10, no. 94
73. Zhū Bì: False Incrimination after Death	*Xjsshj* assigns to j. 9, no. 91
74. Accidentally Hitting a Ghost's Foot	*Xjsshj* assigns to j. 2, no. 12
75. Fàn Qǐ's Wife: Finding the Family Grave	*Xjsshj* assigns to j. 2, no. 13
76. Dharma Master Zhú: Reporting from the Other World	*Xjsshj* assigns to j. 9, no. 90
77. The Ghost in the White Cloth Pants: Susceptible to Poison	*Xjsshj* assigns to j. 9, no. 88

Sshj juàn 7

78. A Man Transformed from a Rainbow	*Xjsshj* assigns to j. 3, no. 25
79. The Mountain Goblin	*Xjsshj* assigns to j. 7, no. 74
80. The Flesh that Fell from the Sky in Píngyáng	*Xjsshj* rejects
81. Zhōu Zǐwén is Stupefied: A Giant Bow	*Xjsshj* assigns to j. 5, no. 46
82. The Hairy Man: A Hidden Forest of Tea	*Xjsshj* assigns to j. 1, no. 4
83. The Man in the Vermillion Gown	*Xjsshj* rejects
84. The Two Headed Man	*Xjsshj* assigns to j. 5, no. 52
85. Something in the Walls: A Deadly House	*Xjsshj* assigns to j. 6, no. 66
86. A Dog Changes Form	*Xjsshj* assigns to j. 6, no. 61

Sshj juàn 8

87. Two Men Wearing Raven Black Clothing	*Xjsshj* rejects
88. Torches Become Butterflies	*Xjsshj* assigns to j. 5, no. 51
89. Zhūgě Chángmín: Haunted by Demons	*Xjsshj* rejects
90. A Dead Person's Head	*Xjsshj* assigns to j. 5, no. 48
91. A Head Falls from Above	*Xjsshj* rejects

92. A Hundred Skulls	*Xjsshj* assigns to j. 9, no. 84
93. The Shallots Shrink Away	*Xjsshj* assigns to j. 4, no. 34
94. Mr. Wú's Catalpa	*Xjsshj* assigns to *Ssj*

Sshj juàn 9

95. The White Clothed Woman	*Xjsshj* assigns to j. 6, no. 63
96. Tigers Divine for Fortune	*Xjsshj* assigns to j. 6, no. 53
97. The Bear Cave	*Xjsshj* assigns to j. 7, no. 70
98. Deer Woman Jerky	*Xjsshj* assigns to j. 6, no. 54
99. Monkeys Violate the Palace Singing Girls	*Xjsshj* assigns to j. 6, no. 53
100. Black Dragon: A Man's Closest Ally	*Xjsshj* assigns to j. 7, no. 72
101. Yáng Shēng's Dog: A Faithful Friend	*Xjsshj* assigns to j. 7, no. 71
102. The Cài Yǒng Family Dogs	*Xjsshj* assigns to j. 6, no. 60
103. Zhāng Píng's Dog	*Xjsshj* assigns to j. 5, no. 47
104. The Old Yellow Dog: Impersonating Old Mr. Wáng	*Xjsshj* assigns to j. 6, no. 62
105. The Dogs at the Traveler's Hut in the Mountains of Línlǜ	*Xjsshj* assigns to j. 6, no. 59
106. Roast Mutton	*Xjsshj* assigns to j. 4, no. 44
107. The Old Fox in an Ancient Grave	*Xjsshj* assigns to j. 6, no. 58
108. The Fox Wearing a Fragrant Pouch	*Xjsshj* assigns to j. 6, no. 57
109. "Let Bóqiú Go!"	*Xjsshj* assigns to j. 6, no. 56

Sshj juàn 10

110. The Baby Crocodiles	*Xjsshj* assigns to j. 7, no. 67
111. The Crocodile Protects the Cottage	*Xjsshj* rejects
112. The Qiú Dragon Dyke	*Xjsshj* assigns to *Ssj*
113. Chopping at the Duke of Thunder	*Xjsshj* assigns to j. 3, no. 23
114. The Men in Black Clothing: A Battle Between Snakes	*Xjsshj* assigns to j. 6, no. 64
115. A Snake Snatches up the Eggs in its Mouth	*Xjsshj* assigns to j. 4, no. 45
116. A Woman Marries a Snake	*Xjsshj* assigns to j. 6, no. 65
117. Letting a Turtle Go	*Xjsshj* assigns to j. 7, no. 73

Xjsshj juàn 1–10: The Twelve Passages added by Lǐ Jiànguó

X7. The Hemp Frocked Monk	*Xjsshj* assigns to j. 1, no. 7
X11. The Shaman Dài Yíng	*Xjsshj* assigns to j. 2, no. 11
X22. Gāo Xún: Repentance	*Xjsshj* assigns to j. 2, no. 22
X37. Xiè Fèng: The Danger of Anger	*Xjsshj* assigns to j. 4, no. 37
X38. Zōng Yuán: Frees the Turtles	*Xjsshj* assigns to j. 4, no. 38
X39. Wáng Méng: Saving the Turtle	*Xjsshj* assigns to j. 4, no. 39
X40. Zhū Gōng: Crime Does Not Pay	*Xjsshj* assigns to j. 4, no. 40
X42. The Monkey Mother	*Xjsshj* assigns to j. 4, no. 42
X43. Huáng Zhé: Ungrateful	*Xjsshj* assigns to j. 4, no. 43

X69. Zǐlù: Bears in Trees	*Xjsshj* assigns to j. 7, no. 69
X81. The Wife of Mǎ Shì	*Xjsshj* assigns to j. 8, no. 81
X99. Gù Kǎizhī: The Life in Paintings	*Xjsshj* assigns to j. 10, no. 99

BIBLIOGRAPHY

Běi shǐ 北史. Compiled by Lǐ Yánshòu 李延壽 (fl. 629). Beijing: Zhonghua shuju, 1975.

Běncǎo gāngmù 本草綱目. Compiled by Lǐ Shízhēn 李時珍 (1518–1592). 3 vols. Beijing: Renmin weisheng chubanshe, 1975.

Bielenstein, Hans. *The Bureaucracy of Han Times*. New York: Cambridge Univ. Press, 1980.

Bishop, Carl Whiting. Rhinoceros and Wild Ox in Ancient China. *China Journal* 18 (1933): 322–30.

Bó Jūyì 白居易 (772–846). *Bó shì liùtiē shìlèi jí* 白氏六帖事類集. Taipei: Xinxing shuju, 1971.

Bodde, Derk. *Festivals in Classical China: New Year and Other Annual Observances during the Han Dynasty, 206 B.C.–A.D. 220*. Princeton: Princeton Univ. Press, 1975.

Boltz, William G. Philological Footnotes to the Han New Year Rites. *JAOS* 99 (1979): 423–39.

Chang, K. C., ed. *Food in Chinese Culture*. New Haven: Yale Univ. Press, 1977.

Chén Yínkè 陳寅恪. 'Táohuā yuán jì' pángzhèng 桃花源記旁證. In *Chén Yínkè xiānshēng lùnwénjí* 陳寅先生論文集, 2: 467–76. Taipei: Sanrenxing chubanshe, 1974.

Chén Yuánliàng 陳元靚. *Suìshí guǎngjì* 歲時廣記. *Cóngshū jíchéng chūbiān* 叢書集成初編 edn. Shanghai: Shangwu yinshuguan, 1929.

Chéng Yìzhōng 程毅中. *Gǔ xiǎoshuō jiǎnmù* 古小說簡目. Beijing: Zhonghua shuju, 1981.

Chou, Yi-liang. Tantrism in China. *Harvard Journal of Asiatic Studies* 8 (1944–45): 242–45.

Dào shì 道世 (fl. 668). *Fǎyuàn zhūlín* 法苑珠林. *Sbck* edn.

DeWoskin, Kenneth J. The 'Sou-shen-chi' and the 'Chih-kuai' Tradition: A Bibliographic and Generic Study. PhD diss., Columbia Univ., 1974.

———. The Six Dynasties *Chih-kuai* and the Birth of Fiction. In *Chinese Narrative: Critical and Theoretical Essays*. Ed. Andrew H. Plaks. Pp. 21–52. Princeton: Princeton Univ. Press, 1977.

———. *Doctors, Diviners, and Magicians of Ancient China: Biographies of* Fang-shih. New York: Columbia Univ. Press, 1983.

Duàn Chéngshì 段成式 (d. 863). *Yǒuyáng zázǔ* 酉陽雜俎. *Cóngshū jíchéng chūbiān* edn.

Duàn Gōnglù 段公路 (n.d.). *Běi hù lù* 北戶錄. Changsha: Shangwu yinshuguan, 1941.

Fàn Níng 范寧. "Lùn Wèi Jìn zhìguài xiǎoshuō de chuánbò hé zhīshìfēnzǐ sīxiǎng fēnhuà de guānxì" 論魏晉志怪小說的傳播和知識分子思想分化的关系. *Běijīng dàxué xuébaò* 1957.2: 75–88.

———. "Guānyú *Sōushén jì*" 关于《搜神記》. *Wénxué pínglùn* 1964.1: 86–92.

Feng, H. Y., and J. K. Shryock. The Black Magic in China Known as *Ku*. *JAOS* 55 (1935): 1–30.

Fēng Yǎn 封演. *Wénjiàn jì* 聞見記. *Xuéjīn tǎoyuán* edn.

Foster, Lawrence Chapin. The *Shih-i chi* and Its Relationship to the Genre Known as *Chih-kuai hsiao-shuo*. PhD diss., Univ. of Washington, 1974.

Fù Xíhuá 傅惜華. Liùcháo zhìguài xiǎoshuō zhī cúnyì 六朝志怪小說知存逸. *Hànxué* 1 (1944): 169–210.

Fujiwara Sukeyo 滕原佐世 (d. 898). *Nihon-koku genzaisho mokuroku kaisetsu kō* 日本國見在書目錄說稿. Ed. Kobase Keikichi 小長谷惠吉 (1865–1944). Tokyo: Komiyamu shoten, 1976.

Gāo Chéng 高承 (fl. 1078–1085). *Shìwù jìyuán* 事物紀原. *Xīyīnxuān cóngshū* 惜陰軒叢書 edn.

Gě Hóng 葛洪 (ca. 250–ca. 330). *Zhǒu hòubèi jífāng* 肘後備急方. Shanghai: Shangwu yinshuguan, 1955.

Granet, Marcel. *Festivals and Songs of Ancient China*. Tr. E. D. Edwards. New York: E.P. Dutton & Company, 1932.

Guō Màoqiàn 郭茂倩 (fl. twelfth century). *Yuèfǔ shījí* 樂府詩集. Beijing: Zhonghua shuju, 1979.

Hàn shū 漢書. Compiled by Bān Gù 班固 (32–92). Beijing: Zhonghua shuju, 1975.

Hanan, Patrick. *The Chinese Vernacular Story*. Cambridge, MA: Harvard Univ. Press, 1981.

Hòu Hàn shū 後漢書. Compiled by Fàn Yè 范曄 (398–446). Beijing: Zhonghua shuju, 1975.

Hú Yīnglín 胡應麟. *Jiǎyǐ shèngyán* 甲乙剩言. *Bǎoyántáng mìjí* 寶顏堂秘笈 edn. N.p.: Wenming shuju, 1922.

———. Jiǔliú xùlùn 九流緒論. In *Shǎoshì shānfáng bǐcóng* 少室山房筆叢, 343–81. Beijing: Zhonghua shuju, 1958.

Hucker, Charles O. *A Dictionary of Official Titles in Imperial China*. Stanford: Stanford Univ. Press, 1985.

Huìjiǎo 慧皎 (497–554). *Gāo sēng zhuàn chūjí* 高僧傳初集. Taipei: Taiwan yinjingchu, 1970.

Jì Yún 紀昀 (1724–1805), et al., eds. *Sìkù quánshū zǒngmù tíyào* 四庫全書總目提要. Shanghai: Shangwu yinshuguan, 1933.

Jiāqìng chóngxiū dàqīng yītǒng zhì 嘉慶重修大清一統志. *Sbck* edn.

Jìn shū 晉書. Compiled by Fáng Xuánlíng 房玄齡 (578–648) et al. Beijing: Zhonghua shuju, 1975.

Jiù Táng shū 舊唐書. Compiled by Liú Xù 劉昫 (887–946). Beijing: Zhonghua shuju, 1975.

Kao, Karl S. Y. *Classical Chinese Tales of the Supernatural and the Fantastic*. Bloomington: Indiana Univ. Press, 1985.

Knechtges, David R. *The Han shu Biography of Yang Xiong (53 B.C.–A.D. 18)*. Occasional Paper no. 14. Tempe: Center for Asian Studies, Arizona State Univ, 1982.

———. *Wen xuan or Selections of Refined Literature*, vol. 1, *Rhapsodies on Metropolises and Capitals*. Princeton: Princeton Univ. Press, 1982.

Lǐ Fǎng 李昉 (925–996), ed. *Tàipíng guǎngjì* 太平廣記. Taipei: Xinxing shuju, 1958.

———. *Tàipíng yùlǎn* 太平御覽. Beijing: Zhonghua shuju, 1960.

Lǐ Fēngmào 李豐楙. Liùcháo jìng jìan chuánshuō yǔ dàojiào fǎshù sīxiǎng 六朝鏡劍傳說與道教法術思想. In *Zhōngguó gǔdiǎn xiǎoshuō yánjiù zhuānjí* 中國古典小說研究專集, 2: 1–28. Ed. Sīlì Jìngyí wénlǐ xuéyuàn Zhōngguó gǔdiǎn xiǎoshuō yánjiù zhōngxīn 私立靜宜文理學院中國古典小說研究中心. Taipei: Lianjing chubanshe, 1980.

———. Liù cháo jīngguài chuánshuō yǔ dàojiào fǎshù sīxiǎng 六朝精怪傳說與道教法術思想. In *Zhōngguó gǔdian xiaoshuo yanjiu zhuanji*, 3: 1–36. Ed. Sili jingyi wénlǐ xuéyuàn Zhōngguó gǔdiǎn xiǎoshuō yánjiū zhōngxīn. Taipei: Lianjing chubanshe, 1981.

Lǐ Gōnghuàn 李公煥, ed. *Jiānzhù Táo Yuānmíng jí* 箋注陶淵明集. *Sbck* edn.

Lǐ Hàn 李翰 (fl. 746). *Méng Qiú jízhù* 蒙求集注. *Xuéjīn tǎoyuán* edn.

Lǐ Jiànguó 李剑国. *Táng qián zhìguài xiǎoshuō shǐ* 唐前志怪小说史. Tianjin: Nankai daxue chubanshe, 1984.

Lǐ Jiànguó 李劍國. *Xīnjí Sōushén jì Xīnjí Sōushén hòujì* 新輯搜神記新輯搜神後記. 2 vols. Beijing: Zhonghua shuju, 2007.

Lǐ Xián 李賢 (1408–1466). *Míng yītǒng zhì* 明一統志. *Sìkù quánshū zhēnběn* 四庫全書珍本 edn.

Liú Lìchuān 刘丽川. Shì lùn *Sōushén jì* zhōng de jiéguǒ bǔyǔ 试论《搜神记》中的结果补语. *Yǔyán yánjiū* 1984.4: 33–39.

Liú Xī 劉熙 (fl. 200). *Shì míng* 釋名. *Hàn Wèi cóngshū* 漢魏叢書 edn.

Liú Yìqìng 劉義慶 (403–444). *Shìhshuō xīnyǔ* 世說新語. Ed. Wāng Zǎo 汪藻 (fl. thirteenth century). Beijing: Zhonghua shuju, 1962.

Liú Zhījǐ 劉知幾 (661–721). *Shǐ tōng* 史通. *Sbck* edn.

Lù Guīméng 陸龜蒙 and Pí Rìxiū. *Sōng Lù jí* 松陸集. *Sìkù quánshū zhēnběn* edn.

Lǔ Xùn魯迅. *Gǔ xiǎoshuō gōuchén* 古小說鈎沈. Beijing: Renmin wenxue chubanshe, 1951.

———. *Zhōnguó xiǎoshuō shǐlüè* 中國小說史略. Taiwan: n.p., n.d.

Lù Yǔ 陸羽. *Chá jīng* 茶經. *Xuéjīn tǎoyuán* edn.

Maenchen-Helfen, Otto. The Ting-ling. *Harvard Journal of Asiatic Studies* 4 (1939): 77–86.

Maspero, Henri. *Mélanges posthumes sur les religions et l'histoire de la Chine: Le Taoïsme*. Paris: Civilisations du sud, 1950.

Mather, Richard. The Mystical Ascent of the T'ient'ai Mountains: Sun Chuo's *Yu-t'ien-t'ai-shan-fu*. *Monumenta Serica* 20 (1961): 226–45.

———. *Shih-shuo Hsin-yü: A New Account of Tales of the World*. 2nd ed. Ann Arbor: Center for Chinese Studies of the Univ. of Michigan, 2002.

Mei Tsu-lin [Méi Zǔlín] 梅祖麟. Xiàndài Hànyǔ wánchéngmào, jùshì hé cíwěi de láiyuán 現代汉语完成貌句式和词尾的来源. *Yǔyán yánjiū* 1 (1981): 65–77.

Morino Shigeo 森野繁夫. *Sōjinkōki* no tsūkōbon 捜神後記の通行本. *Shinagaku kenkyū* 27 (1962): 17–26.

Nán Qí shū 南齊書. Compiled by Xiāo Zǐxiǎn 蕭子顯 (489–537). Beijing: Zhonghua shuju, 1975.

Nán shǐ 南史. Compiled by Lǐ Yánshòu 李延壽 (fl. 629). Beijing: Zhonghua shuju, 1975.

Ogawa Tamaki 小川環樹. Gi Shin jidai igo (san seiki ikō): Senkyō ni asonda setsuwa 魏晉時代以後 (三世紀以降)：仙鄉に遊んだ說話. In *Chūgoku shōsetsu no kenkyu*, 264–73. Tokyo: Iwanami shoten, 1968.

———. Koshosetsu no goho: Toku ni ninsho daimeishi oyobi gimon daimeishi no yoho ni tsuite 古小說の語法：特に人稱代名詞および疑問代名詞の用法について. In *Chūgoku shōsetsu no kenkyu* 中國小說史の研究, 274–92. Tokyo: Iwanami shoten, 1968.

Ōuyáng Xún 歐陽詢 (557–641), ed. *Yìwén lèijù* 藝文類聚. Taipei: Xinxing shuju, 1969.

Qútán Xīdá 瞿曇悉達 (fl. eighth century). *Táng Kāiyuán zhànjīng* 唐開元占經. *Sìkù quánshū zhēnběn* edn.

Read, Bernard E. *Chinese Materia Medica: Animal Drugs*. Peiping: Peking Natural History Bulletin, 1931.

———. *Chinese Materia Medica: Avian Drugs*. Peiping: French Bookstore, 1932.

———. *Chinese Materia Medica: Dragons and Snakes*. Peiping: Peking Natural History Bulletin, 1934.

———. *Chinese Medicinal Plants from the Pen Ts'ao Kang Mu*. Peking: Peking Natural History Bulletin, 1936.

———. *Chinese Materia Medica: Turtle and Shellfish Drugs*. Peiping: Peking Natural History Bulletin, 1937.

———. *Chinese Materia Medica: Scaly and Scaleless Fish*. Peiping: French Bookstore, 1939.

Read, Bernard E., and C. Pak. A Compendium of Minerals and Stones Used in Chinese Medicine from the Pen T'sao Kang Mu. *Peking Society of Natural History Bulletin* 3.2 (December 1928).

Rogers, M. C. *The Chronicle of Fu Chien*. Chinese Dynastic Histories Translations no. 10. Berkeley: Univ. of California Press, 1968.

Pelliot, Paul. Autour d'une traduction sanscrite du *Tao tö king*. *T'oung pao* 13 (1912): 351–430.

Sānguó zhì 三國志. Compiled by Chén Shòu 陳壽 (233–297). Beijing: Zhonghua shuju, 1975.

Schafer, Edward H. *The Golden Peaches of Samarkand*. Berkeley: Univ. of California Press, 1963.

Scholes, Robert. *Elements of Fiction*. New York: Oxford Univ. Press, 1968.

Shān hǎi jīng jiàozhù 山海經校住. Ed. Yuán Kē 袁珂. Shanghai: Guji chubanshe, 1980.

Shǐ jì 史記. Compiled by Sīmǎ Qiān 司馬遷 (145–ca. 86 BCE). Beijing: Zhonghua shuju, 1975.

Shigezawa Toshio 重澤俊朗. Bunken mokuroku o tsujite mita rikuchō no rekishi ishiki 文獻目錄を通して見た六朝の歷史意識. *Toyōshi-kenkyū* 18 (1959): 1–16.

Sīmǎ Guāng 司馬光 (1019–1086). *Zīzhì tōngjiàn* 資治通鑑. Beijing: Guji chubanshe, 1956.

Sòng shǐ 宋史. Compiled by Tuō Tuō 脫脫 (1313–1355) et al. Beijing: Zhonghua shuju, 1977.

Sòng shū 宋書. Compiled by Shěn Yuē 沈約 (441–513). Beijing: Zhonghua shuju, 1975.

Straughair, Anna. *Chang Hua: A Statesman-Poet of the Western Chin Dynasty*. Occasional Paper no. 15, Australian National Univ., Faculty of Asian Studies. Canberra: Australian National Univ., 1973.

Suí shū 隋書. Compiled by Wèi Zhēng 魏徵 (580–643). Beijing: Zhonghua shuju, 1973.

Taishō shinshū Daizōkyō 大正新修大藏經. Ed. Takakusu Junjirō 高楠順次郎 and Watanabe Kaigyoku 渡邊海旭. Tokyo: Taishō issaikyō kankōkai, 1924–32.

Tán Fèngliáng 谈凤樑. Shìlùn Zhōngguó gǔdài xiǎoshuō gàiniàn de yǎnbiàn 试论中国古代小说概念的演变. *Wenyi luncong* 10 (1980): 67–93.

Tán Zhèngbì 譚正璧. *Zhōngguó xiǎoshuō fādá shǐ* 中國小說發達史. Taipei: Qiye shuju, 1978.

Táng xiě Wénxuǎn jìzhù cánběn 唐寫文選記住殘本. Ed. Luó Zhènyù 羅振玉 (1866-1940). *Jiācǎo Xuān cóngshū* 嘉草軒叢書 edn. (1918).

Táo Hóngjǐng 陶弘景 (425–536). *Zhēn gào* 真誥. *Xuéjīn tǎoyuán* edn.

Toyoda Minoru 豐田穰, *Sojinki, Sojinkoki* genryuko 搜神記搜神後記源流考. *Toho gakuho* 12.3 (1941): 43–66. [Translation: Yí Ān 頤安. *Soushen ji, Soushen houji* yuanliukao. *Zhōnghé yuèkān* 3.5 (1942): 40–51 and 3.6 (1942): 45–57.]

Wáng Chōng 王充 (27–ca. 97). *Lùn héng* 論衡. Shanghai: Renmin chubanshe, 1974.

Wáng Guóliáng 王國良. *Sōushén hòujì yánjiū* 搜神後記研究. Taipei: Wenshizhe chubanshe, 1978.

Wáng Guówéi 王國維. *Gǔ hú fú kǎo* 古胡服考. *Xuětáng cóngkè* 雪堂叢刻 edn. N.p.: n.d.

Wáng Lì 王力. *Zhōngguó yǔfǎ lǐlùn* 中國語法理論. Beijing: Zhonghua shuju, 1957.

———. *Hànyǔ shǐgǎo* 漢語史稿. Beijing: Zhonghua shuju, 1982.

Wáng Niànsūn 王念孫 (1744–1832). *Guǎngyǎ shūzhèng* 廣雅疏證. *Jīfǔ cóngshū* 幾輔叢書 edn.

Wāng Shàoyíng 汪紹楹, ed. *Sōushén jì* 搜神記. Compiled by Gān Bǎo 干寶 (d. 336). Beijing: Zhonghua shuju, 1979.

———, ed. *Sōushén hòujì* 搜神後記. Beijing: Zhonghua shuju, 1981.

Wáng Xiàngzhī 王象之 (*jìnshì* 1196). *Yǔdì jìshèng* 輿地紀勝. N.p.: Yueyatang 粤雅堂, 1855; rpt. Taipei: Wénhǎi chubanshe, 1962.

Wáng Yáo 王瑤, ed. and comm. *Táo Yuānmíng jí* 陶淵明集. Beijing: Zuojia chubanshe, 1956.

———. Xiǎoshuō yǔ fāngshù 小說與方術. In *Zhōnggǔ wénxuéshǐ lùnjí* 中古文學史論集, 85–110. Shanghai: Gudian wenxue chubanshe, 1956.

Wáng Yáochén 王堯臣 (1011–1056), ed. *Chóngwén zǒngmù* 崇文總目. N.p.: *Yuèyǎtáng cóngshū*, 1824.

Wèi shū 魏書. Compiled by Wèi Shōu 魏收 (506–572). Beijing: Zhonghua shuju, 1975.

Wèi Zhòngjǔ 魏仲舉 (fl. 1195–1200), ed. *Wǔbǎi jiā zhù Chānglí wénjí* 五百家注昌黎文集. *Sìkù quánshū zhēn běn* edn.

Welch, Holmes, and Anna Seidel, eds. *Facets of Taoism*. New Haven: Yale Univ. Press, 1979.

Wright, Arthur F. Fo-t'u-teng: A Biography. *Harvard Journal of Asiatic Studies* 11 (1948): 321–71.

———. Biography and Hagiography: Hui-chiao's Lives of Eminent Monks. *Silver Jubilee Volume of the Zinbun-kagaku-kenkyusyo Kyoto University* (1954): 383–432.

Wú Hóngyī 吳宏一. Liù cháo guǐshén guàiyì xiǎoshuō yǔ shídài bèijǐng de guānxì 六朝鬼神怪異小說與時代背景的關係. *Xiàndài wénxué* 44 (1971): 37–60.

Wú Shū 吳淑 (947–1002), ed. and comm. *Shì lèi fù* 事類賦. N.p.: n.d.

Wú Yǐng 吳穎. Táo Qián de 'Táohuā yuán jì' 陶潛的《桃花源記》. *Yǔwén xuéxí* 56 (1956): 17–21.

Xīn Táng shū 新唐書. Ōuyáng Xiū 歐陽修 (1007–1072) et al. Beijing: Zhonghua shuju, 1975.

Xú Jiān 徐堅 (659–729). *Chū xué jì* 初學記. Beijing: Zhonghua shuju, 1962.

Xú Zhèn'è 徐震堮. *Hàn Wèi Liùcháo xiǎoshuō xuǎn zhù* 漢魏六朝小說選注. Taipei: Hongshi chubanshe, 1975.

Yán Màoyuán 嚴懋垣. Wèi Jìn Nánběi cháo zhìguài xiǎoshuō shūlù fù kǎozhèng 魏晉南北朝志怪小說書錄附考證. *Wénxué niánbào* 6 (1940): 45–70.

Yang, Hsien-yi, and Gladys Yang, trs. *The Man Who Sold a Ghost*. Peking: Foreign Languages Press, 1958.

Yáo Shúxiáng 姚叔祥. *Jiànzhǐbiān* 見只編. In *Yányì zhìyán* 鹽邑志言. Ed. Fán Wéichéng 樊維城 (*jìnshì* 1616). Shanghai: Shangwu yinshuguan, 1937.

Yè Qìngbǐng 葉慶炳. Wèi Jìn Nánběi cháo de guǐxiǎoshuō yǔ xiǎoshuō guǐ 魏晋南北朝的鬼小說與小說鬼. *Zhongwai wenxue* 3.12 (1975): 100–119.

———. Zhìguài xiǎoshuō zhōng de jī hé quǎn 志怪小說中的雞和犬. *Zhōnghuá wénhuà fùxīng yuèkān* 9.5 (1976): 45–46.

Yīng Shào 應劭 (ca. 140–ca. 206). *Fēngsú tōngyì* 風俗通義. Peking: French Bookstore, 1943.

Yoshikawa Kōjirō 吉川幸次郎. *Sesetsu shingo* no bunshō 世說新語の文章. In *Chūgoku sambun ron* 中國散文論, 74–99. Tokyo: Chikuma shobō, 1966. [Translation: Glen W. Baxter. The *Shih-shuo shin-yü* and Six Dynasties Prose Style. *Harvard Journal of Asiatic Studies* 18 (1955): 124–41; rpt. in *Studies in Chinese Literature*. Ed. John L. Bishop. Pp. 166–83. Cambridge, MA: Harvard Univ. Press, 1966.]

Yóu Guóēn 游国恩 et al. *Zhōngguó wénxuéshǐ* 中国文学史. Beijing: Renmin wenxue chubanshe, 1980.

Yú Shìnán 虞世南 (558–638). *Běitáng shūchāo* 北堂書鈔. N.p.: Nanhai Kongshi sanshi you sanwan juan tang, 1888.

Yuán Kē 袁珂. *Shān hǎi jīng jiàozhù* 山海經校注. Shanghai: Guji chubanshe, 1980.

Yuè Shǐ 樂史 (930–1007). *Tàipíng huányǔ jì* 太平寰宇記. Nanjing: Jinling shuju, 1882.

———. *Yǐng Sòng běn tàipíng huányǔ jì bǔquè* 影宋本太平寰宇記補闕. Taipei: Wenhai chubanshe, 1963.

Zhān Xiùhuì 詹秀惠. Nánběi cháo zhùshì shū sì zhǒng yǔfǎ yánjiù 南北朝著釋書四種語法研究. PhD diss., National Taiwan Univ., 1975.

Zhào Dàoyī 趙道一 (n.d.). *Lìshì zhēnxiān tǐdào tōngjiàn* 歷世真仙體道通鑑. Shanghai: Guangcang xuejun, 1936.

Zhào Kèyáo 赵克尧 and Xǔ Dàoxūn 许道勋. 'Táohuā yuán jì yǔ shī' yǔ lìshǐ shíjì《桃花源记与诗》与历史实际. *Fùdàn xuébào: Shèhuì kēxué* 1981.4: 52–55.

Zhào Yì 趙翼 (1727–1814). *Niànèr shǐ zhājì* 廿二史劄記. *Sìbù bèiyào* 四部備要 edn.

Zhèngtǒng Dàozàng 正統道藏. Taipei: Yiwen yinshuguan, 1964.

Zhōngguó gāoděng zhíwù tújiàn 中国高等植物图鉴. Ed. Zhōngguó kēxuéyuàn, zhíwù yánjiūsuǒ 中國科學院植物研究所. Beijing: Kexue chubanshe, 1972.

INDEX TO PART ONE

INDEX TO PART TWO, THE TRANSLATED STORIES